SUPER COOKERY

Wok & Oriental

This is a Parragon Book
This edition published in 2001

Parragon
Queen Street House
4 Queen Street
Bath BA1 1HE, UK

ISBN: 0-75255-265-1

A copy of the CIP data for this book is available from the British Library, upon request.

Printed in China

Note
Cup measurements used in this book are for American cups. Tablespoons are assumed to be 15 ml. Unless otherwise stated, milk is assumed to be full fat, eggs are medium and pepper is freshly ground black pepper.

Contents

Introduction

Oriental cookery basically requires the use of a wok. If you have one, then a whole array of wonderful dishes are open to you. It is worth buying a wok, rather than using a frying pan (skillet), for more satisfactory results when trying the delicious range of recipes which follow in this book.

Basically, a wok is a curved, shallow, bowl-like cooking implement which is made of metal and has either a single long, wooden handle or two looped handles at opposite sides of the pan. It comes in many sizes, but the most appropriate for a family is approximately 30-35 cm/12-14 inches in diameter. It may be made from stainless steel, cast iron or copper, the cast iron being the better choice as it retains heat more efficiently, especially when well-seasoned. There are numerous advantages to a wok over a frying pan (skillet). The convex shape means that food is easily moved around the wok and tossed (the basis of stir-frying) and cooks much more quickly. It can easily be tilted if required or rotated to reach ingredients easily.

Due to the curved sides of the wok, the heat rises and the whole wok becomes a hot cooking surface. It therefore conserves fuel and is perfect for quick cooking and stir-frying. Cleaning is no problem as there are no corners or edges in which food can become lodged.

USEFUL EQUIPMENT

There are several other pieces of equipment that will be useful with a wok. One of the most important in the Western kitchen is a *collar*. Basically this is a metal crown with angled sides and hollows which aids heat convection from our modern hobs and cooking rings. The wok sits in the collar and gives more even cooking than if it were simply placed on an electric ring. A *long-handled spatula* is useful for cooking and removing foods as the curved edge follows the curve of the wok. Be sure to buy one with a wooden handle to insulate your hands from the heat.

The wok is mainly used for stir-frying, but may also be used for deep-frying and steaming. A *frying strainer* or shallow *wire-meshed basket* is useful to remove foods from fat and a *steaming trivet* will convert your wok to a steamer.

Obviously a *lid* is essential for some wok cooking and should be domed and fitted snugly inside the wok to seal in the flavours during steaming. Many boxed wok sets contain all of these additional pieces of equipment as they are an essential part of wok cooking if it is to be used to its full potential.

USING YOUR WOK

Before using your wok, it is essential to season it as with other pans. Wipe the wok inside and out with oiled kitchen paper and heat it to a high heat in the oven or on the hob. Remove the wok from the heat, allow it to cool and repeat this process several times to give a good coating – this will make it easier to clean and give it a non-stick coating. After the initial seasoning, the wok may be cleaned with soap and water, but it must be dried immediately if made of cast iron, to prevent it from rusting. Generally, the wok is simply wiped clean, and allowed to blacken with use. It is said that the blacker the wok, the better the cook, as it shows how frequently the wok is used.

STIR-FRYING

The wok is most widely used for stir-frying, a cooking method which originated in China, and remains the most recognised form of Chinese cooking. This method has spread throughout East Asia. In China it is called *Ch'au*, which primarily means one or a number of ingredients are sliced thinly and evenly and cooked in 1–2 tablespoons of fat. The food is stirred with long bamboo chopsticks or a spatula and seasonings and sauces are added.

Stir-frying is often done in stages. This allows foods which have longer cooking times to be stir-fried and removed and then returned to the wok at a later stage, and also for individual flavours to be kept distinct. The dish is always brought together at the end of cooking in the wok and served as a whole. Usually peanut or corn oil are used to fry the foods, but occasionally chicken fat and sometimes lard will be used for more delicate flavours.

There are different types of stir-frying which are described below:

Liu is wet-frying with less vigorous stirring and more turning of the foods. A cornflour (cornstarch) and stock mixture is added with sugar, vinegar and soy sauce at the end of cooking for a delicious coating sauce.

Pao, or 'explosion', requires foods to be fried at the highest heat, and it is a very short, sharp method of cooking, usually lasting only 1 minute. Foods cooked in this way are generally marinated beforehand for flavour and tenderness.

WOK COOKING AROUND THE WORLD

Across the Far East woks are used in various guises for many dishes. In India, a large pan or *karahi* is used which sits over a hole in a brick or earth oven. This wok-like vessel is used for braising and frying, the infamous curry or *karahi* deriving its name from the pan. In Indonesia, a *wajan* or wok is used over wood or charcoal for curries, rice dishes and quick stir-fries – the same applies in Japan, Thailand, Singapore and Malaysia, all of which have been influenced by Chinese cooking. Even a Mongolian barbecue resembles a wok, being a convex iron griddle.

You will gather from the preceding information that the wok and the stir-frying cooking methods are both essential and unique to Asian and Far Eastern cooking, being swift, light, healthy and extremely versatile. The following recipes take you on a magical journey of the Far East, covering soups, starters, meat and poultry, fabulous fish dishes, vegetarian dishes and, of course, rice and noodles, the staples in these countries. So get out your wok and prepare yourself for the feast of flavours now open to you!

In the West we tend to talk about Chinese cooking as a generalization, as though it were the same throughout China. In fact, China is a vast country, with a range of topography and climates that produce distinct regional differences.

This book, contains recipes that are popular in both China and the west. Dishes from Szechuan in the West, Canton in the south, Beijing in the north and Shanghai in the east offer an array of different flavours and cooking methods. The dishes included in this book range from hot and spicy to delicate flavours using fish and vegetables, with a mid-range of sweet-and-sour dishes, rice, noodles and a small section of desserts.

One of the most important features of Chinese cooking is texture. Vegetables should remain crisp, and rice and noodles should be treated like pasta and retain their 'bite' after cooking. Ingredients such as tofu (bean curd) are used for texture, even though they have little flavour. Bamboo shoots, a common ingredient, are included purely for texture.

Although the Chinese make use of fresh foods, they also use dried foodstuffs in their recipes, in particular mushrooms, tofu (bean curd), noodles and spices.

COOKING METHODS

The Chinese combine a couple of cooking methods in one dish, such as steaming and then frying, or frying and roasting, but little special equipment is required.

Steaming is widely used in Chinese cookery. Traditionally bamboo steamers are used, so that a whole meal may be cooked in one stack of bamboo racks. The rice is usually placed in the bottom and different dishes stacked on top, those taking the longest to cook being placed at the bottom. If you do not have a steamer, invert a heatproof plate in a large saucepan and cover it with a lid or foil. Boiling water is added to the steamer, to cover one third of the depth of the dish. This water may need topping up during cooking, although many of the dishes cook very quickly. Steaming is a very healthy method of cooking, not using any fat, and it traps the flavours of the dish.

Stir-frying is done in a wok that must be heated before use. Foods of similar size (all small) are stirred constantly, so that as they come into contact with the wok, they cook quickly. Sometimes foods are cooked in batches and removed. This is to preserve flavours. The dishes are always brought together in the wok at the end of cooking and may have sauces added during or at the end of the cooking time, depending on the region from which they originated. Peanut oil is usually used for stir-frying, but vegetable oil may be used in its place.

Deep-frying is also done in the wok, which uses less oil than a deep-fryer. The shape of the wok allows oil to drain from the food into the centre of the wok. The foods are often marinated first or coated in a light batter. Quick-frying is also used, whereby foods are either fried on one side (used for noodles) and not turned, or turned once and sliced for serving.

USEFUL CHINESE INGREDIENTS

Bamboo shoots *These are added for texture, as they have very little flavour. Available in cans, they are a common ingredient in Chinese cooking.*

Beansprouts *These are mung bean shoots, which are very nutritious, containing many vitamins. They add crunch to a recipe and are widely available. Do not overcook them, as they wilt and do not add texture to the dish.*

Black beans *These are soy beans and are very salty. They can be bought and crushed with salt and then rinsed or used in the form of a ready-made sauce for convenience.*

Chinese beans *These long beans may be eaten whole and are very tender. French (green) beans may also be used.*

Chinese five-spice powder *An aromatic blend of cinnamon, cloves, star anise, fennel and brown peppercorns. It is often used in marinades.*

Chinese leaves *A light green leaf with a sweet flavour. It can be found readily in most supermarkets.*

Hoisin sauce *A dark brown, sweet, thick sauce that is widely available. It is made from spices, soy sauce, garlic and chilli, and is often served as a dipping sauce.*

Lychees *These are worth buying fresh, as they are easy to prepare. Inside the inedible skin is a fragrant white fruit. Lychees are available canned and are a classic ingredient.*

Mango *Choose a ripe mango for its sweet, scented flesh. If a mango is underripe when bought, leave it in a sunny place for a few days before using.*

Noodles *The Chinese use several varieties of noodle. You will probably find it easier to use the readily available dried varieties, such as egg noodles, which are yellow, rice stick noodles, which are white and very fine, or transparent noodles, which are opaque when dry and turn transparent on cooking. However, cellophane or rice noodles may be used instead.*

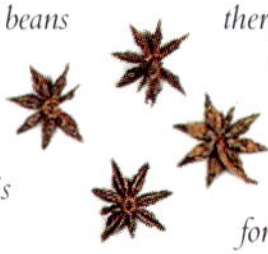

Oyster sauce *Readily available, this sauce is made from oysters, salt, seasonings and cornflour (cornstarch) and is brown in colour.*

Pak choi *Also known as Chinese cabbage, this has a mild, slightly bitter flavour.*

Rice vinegar *This has a mild, sweet taste that is quite delicate. It is available in some supermarkets, but if not available use cider vinegar instead.*

Rice wine *This is similar to dry sherry in colour, alcohol content and smell, but it is worth buying rice wine for its distinctive flavour.*

Sesame oil *This is made from roasted sesame seeds and has an intense flavour. It burns easily and is therefore added at the end of cooking for flavour, and is not used for frying.*

Soy sauce *This is widely available, but it is worth buying a good grade of sauce. It is produced in both light and dark varieties – the former is used with fish and vegetables for a lighter colour and flavour, while the latter, being darker, richer, saltier and more intense, is used as a dipping sauce or with strongly flavoured dark meats.*

Star anise *This is an eight-pointed, star-shaped pod with a strong aniseed flavour. The spice is also available ground. If a pod is added to a dish, it should be removed before serving.*

Szechuan pepper *This is quite hot and spicy and should be used sparingly. It is red in colour and is readily available.*

Tofu (bean curd) *This soya bean paste is available in several forms. The cake variety, which is soft and spongy and a white-grey colour, is used in this book. It is very bland, but adds texture to dishes and is perfect for absorbing all the other flavours in the dish.*

Water chestnuts *These are flat and round and can usually only be purchased in cans, already peeled. They add a delicious crunch to dishes and have a sweet flavour.*

Yellow beans *Again a soy bean and very salty. Use a variety that is chunky rather than smooth.*

Soups & Starters

Soup is indispensable at Asian tables, especially in China, Japan, Korea and South East Asia. Chicken soup, for example, is sometimes served in China, Malaysia and Thailand for breakfast! However, it is generally eaten part way through a main meal to clear the palate for further dishes, but it is never served as a starter as in the Western world. There are many different types of delicious soups, both thick and thin, and, of course, the clear soups which are often served with wontons or dumplings in them. In Japan, the clear soups are exquisite arrangements of fish, meat and vegetables in a clear broth.

Starters or snacks are drier foods in general, such as spring rolls, which come in many variations and shapes across the Far East. Satay is served in Indonesia, Malaysia and Thailand and other delights are wrapped in pastry, bread, rice paper or skewered for ease of eating. Again these are generally served as snacks in their native countries, but are frequent starters in Western restaurants.

The following chapter contains many delicious recipes for both soups and starters, all of which are the perfect way to begin a meal and whet the appetite for the delicious dishes that follow.

Spicy Chicken Noodle Soup

Serves 4

INGREDIENTS

2 tbsp tamarind paste
4 red Thai chillies, finely chopped
2 cloves garlic, crushed
2.5 cm/1-inch piece Thai ginger, peeled and very finely chopped
4 tbsp fish sauce
2 tbsp palm sugar or caster (superfine) sugar
8 lime leaves, roughly torn
1.2 litres/2 pints/5 cups chicken stock
350 g/12 oz boneless chicken breast
100 g/3½ oz carrots, very thinly sliced
350 g/12 ozsweet potato, diced
100 g/3½ oz baby corn cobs, halved
3 tbsp fresh coriander (cilantro), roughly chopped
100 g/3½ oz cherry tomatoes, halved
150 g/5½ oz flat rice noodles
fresh coriander (cilantro), chopped,to garnish

1 Place the tamarind paste, Thai chillies, garlic, Thai ginger, fish sauce, sugar, lime leaves and chicken stock in a large preheated wok and bring to the boil, stirring constantly. Reduce the heat and cook for about 5 minutes.

2 Using a sharp knife, thinly slice the chicken. Add the chicken to the wok and cook for a further 5 minutes, stirring the mixture well.

3 Reduce the heat and add the carrots, sweet potato and baby corn cobs to the wok. Leave to simmer, uncovered, for 5 minutes, or until the vegetables are just tender and the chicken is completely cooked through.

4 Stir in the coriander (cilantro), cherry tomatoes and noodles. Leave the soup to simmer for about 5 minutes, or until the noodles are tender. Garnish and serve hot.

COOK'S TIP

Tamarind paste is produced from the seed pod of the tamarind tree. It adds both a brown colour and tang to soups and gravies. If unavailable, dilute molasses (dark muscovado) sugar or treacle with lime juice.

Crab & Sweetcorn Noodle Soup

Serves 4

INGREDIENTS

1 tbsp sunflower oil
1 tsp Chinese five-spice powder
225 g/8 oz carrots, cut into sticks
150 g/5½ oz/½ cup canned or frozen sweetcorn
75 g/2¾ oz/¼ cup peas
6 spring onions (scallions), trimmed and sliced
1 red chilli, deseeded and very thinly sliced
2 x 200 g/7 oz can white crab meat
175 g/6 oz egg noodles
1.7 litres/3 pints/7½ cups fish stock
3 tbsp soy sauce

1 Heat the sunflower oil in a large preheated wok.

2 Add the Chinese five-spice powder, carrots, sweetcorn, peas, spring onions (scallions) and chilli to the wok and stir fry for about 5 minutes.

3 Add the crab meat to the wok and stir-fry the mixture for 1 minute.

4 Roughly break up the egg noodles and add to the wok.

5 Pour the stock and soy sauce into the mixture in the wok, bring to the boil, cover and leave to simmer for 5 minutes.

6 Transfer the soup to warm serving bowls and serve at once.

COOK'S TIP

Chinese five-spice powder is a mixture of star anise, fennel, cloves, cinnamon and Szechuan pepper.

COOK'S TIP

Use thin egg noodles for the best result in this recipe.

Spicy Thai Soup with Prawns

Serves 4

INGREDIENTS

2 tbsp tamarind paste
4 red Thai chilies, very finely chopped
2 cloves garlic, crushed
2.5 cm/1 inch piece Thai ginger, peeled and very finely chopped
4 tbsp fish sauce
2 tbsp palm sugar or caster (superfine) sugar
8 lime leaves, roughly torn
1.2 litres/2 pints/5 cups fish stock
100 g/3½ oz carrots, very thinly sliced
350 g/12 oz sweet potato, diced
100 g/3½ oz/1 cup baby corn cobs, halved
3 tbsp fresh coriander (cilantro), roughly chopped
100g/3½ oz cherry tomatoes, halved
225 g/8 oz fan-tail prawns (shrimp)

1 Place the tamarind paste, chillies, garlic, ginger, fish sauce, sugar, lime leaves and stock in a large preheated wok. Bring to the boil, stirring constantly.

2 Reduce the heat and add the carrot, sweet potato and baby corn to the mixture in the wok.

3 Leave the soup to simmer, uncovered, for about 10 minutes, or until the vegetables are just tender.

4 Stir the coriander, cherry tomatoes and prawns (shrimp) into the soup and heat through for 5 minutes.

5 Transfer the soup to warm serving bowls and serve hot.

COOK'S TIP

Baby corn cobs have a sweet fragrance and flavour. They are available both fresh and canned.

COOK'S TIP

Thai ginger or galangal is a member of the ginger family, but it is yellow in colour with pink sprouts. The flavour is aromatic and less pungent than ginger.

Coconut & Crab Soup

Serves 4

INGREDIENTS

- 1 tbsp groundnut oil
- 2 tbsp Thai red curry paste
- 1 red (bell) pepper, deseeded and sliced
- 600 ml/1 pint/2½ cups coconut milk
- 600 ml/1 pint/2½ cups fish stock
- 2 tbsp fish sauce
- 225 g/8 oz canned or fresh white crab meat
- 225 g/8 oz fresh or frozen crab claws
- 2 tbsp chopped fresh coriander (cilantro)
- 3 spring onions (scallions), trimmed and sliced

1 Heat the oil in a large preheated wok.

2 Add the red curry paste and red (bell) pepper to the wok and stir-fry for 1 minute.

3 Add the coconut milk, fish stock and fish sauce to the wok and bring to the boil.

4 Add the crab meat, crab claws, coriander (cilantro) and spring onions (scallions) to the wok. Stir the mixture well and heat thoroughly for 2–3 minutes.

5 Transfer the soup to warm bowls and serve hot.

COOK'S TIP

Coconut milk adds a sweet and creamy flavour to the dish. It is available in powdered form or in tins ready to use.

COOK'S TIP

Clean the wok after each use by washing it with water, using a mild detergent if necessary, and a soft cloth or brush. Do not scrub or use any abrasive cleaner as this will scratch the surface. Dry thoroughly with paper towels or over a low heat, then wipe the surface all over with a little oil. This forms a sealing layer to protect the surface of the wok from moisture and prevents it rusting.

Chilli Fish Soup

Serves 4

INGREDIENTS

- 15 g/½ oz Chinese dried mushrooms
- 2 tbsp sunflower oil
- 1 onion, sliced
- 100 g/3½ oz/1½ cups mangetout (snow peas)
- 100 g/3½ oz/1½ cups bamboo shoots
- 3 tbsp sweet chilli sauce
- 1.2 litres/2 pints/5 cups fish or vegetable stock
- 3 tbsp light soy sauce
- 2 tbsp fresh coriander (cilantro)
- 450 g/1 lb cod fillet, skinned and cubed

1 Place the mushrooms in a large bowl. Pour over enough boiling water to cover and leave to stand for 5 minutes. Drain the mushrooms thoroughly. Using a sharp knife, roughly chop the mushrooms.

2 Heat the sunflower oil in a preheated wok. Add the onion to the wok and stir-fry for 5 minutes, or until softened.

3 Add the mangetout (snow peas), bamboo shoots, chilli sauce, stock and soy sauce to the wok and bring to the boil.

4 Add the coriander (cilantro) and cubed fish to the wok. Leave to simmer for 5 minutes or until the fish is cooked through.

5 Transfer the soup to warm bowls, garnish with extra coriander (cilantro) if wished and serve hot.

VARIATION

Cod is used in this recipe as it is a meaty white fish. For real luxury, use monkfish tail instead.

COOK'S TIP

There are many different varieties of dried mushrooms, but shiitake are best. They are not cheap, but a small amount will go a long way.

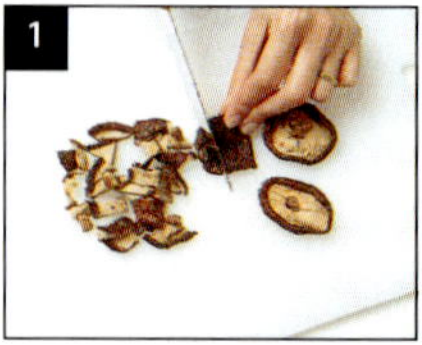

Hot & Sour Mushroom Soup

Serves 4

INGREDIENTS

2 tbsp tamarind paste
4 red Thai chilies, very finely chopped
2 cloves garlic, crushed
2.5 cm/1 inch piece of Thai ginger, peeled and very finely chopped
4 tbsp fish sauce
2 tbsp palm sugar or caster (superfine) sugar
8 lime leaves, roughly torn
1.2 litres/2 pints/5 cups vegetable stock
100 g/3½ oz carrots, very thinly sliced
225 g/8 oz button mushrooms, halved
350 g/12 oz shredded white cabbage
100 g/3½ oz fine green beans, halved
3 tbsp fresh coriander (cilantro), roughly chopped
100 g/3½ oz cherry tomatoes, halved

1 Place the tamarind paste, Thai chillies, garlic, Thai ginger, fish sauce, palm or caster (superfine) sugar, lime leaves and stock in a large preheated wok. Bring the mixture to the boil, stirring occasionally.

2 Reduce the heat and add the carrots, mushrooms, cabbage and green beans. Leave the soup to simmer, uncovered, for about 10 minutes, or until the vegetables are just tender.

3 Stir the coriander (cilantro) and cherry tomatoes into the mixture in the wok and heat through for 5 minutes.

4 Transfer the soup to warm bowls and serve hot.

COOK'S TIP

Tamarind is one of the ingredients that gives Thai cuisine its special sweet and sour flavour.

VARIATION

Instead of the white cabbage, try using Chinese leaves for a sweeter flavour. Add the Chinese leaves with the coriander (cilantro) and cherry tomatoes in step 3.

Chicken Wonton Soup

Serves 4–6

INGREDIENTS

FILLING:

350 g/12 oz minced (ground) chicken

1 tbsp soy sauce

1 tsp grated, fresh ginger root

1 garlic clove, crushed

2 tsp sherry

2 spring onions (scallions), chopped

1 tsp sesame oil

1 egg white

½ tsp cornflour (cornstarch)

½ tsp sugar

about 35 wonton wrappers

SOUP:

1.5 litres/2¾ pints/6 cups chicken stock

1 tbsp light soy sauce

1 spring onion (scallion), shredded

1 small carrot, cut into very thin slices

1 Combine all the ingredients for the filling and mix well.

2 Place a small spoonful of the filling in the centre of each wonton wrapper.

3 Dampen the edges and gather up the wonton wrapper to form a pouch enclosing the filling.

4 Cook the filled wontons in boiling water for 1 minute or until they float to the top.

5 Remove with a slotted spoon. Bring the chicken stock to the boil.

6 Add the soy sauce, spring onion (scallion), carrot and wontons to the soup. Simmer gently for 2 minutes then serve.

VARIATION

Substitute the chicken for minced (ground) pork.

COOK'S TIP

Look for wonton wrappers in Chinese or oriental supermarkets. Fresh wrappers can be found in the chilled compartment and they can be frozen if you wish. Wrap in cling film (plastic wrap) before freezing.

Clear Chicken & Egg Soup

Serves 4

INGREDIENTS

1 tsp salt
1 tbsp rice wine vinegar
4 eggs
850 ml/1 1/2 pints/3 3/4 cups chicken stock
1 leek, sliced
125 g/4 1/2 oz broccoli florets
125 g/4 1/2 oz/1 cup shredded cooked chicken
2 open-cap mushrooms, sliced
1 tbsp dry sherry
dash of chilli sauce
chilli powder, to garnish

1 Bring a large saucepan of water to the boil and add the salt and rice wine vinegar. Reduce the heat so that it is just simmering and carefully break the eggs into the water, one at a time. Poach the eggs for 1 minute. Remove the poached eggs with a slotted spoon and set aside.

2 Bring the stock to the boil in a separate pan and add the leek, broccoli, chicken, mushrooms and sherry and season with chilli sauce to taste. Cook for 10–15 minutes.

3 Add the poached eggs to the soup and cook for a further 2 minutes. Carefully transfer the soup and poached eggs to 4 individual soup bowls. Dust with a little chilli powder to garnish and serve immediately.

COOK'S TIP

You could use 4 dried Chinese mushrooms, rehydrated according to the packet instructions, instead of the open-cap mushrooms, if you prefer.

VARIATION

You could substitute 125 g/4 1/2 oz fresh or canned crabmeat or the same quantity of fresh or frozen cooked prawns (shrimp) for the chicken, if desired.

Curried Chicken & Sweetcorn (Corn) Soup

Serves 4

INGREDIENTS

175 g/6 oz can sweetcorn (corn), drained
850 ml/1 1/2 pints/3 3/4 cups chicken stock
350 g/12 oz cooked, lean chicken, cut into strips
16 baby corn cobs
1 tsp Chinese curry powder
1-cm/1/2-inch piece fresh root ginger (ginger root), grated
3 tbsp light soy sauce
2 tbsp chopped chives

1 Place the canned sweetcorn (corn) in a food processor, together with 150 ml/¼ pint/⅔ cup of the chicken stock and process until the mixture forms a smooth purée.

2 Pass the sweetcorn purée through a fine sieve, pressing with the back of a spoon to remove any husks.

3 Pour the remaining chicken stock into a large pan and add the strips of cooked chicken. Stir in the sweetcorn (corn) purée.

4 Add the baby corn cobs and bring the soup to the boil. Boil the soup for 10 minutes.

5 Add the curry powder, ginger and soy sauce and cook for 10–15 minutes. Stir in the chives.

6 Transfer the soup to warm bowls and serve.

COOK'S TIP

Prepare the soup up to 24 hours in advance without adding the chicken, let cool, cover and store in the refrigerator. Add the chicken and heat the soup through thoroughly before serving.

2

4

5

Hot & Sour Soup

Serves 4

INGREDIENTS

2 tbsp cornflour (cornstarch)
4 tbsp water
2 tbsp light soy sauce
3 tbsp rice wine vinegar
1/2 tsp ground black pepper
1 small fresh red chilli, finely chopped
1 egg
2 tbsp vegetable oil
1 onion, chopped
850 ml/1 1/2 pints/3 3/4 cups chicken or beef consommé
1 open-cap mushroom, sliced
50 g/1 3/4 oz skinless chicken breast, cut into very thin strips
1 tsp sesame oil

1 Blend the cornflour (cornstarch) with the water to form a smooth paste. Add the soy sauce, rice wine vinegar, pepper and chilli and mix together.

2 Break the egg into a separate bowl and beat well.

3 Heat the oil in a preheated wok and fry the onion for 1–2 minutes.

4 Stir in the consommé, mushroom and chicken and bring to the boil. Cook for 15 minutes or until the chicken is tender.

5 Pour the cornflour (cornstarch) mixture into the soup and cook, stirring, until it thickens.

6 As you are stirring, gradually drizzle the egg into the soup, to create threads of egg.

7 Sprinkle with the sesame oil and serve immediately.

COOK'S TIP

Make sure that the egg is poured in very slowly and that you stir continuously to create threads of egg and not large pieces.

Peking Duck Soup

Serves 4

INGREDIENTS

125 g/4 1/2 oz lean duck breast meat
225 g/8 oz Chinese leaves (cabbage)
850 ml/1 1/2 pints/3 3/4 cups chicken or duck stock
1 tbsp dry sherry or rice wine
1 tbsp light soy sauce
2 garlic cloves, crushed
pinch of ground star anise
1 tbsp sesame seeds
1 tsp sesame oil
1 tbsp chopped fresh parsley

1 Remove the skin from the duck breast and finely dice the flesh.

2 Using a sharp knife, shred the Chinese leaves (cabbage).

3 Put the stock in a large saucepan and bring to the boil.

4 Add the sherry or rice wine, soy sauce, diced duck meat and shredded Chinese leaves and stir to mix thoroughly. Reduce the heat and leave to simmer for 15 minutes.

5 Stir in the garlic and star anise and cook over a low heat for 10–15 minutes, or until the duck is tender.

6 Dry-fry the sesame seeds in a preheated, heavy-based frying pan (skillet) or wok, stirring.

7 Remove the sesame seeds from the pan and stir them into the soup, together with the sesame oil and parsley.

8 Spoon the soup into warm bowls and serve.

COOK'S TIP

If Chinese leaves (cabbage) are unavailable, use leafy green cabbage instead. You may wish to adjust the quantity to taste, as Western cabbage has a stronger flavour and odour than Chinese leaves (cabbage).

Beef & Vegetable Noodle Soup

Serves 4

INGREDIENTS

225 g/8 oz lean beef
1 garlic clove, crushed
2 spring onions (scallions), chopped
3 tbsp soy sauce
1 tsp sesame oil
225 g/8 oz egg noodles
850 ml/1 $^{1}/_{2}$ pints/3 $^{3}/_{4}$ cups beef stock
3 baby corn cobs, sliced
$^{1}/_{2}$ leek, shredded
125 g/4 $^{1}/_{2}$ oz broccoli, cut into florets (flowerets)
pinch of chilli powder

1 Using a sharp knife, cut the beef into thin strips and place them in a shallow glass bowl.

2 Add the garlic, spring onions (scallions), soy sauce and sesame oil and mix together well, turning the beef to coat. Cover and leave to marinate in the refrigerator for 30 minutes.

3 Cook the noodles in a saucepan of boiling water for 3–4 minutes. Drain the noodles thoroughly and set aside until required.

4 Put the beef stock in a large saucepan and bring to the boil.

5 Add the beef, together with the marinade, the baby corn, leek and broccoli. Cover and leave to simmer over a low heat for 7–10 minutes, or until the beef and vegetables are tender and cooked through.

6 Stir in the noodles and chilli powder and cook for a further 2–3 minutes. Transfer to bowls and serve immediately.

COOK'S TIP

Vary the vegetables used, or use those to hand. If preferred, use a few drops of chilli sauce instead of chilli powder, but remember it is very hot!

Lamb & Rice Soup

Serves 4

INGREDIENTS

- 150 g/5½ oz lean lamb
- 50 g/1¾ oz/¼ cup rice
- 850 ml/1½ pints/3¾ cups lamb stock
- 1 leek, sliced
- 1 garlic clove, thinly sliced
- 2 tsp light soy sauce
- 1 tsp rice wine vinegar
- 1 medium open-cap mushroom, thinly sliced
- salt

1 Using a sharp knife, trim any fat from the lamb and cut the meat into thin strips. Set aside until required.

2 Bring a large pan of lightly salted water to the boil and add the rice. Bring back to the boil, stir once, reduce the heat and cook for 10–15 minutes, until tender. Drain, rinse under cold running water, drain again and set aside until required.

3 Meanwhile, put the lamb stock in a large saucepan and bring to the boil.

4 Add the lamb strips, leek, garlic, soy sauce and rice wine vinegar to the stock in the pan. Reduce the heat, cover and leave to simmer for 10 minutes, or until the lamb is tender and cooked through.

5 Add the mushroom slices and the rice to the pan and cook for a further 2–3 minutes, or until the mushroom is completely cooked through.

6 Ladle the soup into 4 individual warmed soup bowls and serve immediately.

COOK'S TIP

Use a few dried Chinese mushrooms, rehydrated according to the packet instructions and chopped, as an alternative to the open-cap mushroom. Add the Chinese mushrooms with the lamb in step 4.

Fish Soup with Wontons

Serves 4

INGREDIENTS

125 g/4 1/2 oz large, cooked, peeled prawns (shrimp)
1 tsp chopped chives
1 small garlic clove, finely chopped
1 tbsp vegetable oil
12 wonton wrappers
1 small egg, beaten
850 ml/1 1/2 pints/3 3/4 cups fish stock
175 g/6 oz white fish fillet, diced
dash of chilli sauce
sliced fresh red chilli and chives, to garnish

1 Roughly chop a quarter of the prawns (shrimp) and mix together with the chopped chives and garlic.

2 Heat the oil in a preheated wok and stir-fry the prawn (shrimp) mixture for 1–2 minutes. Remove from the heat and set aside to cool completely.

3 Spread out the wonton wrappers on a work surface (counter). Spoon a little of the prawn (shrimp) filling into the centre of each wonton wrapper. Brush the edges of the wonton wrappers with beaten egg and press the edges together, scrunching them to form a 'moneybag' shape. Set aside while you are preparing the soup.

4 Pour the fish stock into a large saucepan and bring to the boil. Add the diced white fish and the remaining prawns (shrimp) and cook for 5 minutes.

5 Season to taste with the chilli sauce. Add the wontons and cook for a further 5 minutes. Spoon into warmed serving bowls, garnish with sliced red chilli and chives and serve immediately.

VARIATION

Replace the prawns (shrimp) with cooked crabmeat for an alternative flavour.

3

4

5

Crab & Ginger Soup

Serves 4

INGREDIENTS

1 carrot, chopped
1 leek, chopped
1 bay leaf
850 ml/1 1/2 pints/3 3/4 cups fish stock
2 medium-sized cooked crabs
2.5-cm/1-inch piece fresh root ginger (ginger root), grated
1 tsp light soy sauce
1/2 tsp ground star anise
salt and pepper

1 Put the carrot, leek, bay leaf and stock into a large pan and bring to the boil. Reduce the heat, cover and simmer for 10 minutes, or until the vegetables are nearly tender.

2 Meanwhile, remove all of the meat from the cooked crabs. Break off the claws, break the joints and remove the meat (you may require a fork or skewer for this). Add the crabmeat to the saucepan of fish stock.

3 Add the ginger, soy sauce and star anise to the fish stock and bring to the boil. Leave to simmer for about 10 minutes, or until the vegetables are tender and the crab is heated through. Season.

4 Ladle the soup into warmed serving bowls and garnish with crab claws. Serve at once.

COOK'S TIP

If fresh crabmeat is unavailable, use drained canned crabmeat or thawed frozen crabmeat instead.

COOK'S TIP

To prepare cooked crab, loosen the meat from the shell by banging the back of the underside with a clenched fist. Stand the crab on its edge with the shell towards you. Force the shell from the body with your thumbs. Twist off the legs and claws and remove the meat. Twist off the tail; discard. Remove and discard the gills. Cut the body in half along the centre and remove the meat. Scoop the brown meat from the shell with a spoon.

Shrimp Dumpling Soup

Serves 4

INGREDIENTS

DUMPLINGS:
- 150 g/5 1/2 oz/1 5/8 cups plain (all-purpose) flour
- 50 ml/2 fl oz/1/4 cup boiling water
- 25 ml/1 fl oz/1/8 cup cold water
- 1 1/2 tsp vegetable oil

FILLING:
- 125 g/4 1/2 oz minced (ground) pork
- 125 g/4 1/2 oz cooked peeled shrimp, chopped
- 50 g/1 3/4 oz canned water chestnuts, drained, rinsed and chopped
- 1 celery stick, chopped
- 1 tsp cornflour (cornstarch)
- 1 tbsp sesame oil
- 1 tbsp light soy sauce

SOUP:
- 850 ml/1 1/2 pints/3 3/4 cups fish stock
- 50 g/1 3/4 oz cellophane noodles
- 1 tbsp dry sherry
- chopped chives, to garnish

1 To make the dumplings, mix the flour, boiling water, cold water and oil in a bowl until a pliable dough is formed.

2 Knead the dough on a floured surface for 5 minutes. Cut the dough into 16 equal-sized pieces.

3 Roll the dough pieces into rounds 7.5 cm/3 inches in diameter.

4 Mix the filling ingredients together.

5 Spoon a little of the filling mixture into the centre of each round. Bring the edges of the dough together, scrunching them up to form a 'moneybag' shape. Twist to seal.

6 Pour the fish stock into a large saucepan and bring to the boil.

7 Add the cellophane noodles, dumplings and dry sherry to the pan and cook for 4–5 minutes, until the noodles and dumplings are tender. Garnish and serve.

COOK'S TIP

Wonton wrappers may be used instead of the dumpling dough if time is short.

3

5

7

Chinese Cabbage Soup

Serves 4

INGREDIENTS

450 g/1 lb pak choi
600 ml/1 pint/$2^1/_2$ cups vegetable stock
1 tbsp rice wine vinegar
1 tbsp light soy sauce
1 tbsp caster (superfine) sugar
1 tbsp dry sherry
1 fresh red chilli, thinly sliced
1 tbsp cornflour (cornstarch)
2 tbsp water

1 Trim the stems of the pak choi and shred the leaves.

2 Heat the stock in a large saucepan. Add the pak choi and cook for 10–15 minutes.

3 Mix the rice wine vinegar, soy sauce, sugar and sherry together. Add this mixture to the stock, together with the sliced chilli. Bring to the boil, lower the heat and cook for 2–3 minutes.

4 Blend the cornflour (cornstarch) with the water to form a smooth paste. Gradually stir the cornflour (cornstarch) mixture into the soup. Cook, stirring constantly, until it thickens. Cook for a further 4–5 minutes. Ladle the soup into individual warm serving bowls and serve immediately.

VARIATION

Boil about 2 tbsp rice in lightly salted water until tender. Drain and spoon into the base of the soup bowls. Ladle the soup over the rice and serve immediately.

COOK'S TIP

Pak choi, *also known as* bok choi *or spoon cabbage, has long, white leaf stalks and fleshy, spoon-shaped, shiny green leaves. There are a number of varieties available, which differ mainly in size rather than flavour.*

1

3

4

Thai-Style Spicy Sweetcorn Fritters

Serves 4

INGREDIENTS

225 g/8 oz/¾ cup canned or frozen sweetcorn
2 red Thai chillies, deseeded and very finely chopped
2 cloves garlic, crushed
10 lime leaves, very finely chopped
2 tbsp fresh coriander (cilantro), chopped
1 large egg
75 g/2¾ oz/½ cup cornmeal
100 g/3½ oz fine green beans, very finely sliced
groundnut oil, for frying

1 Place the sweetcorn, chillies, garlic, lime leaves, coriander (cilantro), egg and cornmeal in a large mixing bowl, and stir to combine.

2 Add the green beans to the ingredients in the bowl and mix well, using a wooden spoon.

3 Divide the mixture into small balls. Flatten the balls of mixture between the palms of your hands to form rounds.

4 Heat a little groundnut oil in a preheated wok.

5 Cook the fritters, in batches, until brown and crispy on the outside, turning occasionally.

6 Transfer the fritters to warm serving plates and serve immediately.

COOK'S TIP

If using canned sweetcorn, drain thoroughly and then rinse and drain thoroughly again before use.

COOK'S TIP

Kaffir lime leaves are dark green, glossy leaves that have a lemony-lime flavour. They can be bought from specialist Asian stores either fresh or dried. Fresh leaves impart the most delicious flavour.

1

2

3

Vegetable Spring Rolls

Serves 4

INGREDIENTS

225 g/8 oz carrots
1 red (bell) pepper
1 tbsp sunflower oil, plus extra for frying
75 g/2¾ oz/¾ cup beansprouts
finely grated zest and juice of 1 lime
1 red chilli, deseeded and very finely chopped
1 tbsp soy sauce
½ tsp arrowroot
2 tbsp chopped fresh coriander (cilantro)
8 sheets filo pastry
25 g/1 oz butter
2 tsp sesame oil

TO SERVE:
chili sauce
spring onion (scallion) tassels

1 Using a sharp knife, cut the carrots into thin sticks. Deseed the red (bell) pepper and cut into thin slices.

2 Heat the sunflower oil in a large preheated wok.

3 Add the carrot, red (bell) pepper and beansprouts and cook, stirring, for 2 minutes, or until softened. Remove the wok from the heat and toss in the lime zest and juice, and the red chilli.

4 Mix the soy sauce with the arrowroot. Stir the mixture into the wok, return to the heat and cook for 2 minutes or until the juices thicken. Add the coriander (cilantro) and mix well.

5 Lay the sheets of filo pastry out on a board. Melt the butter and sesame oil and brush each sheet with the mixture. Spoon a little of the vegetable filling at the top of each sheet, fold over each long side, and roll up.

6 Add a little oil to the wok and cook the spring rolls in batches, for 2–3 minutes, or until crisp and golden. Garnish with spring onion (scallion) tassels and serve hot with chilli dipping sauce.

COOK'S TIP

Use prepared spring roll skins available from Chinese supermarkets or health food shops instead of the filo pastry if liked.

1

4

5

Seven-Spice Aubergines (Eggplant)

Serves 4

INGREDIENTS

450 g/1 lb aubergines (eggplants), wiped
1 egg white
50 g/1¾ oz/3½ tbsp cornflour (cornstarch)
1 tsp salt
1 tbsp Thai seven spice seasoning
oil, for deep-frying

1 Using a sharp knife, slice the aubergines (eggplants) into thin rings.

2 Place the egg white in a small bowl and whip until light and foamy.

3 Mix together the cornflour, salt and seven-spice powder on a large plate.

4 Heat the oil for deep-frying in a large wok.

5 Dip each piece of aubergine (eggplant) into the beaten egg white then coat in the cornflour and seven spice mixture.

6 Deep-fry the coated aubergine (eggplant) slices, in batches, for 5 minutes, or until pale golden and crispy.

7 Transfer the aubergines (eggplants) to absorbent kitchen paper and leave to drain. Transfer to serving plates and serve hot.

COOK'S TIP

Thai seven spice seasoning can be found in the spice racks of most large supermarkets.

COOK'S TIP

The best oil to use for deep-frying is groundnut oil which has a high smoke point and mild flavour, so it will neither burn or taint the food. About 600 ml/1 pint oil is sufficient.

Stir-Fried Tofu (Bean Curd) with Peanut & Chilli Sauce

Serves 4

INGREDIENTS

450 g/1 lb tofu (bean curd), cubed
oil, for frying

SAUCE:
6 tbsp crunchy peanut butter
1 tbsp sweet chilli sauce
150 ml/¼ pint/⅔ cup coconut milk
1 tbsp tomato purée
25 g/1 oz/¼ cup chopped salted peanuts

1 Pat away any moisture from the tofu (bean curd), using absorbent kitchen paper.

2 Heat the oil in a large wok until very hot. Cook the tofu (bean curd), in batches, for about 5 minutes, or until golden and crispy. Remove the tofu (bean curd) with a slotted spoon, transfer to absorbent kitchen paper and leave to drain.

3 To make the sauce, mix together the crunchy peanut butter, sweet chilli sauce, coconut milk, tomato purée and chopped peanuts in a bowl. Add a little boiling water if necessary to achieve a smooth consistency.

4 Transfer the crispy fried tofu (bean curd) to serving plates and serve with the peanut and chilli sauce.

COOK'S TIP

Cook the peanut and chilli sauce in a saucepan over a gentle heat before serving, if you prefer.

COOK'S TIP

Make sure that all of the moisture has been absorbed from the tofu (bean curd) before frying, otherwise it will not crispen.

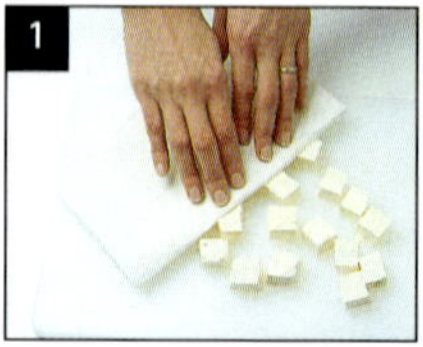

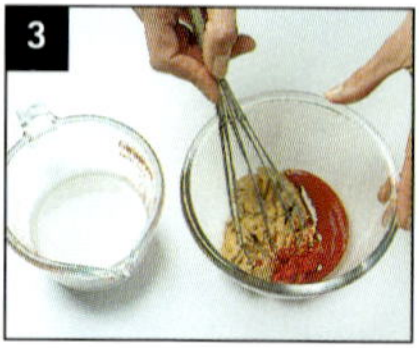

Crispy Seaweed

Serves 4

INGREDIENTS

1 kg/2.4 lb pak choi
groundnut oil, for deep frying (about 850 ml/1½ pints/3¾ cups)
1 tsp salt
1 tbsp caster (superfine) sugar
50 g/1¾ oz/2½ tbsp toasted pine kernels (nuts)

1 Rinse the pak choi leaves under cold running water, then pat dry thoroughly with absorbent kitchen paper.

2 Roll each pak choi leaf up, then slice through thinly so that the leaves are finely shredded.

3 Heat the oil in a large wok. Carefully add the shredded leaves and fry for about 30 seconds or until they shrivel up and become crispy (you may need to do this in about 4 batches).

4 Remove the crispy seaweed from the wok with a slotted spoon and leave to drain on absorbent kitchen paper.

5 Transfer the crispy seaweed to a large bowl and toss with the salt, sugar and pine kernels (nuts). Serve immediately.

VARIATION

Use savoy cabbage instead of the pak choi if it is unavailable, making sure the leaves are well dried before frying.

COOK'S TIP

As a time-saver you can use a food processor to shred the pak choi finely. Make sure you use only the best leaves; sort through the pak choi and discard any tough, outer leaves as these will spoil the overall taste and texture of the dish.

1

2

4

Spicy Chicken Livers with Pak Choi

Serves 4

INGREDIENTS

350 g/12 oz chicken livers
2 tbsp sunflower oil
1 red chilli, deseeded and finely chopped
1 tsp fresh grated ginger
2 cloves garlic, crushed
2 tbsp tomato ketchup
3 tbsp sherry
3 tbsp soy sauce
1 tsp cornflour (cornstarch)
450 g/1 lb pak choi
egg noodles, to serve

1 Using a sharp knife, trim the fat from the chicken livers and slice into small pieces.

2 Heat the oil in a large wok. Add the chicken liver pieces and stir-fry over a high heat for 2–3 minutes.

3 Add the chilli, ginger and garlic and stir-fry for about 1 minute.

4 Mix together the tomato ketchup, sherry, soy sauce and cornflour (cornstarch) in a small bowl and set aside.

5 Add the pak choi to the wok and stir-fry until it just wilts.

6 Add the reserved tomato ketchup mixture to the wok and cook, stirring to mix, until the juices start to bubble.

7 Transfer to serving bowls and serve hot with noodles.

COOK'S TIP

Fresh ginger root will keep for several weeks in a dry, cool place.

COOK'S TIP

Chicken livers are available fresh or frozen from most supermarkets.

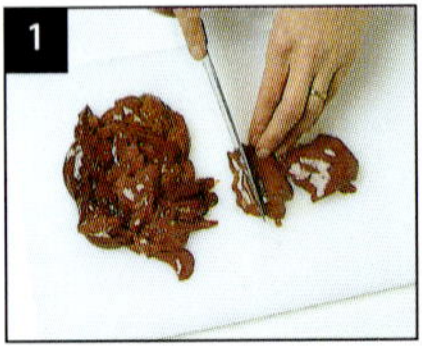

Thai-Style Fish Cakes

Serves 4

INGREDIENTS

450 g/1 lb cod fillets, skinned
2 tbsp fish sauce
2 red Thai chilies, deseeded and very finely chopped
2 cloves garlic, crushed
10 lime leaves, very finely chopped
2 tbsp fresh coriander (cilantro), chopped
1 large egg
25 g/1 oz/¼ cup plain (all-purpose) flour
100 g/3½ oz fine green beans, very finely sliced
groundnut oil, for frying

1 Using a sharp knife, roughly cut the cod fillets into bite-sized pieces.

2 Place the cod pieces in a food processor together with the fish sauce, chillies, garlic, lime leaves, coriander (cilantro), egg and plain (all-purpose) flour. Process until finely chopped and turn out into a large mixing bowl.

3 Add the green beans to the cod mixture and combine.

4 Divide the mixture into small balls. Flatten the balls between the palms of your hands to form rounds.

5 Heat a little oil in a preheated wok. Fry the fish cakes on both sides until brown and crispy on the outside.

6 Transfer the fish cakes to serving plates and serve hot.

VARIATION

Almost any kind of fish fillets and seafood can used in this recipe, try haddock, crab meat or lobster.

COOK'S TIP

Fish sauce is a salty, brown liquid which is a must for authentic flavour. It is used to salt dishes but is milder in flavour than soy sauce. It is available from Asian food stores or health food shops.

2

3

4

Crispy Chilli & Peanut Prawns (Shrimp)

Serves 4

INGREDIENTS

450 g/1 lb king prawns (shrimp) (peeled apart from tail end)
3 tbsp crunchy peanut butter
1 tbsp chilli sauce
10 sheets filo pastry
25 g/1 oz butter, melted
50 g/1¾ oz fine egg noodles
oil, for frying

1 Using a sharp knife, make a small horizontal slit across the back of each prawn (shrimp). Press down on the prawns (shrimps) so that they lie flat.

2 Mix together the peanut butter and chilli sauce in a small bowl. Spread a little of the sauce on to each prawn (shrimp).

3 Cut each pastry sheet in half and brush with melted butter.

4 Wrap each prawn (shrimp) in a piece of pastry, tucking the edges under to fully enclose the prawn (shrimp).

5 Place the egg noodles in a bowl, pour over enough boiling water to cover and leave to stand for 5 minutes. Drain the noodles thoroughly. Use 2–3 cooked noodles to tie around each prawn (shrimp).

6 Heat the oil in a preheated wok. Cook the prawns (shrimp) for 3–4 minutes, or until golden and crispy.

7 Remove the prawns (shrimp) with a slotted spoon, transfer to absorbent kitchen paper and leave to drain. Transfer to serving plates and serve warm.

COOK'S TIP

When using filo pastry, keep any unused pastry covered to prevent it drying out and becoming brittle.

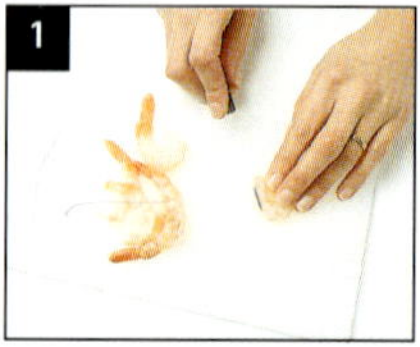

1

2

5

Prawn (Shrimp) Parcels

Serves 4

INGREDIENTS

1 tbsp sunflower oil
1 red (bell) pepper, deseeded and very thinly sliced
75 g/2¾ oz/¾ cup beansprouts
finely grated zest and juice of 1 lime
1 red Thai chili, deseeded and very finely chopped
1 cm/½ inch piece of root ginger, peeled and grated
225 g/8 oz peeled prawns (shrimp)
1 tbsp fish sauce
½ tsp arrowroot
2 tbsp chopped fresh coriander (cilantro)
8 sheets filo pastry
25 g/1 oz/2 tbsp butter
2 tsp sesame oil
oil, for frying
spring onion (scallion) tassels, to garnish
chilli sauce, to serve

1 Heat the sunflower oil in a large preheated wok. Add the red (bell) pepper and beansprouts and stir-fry for 2 minutes, or until the vegetables have softened.

2 Remove the wok from the heat and toss in the lime zest and juice, red chilli, ginger and prawns (shrimp), stirring well.

3 Mix the fish sauce with the arrowroot and stir the mixture into the wok juices. Return the wok to the heat and cook, stirring, for 2 minutes, or until the juices thicken. Toss in the coriander (cilantro) and mix well.

4 Lay the sheets of filo pastry out on a board. Melt the butter and sesame oil and brush each pastry sheet with the mixture.

5 Spoon a little of the prawn (shrimp) filling on to the top of each sheet, fold over each end, and roll up to enclose the filling.

6 Heat the oil in a large wok. Cook the parcels, in batches, for 2–3 minutes, or until crisp and golden. Garnish with spring onion (scallion) tassels and serve hot with a chilli dipping sauce.

COOK'S TIP

If using cooked prawns (shrimp), cook for 1 minute only otherwise the prawns (shrimp) will toughen.

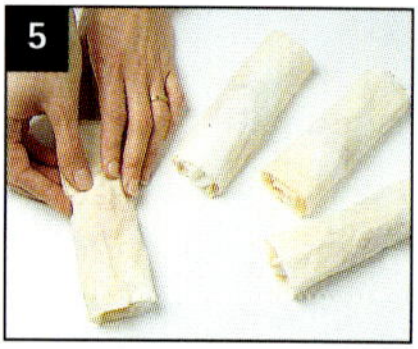

Chinese Prawn (Shrimp) Salad

Serves 4

INGREDIENTS

- 250 g/9 oz fine egg noodles
- 3 tbsp sunflower oil
- 1 tbsp sesame oil
- 1 tbsp sesame seeds
- 150 g/5½ oz/1½ cups beansprouts
- 1 ripe mango, sliced
- 6 spring onions (scallions), sliced
- 75 g/2¾ oz radish, sliced
- 350 g/12 oz peeled cooked prawns (shrimp)
- 2 tbsp light soy sauce
- 1 tbsp sherry

1 Place the egg noodles in a large bowl and pour over enough boiling water to cover. Leave to stand for 10 minutes.

2 Drain the noodles thoroughly and pat away any moisture with absorbent kitchen paper.

3 Heat the sunflower oil in a large wok. Add the noodles and stir-fry for 5 minutes, tossing frequently.

4 Remove the wok from the heat and add the sesame oil, sesame seeds and beansprouts, tossing to mix well.

5 In a separate bowl, mix together the sliced mango, spring onions (scallions), radish, prawns (shrimp), light soy sauce and sherry.

6 Toss the prawn (shrimp) mixture with the noodles or alternatively, arrange the noodles around the edge of a serving plate and pile the prawn (shrimp) mixture into the centre. Serve immediately.

VARIATION

If fresh mango is unavailable, use canned mango slices, rinsed and drained, instead.

Sesame Prawn (Shrimp) Toasts

Serves 4

INGREDIENTS

4 slices medium, thick-sliced white bread
225 g/8 oz cooked peeled prawns (shrimp)
1 tbsp soy sauce
2 cloves garlic, crushed
1 tbsp sesame oil
1 egg
25 g/1 oz/2 tbsp sesame seeds
oil, for frying
sweet chilli sauce, to serve

1 Remove the crusts from the bread if desired, then set the slices of bread aside until required.

2 Place the peeled prawns (shrimp), soy sauce, crushed garlic, sesame oil and egg into a food processor and blend until a smooth paste has formed.

3 Spread the prawn (shrimp) paste evenly over the 4 slices of bread.

4 Sprinkle the sesame seeds over the top of the prawn (shrimp) mixture and press the seeds down with your hands so that they stick to the mixture.

5 Cut each slice in half and in half again to form 4 triangles.

6 Heat the oil in a large wok and deep-fry the toasts, sesame seed-side up, for 4-5 minutes, or until golden and crispy.

7 Remove the toasts with a slotted spoon and transfer to absorbent kitchen paper and leave to drain thoroughly.

8 Serve warm with sweet chilli sauce for dipping.

VARIATION

Add two chopped spring onions (scallions) to the mixture in step 2 for added flavour and crunch.

2

3

4

Prawn & Mushroom Omelette

Serves 4

INGREDIENTS

3 tbsp sunflower oil
2 leeks, trimmed and sliced
350 g/12 oz raw tiger prawns (shrimp)
25 g/1 oz/4 tbsp cornflour (cornstarch)
1 tsp salt
175 g/6 oz mushrooms, sliced
175 g/6 oz/1½ cups beansprouts
6 eggs
deep-fried leeks, to garnish (optional)

1 Heat the sunflower oil in a preheated wok. Add the leeks and stir-fry for 3 minutes.

2 Rinse the prawns (shrimp) under cold running water and then pat dry with absorbent kitchen paper.

3 Mix together the cornflour (cornstarch) and salt in a large bowl.

4 Add the prawns (shrimp) to the cornflour (cornstarch) and salt mixture and toss to coat all over.

5 Add the prawns (shrimp) to the wok and stir-fry for 2 minutes, or until the prawns (shrimp) are almost cooked through.

6 Add the mushrooms and beansprouts to the wok and stir-fry for a further 2 minutes.

7 Beat the eggs with 3 tablespoons of cold water. Pour the egg mixture into the wok and cook until the egg sets, carefully turning over once. Turn the omelette out on to a clean board, divide into 4 and serve hot, garnished with deep-fried leeks (if using).

COOK'S TIP

If liked, divide the mixture into 4 once the initial cooking has taken place in step 6 and cook 4 individual omelettes.

Salt & Pepper Prawns

Serves 4

INGREDIENTS

2 tsp salt
1 tsp black pepper
2 tsp Szechuan peppercorns
1 tsp sugar
450 g/1 lb peeled raw tiger prawns (shrimp)
2 tbsp groundnut oil
1 red chilli, deseeded and finely chopped
1 tsp freshly grated ginger
3 cloves garlic, crushed
spring onions (scallions), sliced, to garnish
prawn (shrimp) crackers, to serve

1 Grind the salt, black pepper and Szechuan peppercorns in a pestle and mortar. Mix the salt and pepper mixture with the sugar and set aside until required.

2 Rinse the prawns (shrimp) under cold running water and pat dry with absorbent kitchen paper.

3 Heat the oil in a preheated wok. Add the prawns (shrimp), chilli, ginger and garlic and stir-fry for 4–5 minutes, or until the prawns (shrimp) are cooked through.

4 Add the salt and pepper mixture to the wok and stir-fry for 1 minute.

5 Transfer to warm serving bowls and garnish with spring onions (scallion). Serve hot with prawn (shrimp) crackers.

COOK'S TIP

Szechuan peppercorns are also known as farchiew. *These wild reddish-brown peppercorns from the Szechuan region of China add an aromatic flavour to a dish.*

COOK'S TIP

Tiger prawns (shrimps) are widely available and are not only colourful and tasty, but they have a meaty texture, too. If cooked tiger prawns (shrimp) are used, add them with the salt and pepper mixture in step 4 – if the cooked prawns (shrimp) are added any earlier they will toughen up and be inedible.

1

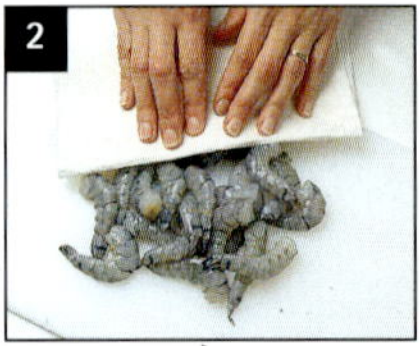
2

3

Spring Rolls

Serves 4

INGREDIENTS

175 g/6 oz cooked pork, chopped
75 g/$2^3/_4$ oz cooked chicken, chopped
1 tsp light soy sauce
1 tsp light brown sugar
1 tsp sesame oil
1 tsp vegetable oil
225 g/8 oz beansprouts
25 g/1 oz canned bamboo shoots, drained, rinsed and chopped
1 green (bell) pepper, seeded and chopped
2 spring onions (scallions), sliced
1 tsp cornflour (cornstarch)
2 tsp water
vegetable oil, for deep-frying

SKINS:
125 g/$4^1/_2$ oz/$1^1/_8$ cups plain (all-purpose) flour
5 tbsp cornflour (cornstarch)
450 ml/16 fl oz/2 cups water
3 tbsp vegetable oil

1 Mix the pork, chicken, soy, sugar and sesame oil. Cover and marinate for 30 minutes. Heat the vegetable oil in a wok. Add the beansprouts, bamboo shoots, (bell) pepper and spring onions (scallions) and stir-fry for 2–3 minutes. Add the meat and the marinade to the wok and stir-fry for 2–3 minutes. Blend the cornflour (cornstarch) with the water and stir the mixture into the wok. Cool.

2 To make the skins, mix the flour and cornflour (cornstarch) and gradually stir in the water, to make a smooth batter. Heat a small, oiled frying pan (skillet). Swirl one-eighth of the batter over the base and cook for 2–3 minutes. Repeat with the remaining batter. Cover with a damp tea towel (dish cloth).

3 Spread out the skins and spoon one-eighth of the filling along the centre of each. Brush the edges with water and fold in the sides, then roll up.

4 Heat the oil for deep-frying in a wok to 180°C/350°F. Cook the spring rolls, in batches, for 2–3 minutes, or until golden and crisp. Remove from the oil with a slotted spoon and drain on absorbent kitchen paper (paper towels). Serve.

Pork Dim Sum

Serves 4

INGREDIENTS

400 g/14 oz minced (ground) pork
2 spring onions (scallions), chopped
50 g/1$^{3}/_{4}$ oz canned bamboo shoots, drained, rinsed and chopped
1 tbsp light soy sauce
1 tbsp dry sherry
2 tsp sesame oil
2 tsp caster (superfine) sugar
1 egg white, lightly beaten
4$^{1}/_{2}$ tsp cornflour (cornstarch)
24 wonton wrappers

1 Mix together the minced (ground) pork, spring onions (scallions), bamboo shoots, soy sauce, dry sherry, sesame oil, sugar and beaten egg white in a bowl until well combined.

2 Stir in the cornflour (cornstarch), mixing well to combine.

3 Spread out the wonton wrappers on a work surface (counter). Place a spoonful of the pork and vegetable mixture in the centre of each wonton wrapper and lightly brush the edges of the wrappers with water.

4 Bring the sides of the wrappers together in the centre of the filling, pinching firmly together.

5 Line a steamer with a clean, damp tea towel (dish cloth) and arrange the wontons inside. Cover and steam for 5–7 minutes, until cooked through. Serve.

COOK'S TIP

Bamboo steamers are designed to rest on the sloping sides of a wok above the water. They are available in a range of sizes.

VARIATION

Use prawns (shrimp), minced (ground) chicken or crabmeat for the filling, with other vegetables, such as chopped carrot, and flavourings, such as chilli or ginger, if you prefer.

Crispy Crab Wontons

Serves 4

INGREDIENTS

175 g/6 oz white crabmeat, flaked
50 g/1 3/4 oz canned water chestnuts, drained, rinsed and chopped
1 small fresh red chilli, chopped
1 spring onion (scallion), chopped
1 tbsp cornflour (cornstarch)
1 tsp dry sherry
1 tsp light soy sauce
1/2 tsp lime juice
24 wonton wrappers
vegetable oil, for deep-frying
sliced lime, to garnish

1 To make the filling, mix together the crabmeat, water chestnuts, chilli, spring onion (scallion), cornflour (cornstarch), sherry, soy sauce and lime juice.

2 Spread out the wonton wrappers on a work surface (counter) and spoon one portion of the filling into the centre of each wonton wrapper.

3 Dampen the edges of the wonton wrappers with a little water and fold them in half to form triangles. Fold the two pointed ends in towards the centre, moisten with a little water to secure and then pinch together to seal.

4 Heat the oil for deep-frying in a wok or deep-fryer to 180°C–190°C/350°F–375°F, or until a cube of bread browns in 30 seconds. Fry the wontons, in batches, for 2–3 minutes, until golden and crisp. Remove the wontons from the oil and leave to drain on kitchen paper (paper towels).

5 Serve the wontons hot, garnished with slices of lime.

COOK'S TIP

Wonton wrappers, available from Chinese supermarkets, are paper-thin squares made from wheat-flour and egg. They can be easily damaged, so handle them carefully. Make sure that the wontons are sealed well and secured before deep-frying to prevent the filling coming out and the wontons unwrapping.

1

3

4

Pot Sticker Dumplings

Serves 4

INGREDIENTS

DUMPLINGS:
- 175 g/6 oz/1 1/2 cups plain (all-purpose) flour
- pinch of salt
- 3 tbsp vegetable oil
- 6–8 tbsp boiling water
- oil, for deep-frying
- 125 ml/4 fl oz/1/2 cup water, for steaming
- sliced spring onions (scallions) and chives, to garnish
- soy sauce or hoisin sauce, to serve

FILLING:
- 150 g/5 1/2 oz lean chicken, very finely chopped
- 25 g/1 oz canned bamboo shoots, drained and chopped
- 2 spring onions (scallions), finely chopped
- 1/2 small red (bell) pepper, seeded and finely chopped
- 1/2 tsp Chinese curry powder
- 1 tbsp light soy sauce
- 1 tsp caster (superfine) sugar
- 1 tsp sesame oil

1 To make the dumplings, mix together the flour and salt in a bowl. Make a well in the centre, add the oil and water and mix well to form a soft dough. Knead the dough on a lightly floured surface, wrap in cling film (plastic wrap) and let stand for 30 minutes.

2 Meanwhile, mix all of the filling ingredients.

3 Divide the dough into 12 equal-sized pieces and roll each piece into a 12.5-cm/5-inch round. Spoon a portion of the filling on to one half of each round. Fold the dough over the filling to form a 'pasty', sealing the edges together.

4 Pour a little oil into a heavy-based frying pan (skillet) and cook the dumplings, in batches, until browned and crisp. Return all of the dumplings to the pan (skillet) and add about 125 ml/4 fl oz/½ cup water. Cover and steam for 5 minutes, or until the dumplings are cooked through. Remove with a slotted spoon and garnish with sliced spring onions (scallions) and chives. Serve with soy or hoisin sauce.

3

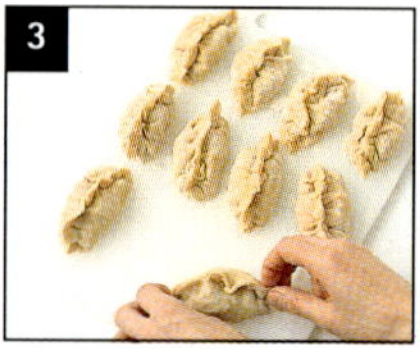
3

4

Pancake Rolls

Serves 4

INGREDIENTS

4 tsp vegetable oil
1–2 garlic cloves, crushed
225 g/8 oz minced (ground) pork
225/8 oz pak choi, shredded
$4^1/_2$ tsp light soy sauce
$^1/_2$ tsp sesame oil
8 spring roll skins, 25 cm/ 10 inches square, thawed if frozen
oil, for deep-frying
chilli sauce (see Cook's Tip, below), to serve

1 Heat the vegetable oil in a preheated wok. Add the garlic and stir-fry for 30 seconds. Add the pork and stir-fry for 2–3 minutes, until just lightly coloured. Add the shredded pak choi, soy sauce and sesame oil to the wok and stir-fry for 2–3 minutes. Remove from the heat and set aside to cool.

2 Spread out the spring roll skins on a work surface (counter) and spoon 2 tbsp of the pork mixture along one edge of each. Roll the skin over once and fold in the sides. Roll up completely to make a sausage shape, brushing the edges with a little water to seal. If you have time, set the pancake rolls aside for 10 minutes to seal firmly.

3 Heat the oil for deep-frying in a wok until almost smoking. Reduce the heat slightly and fry the pancake rolls, in batches if necessary, for 3–4 minutes, until golden. Remove from the oil with a slotted spoon and drain on kitchen paper (paper towels). Serve with chilli sauce.

COOK'S TIP

To make chilli sauce, heat 60 g/2 oz/¼ cup caster (superfine) sugar, 50 ml/2 fl oz/¼ cup rice vinegar and 2 tbsp water in a small pan, stirring until the sugar has dissolved. Bring the mixture to the boil and boil rapidly until a light syrup forms. Remove the pan from the heat and stir in 2 finely chopped, fresh red chillies. Leave the sauce to cool before serving. If you prefer a milder sauce, deseed the chillies before chopping them.

Sweet & Sour Battered Prawns (Shrimp)

Serves 4

INGREDIENTS

16 large raw prawns (shrimp), peeled
1 tsp grated fresh root ginger
1 garlic clove, crushed
2 spring onions (scallions), sliced
2 tbsp dry sherry
2 tsp sesame oil
1 tbsp light soy sauce
vegetable oil, for deep-frying
shredded spring onion (scallion), to garnish

BATTER:
4 egg whites
4 tbsp cornflour (cornstarch)
2 tbsp plain (all-purpose) flour

SAUCE:
2 tbsp tomato purée (tomato paste)
3 tbsp white wine vinegar
4 tsp light soy sauce
2 tbsp lemon juice
3 tbsp light brown sugar
1 green (bell) pepper, seeded and cut into thin matchsticks
½ tsp chilli sauce
300 ml/½ pint/1¼ cups vegetable stock
2 tsp cornflour (cornstarch)

1 Using tweezers, devein the prawns (shrimp), then flatten them with a knife.

2 Place the prawns (shrimp) in a dish and add the ginger, garlic, spring onions (scallions), sherry, oil and soy. Cover and marinate for 30 minutes.

3 Make the batter by beating the egg whites until thick. Fold in the cornflour (cornstarch) and flour to form a light batter.

4 Place all of the sauce ingredients in a pan and bring to the boil. Reduce the heat and leave to simmer for 10 minutes.

5 Remove the prawns (shrimp) from the marinade and dip them into the batter to coat.

6 Heat the oil until almost smoking. Reduce the heat and fry the prawns (shrimp) for 3–4 minutes, until crisp. Serve with the sauce.

1

1

5

Prawn (Shrimp) Rice Paper Parcels

Serves 4

INGREDIENTS

1 egg white
2 tsp cornflour (cornstarch)
2 tsp dry sherry
1 tsp caster (superfine) sugar
2 tsp hoisin sauce
225 g/8 oz peeled, cooked prawns (shrimp)
4 spring onions (scallions), sliced
25 g/1 oz canned water chestnuts, drained, rinsed and chopped
8 Chinese rice paper wrappers
vegetable oil, for deep-frying
hoisin sauce or plum sauce, to serve

1 Lightly beat the egg white, then mix in the cornflour (cornstarch), dry sherry, sugar and hoisin sauce. Add the prawns (shrimp), spring onions (scallions) and water chestnuts, mixing well.

2 Soften the rice papers by dipping them in a bowl of water one at a time. Spread them out on a work surface (counter).

3 Spoon a little of the prawn (shrimp) mixture into the centre of each rice paper and wrap the paper around the filling to make a secure parcel.

4 Heat the oil in a wok until it is almost smoking. Reduce the heat slightly, add the parcels, in batches, and deep-fry for 4–5 minutes, until crisp. Remove from the oil with a slotted spoon and drain on kitchen paper (paper towels).

5 Transfer the parcels to a warmed serving dish and serve immediately with a little hoisin or plum sauce.

COOK'S TIP

Use this filling inside wonton wrappers if the rice paper wrappers are unavailable.

Crab Ravioli

Serves 4

INGREDIENTS

450 g/1 lb crabmeat (fresh or canned and drained)
$^{1}/_{2}$ red (bell) pepper, seeded and finely diced
125 g/4$^{1}/_{2}$ oz Chinese leaves (cabbage), shredded
25 g/1 oz beansprouts, roughly chopped
1 tbsp light soy sauce
1 tsp lime juice
16 wonton wrappers
1 small egg, beaten
2 tbsp peanut oil
1 tsp sesame oil
salt and pepper

1 Mix together the crabmeat, (bell) pepper, Chinese leaves (cabbage), beansprouts, soy sauce and lime juice in a bowl. Season and leave to stand for 15 minutes, stirring occasionally.

2 Spread out the wonton wrappers on a work surface (counter). Spoon a little of the crabmeat mixture into the centre of each wrapper, dividing it equally between them. Reserve the remaining crabmeat filling.

3 Brush the edges of the wrappers with the beaten egg and fold in half, pushing out any air. Press the edges together with your fingers to seal tightly.

4 Heat the peanut oil in a preheated wok or frying pan (skillet). Fry the ravioli, in batches, for 3–4 minutes, turning until browned. Remove with a slotted spoon and drain on paper towels.

5 Heat the remaining filling in the wok or frying pan (skillet) over a gentle heat until hot. Serve the ravioli with the hot filling and sprinkled with sesame oil.

COOK'S TIP

Make sure that the edges of the ravioli are sealed well and that all of the air is pressed out to prevent them from opening during cooking.

2

3

4

Spare Ribs

Serves 4

INGREDIENTS

900 g/2 lb pork spare ribs
2 tbsp dark soy sauce
3 tbsp hoisin sauce
1 tbsp Chinese rice wine or dry sherry
pinch of Chinese five-spice powder
2 tsp dark brown sugar
1/4 tsp chilli sauce
2 garlic cloves, crushed
coriander (cilantro) sprigs, to garnish (optional)

1 Cut the spare ribs into separate pieces if they are joined together. If desired, you can chop them into 5 cm/2-inch lengths, using a cleaver.

2 Mix together the soy sauce, hoisin sauce, Chinese rice wine or sherry, Chinese five-spice powder, dark brown sugar, chilli sauce and garlic.

3 Place the ribs in a shallow dish and pour the mixture over them, turning to coat them well. Cover and marinate in the refrigerator, turning the ribs from time to time, for at least 1 hour.

4 Remove the ribs from the marinade and arrange them in a single layer on a wire rack placed over a roasting tin (pan) half filled with warm water. Brush with the marinade, reserving the remainder.

5 Cook in a preheated oven, at 180°C/350°F/ Gas Mark 4, for 30 minutes. Remove the roasting tin (pan) from the oven and turn the ribs over. Brush with the remaining marinade and return to the oven for a further 30 minutes, or until cooked through. Transfer to a warmed serving dish, garnish with the coriander (cilantro) sprigs (if using) and serve immediately.

COOK'S TIP

Add more hot water to the roasting tin (pan) during cooking if required. Do not allow it to dry out as the water steams the ribs and aids in their cooking.

2

3

4

Honeyed Chicken Wings

Serves 4

INGREDIENTS

450 g/1 lb chicken wings
2 tbsp peanut oil
2 tbsp light soy sauce
2 tbsp hoisin sauce
2 tbsp clear honey
2 garlic cloves, crushed
1 tsp sesame seeds

MARINADE:
1 dried red chilli
1/2–1 tsp chilli powder
1/2–1 tsp ground ginger
finely grated rind of 1 lime

1 To make the marinade, crush the dried chilli in a pestle and mortar. Mix together the crushed dried chilli, chilli powder, ground ginger and lime rind in a small bowl.

2 Rub the spice mixture into the chicken wings with your fingertips. Set aside for at least 2 hours to allow the flavours to penetrate the chicken wings.

3 Heat the peanut oil in a preheated wok.

4 Add the chicken wings to the wok and fry, turning frequently, for 10–12 minutes, until golden and crisp. Drain off any excess oil.

5 Add the soy sauce, hoisin sauce, honey, garlic and sesame seeds to the wok, turning the chicken wings to coat them with the mixture.

6 Reduce the heat and cook for 20–25 minutes, turning the chicken wings frequently, until completely cooked through. Serve hot.

COOK'S TIP

Make the dish in advance and freeze the chicken wings. Defrost thoroughly, cover with foil and heat right through in a moderate oven.

Steamed Duck Dumplings

Serves 4

INGREDIENTS

DUMPLING DOUGH:
300 g/10½ oz/2⅔ cups plain (all-purpose) flour
15 g/½ oz dried yeast
1 tsp caster (superfine) sugar
2 tbsp warm water
175 ml/6 fl oz/¾ cup warm milk

FILLING:
300 g/10½ oz duck breast
1 tbsp light brown sugar
1 tbsp light soy sauce
2 tbsp clear honey
1 tbsp hoisin sauce
1 tbsp vegetable oil
1 leek, finely chopped
1 garlic clove, crushed
1-cm/½-inch piece fresh root ginger (ginger root), grated

1 To make the filling, place the duck breast in a bowl. Mix the sugar, soy sauce, honey and hoisin sauce. Pour the mixture over the duck and marinate for 20 minutes. Remove the duck from the marinade and cook on a rack set over a roasting tin (pan) in a preheated oven, at 200°C/400°F/Gas Mark 6, for 35–40 minutes, or until cooked through. Let cool, remove the meat from the bones and cut into small cubes.

2 Heat the oil in a wok and fry the leek, garlic and ginger for 3 minutes. Mix with the duck meat.

3 To make the dough, sift the flour into a bowl. Mix the yeast, sugar and water in a separate bowl and leave in a warm place for 15 minutes. Pour the yeast mixture into the flour, with the warm milk, mixing to form a firm dough. Knead the dough on a floured surface for 5 minutes. Roll into a sausage shape, 2.5 cm/1 inch in diameter. Cut into 16 pieces, cover and let stand for 20–25 minutes. Flatten the pieces into 10-cm/4-inch rounds. Place a spoonful of filling in the centre of each, draw up the sides to form a 'moneybag' shape and twist to seal.

4 Place the dumplings on a clean, damp tea towel (dish cloth) in the base of a steamer, cover and steam for 20 minutes.

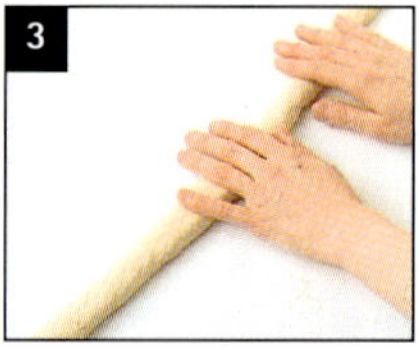

Spinach Meatballs

Serves 4

INGREDIENTS

125 g/4½ oz pork
1 small egg
1-cm/½-inch piece fresh root ginger (ginger root), chopped
1 small onion, finely chopped
1 tbsp boiling water
25 g/1 oz canned bamboo shoots, drained, rinsed and chopped
2 slices smoked ham, chopped
2 tsp cornflour (cornstarch)
450 g/1 lb fresh spinach
2 tsp sesame seeds

SAUCE:
150 ml/¼ pint/⅔ cup vegetable stock
½ tsp cornflour (cornstarch)
1 tsp cold water
1 tsp light soy sauce
½ tsp sesame oil
1 tbsp chopped chives

1 Mince (grind) the pork very finely in a food processor or meat mincer (grinder). Lightly beat the egg in a bowl and stir into the pork.

2 Put the ginger and onion in a separate bowl, add the boiling water and let stand for 5 minutes. Drain and add to the pork mixture with the bamboo shoots, ham and cornflour (cornstarch). Mix well and roll into 12 balls.

3 Wash the spinach and remove the stalks. Blanch in boiling water for 10 seconds and drain well, pressing out as much moisture as possible. Slice the spinach into very thin strips, then mix with the sesame seeds. Spread out the mixture in a shallow baking tin (pan). Roll the meatballs in the mixture to coat.

4 Place the meatballs on a heatproof plate in the base of a steamer. Cover and steam for 8–10 minutes, until cooked through and tender.

5 Meanwhile, make the sauce. Put the stock in a saucepan and bring to the boil. Mix together the cornflour (cornstarch) and water to a smooth paste and stir it into the stock. Stir in the soy sauce, sesame oil and chives. Transfer the cooked meatballs to a warm plate and serve with the sauce.

Steamed Cabbage Rolls

Serves 4

INGREDIENTS

- 8 cabbage leaves, trimmed
- 225 g/8 oz skinless, boneless chicken
- 175 g/6 oz peeled raw or cooked prawns (shrimp)
- 1 tsp cornflour (cornstarch)
- 1/2 tsp chilli powder
- 1 egg, lightly beaten
- 1 tbsp vegetable oil
- 1 leek, sliced
- 1 garlic clove, thinly sliced
- sliced fresh red chilli, to garnish

1 Bring a large saucepan of water to the boil. Blanch the cabbage leaves for 2 minutes. Drain, rinse under cold water and drain again. Pat dry with kitchen paper (paper towels) and spread out on a work surface (counter).

2 Put the chicken and prawns (shrimp) into a food processor and process until finely minced (ground). Alternatively, mince (grind) in a meat mincer (grinder). Transfer to a bowl and add the cornflour (cornstarch), chilli powder and egg, mixing together well.

3 Place 2 tablespoons of the chicken and prawn (shrimp) mixture towards one end of each cabbage leaf. Fold the sides of the cabbage leaf around the filling and roll up to form a firm parcel.

4 Arrange the cabbage parcels, seam-side down, in a single layer on a heatproof plate and cook in a steamer for 10 minutes, or until cooked through.

5 Heat the vegetable oil in a preheated wok. Add the leek and garlic and sauté for 1–2 minutes.

6 Transfer the cabbage parcels to warmed individual serving plates and garnish with red chilli slices. Serve with the leek and garlic sauté.

COOK'S TIP

Use Chinese cabbage or Savoy cabbage for this recipe, choosing leaves of a similar size for the parcels.

1

3

3

Chinese Omelette

Serves 4

INGREDIENTS

8 eggs
225 g/8 oz/2 cups cooked chicken, shredded
12 tiger prawns (jumbo shrimp), peeled and deveined
2 tbsp chopped chives
2 tsp light soy sauce
dash of chilli sauce
2 tbsp vegetable oil

1 Lightly beat the eggs in a large mixing bowl.

2 Add the shredded chicken and tiger prawns (jumbo shrimp) to the eggs, mixing well.

3 Stir in the chopped chives, soy sauce and chilli sauce, mixing well.

4 Heat the oil in a large frying pan (skillet) over a medium heat and add the egg mixture, tilting the pan to coat the base completely. Cook over a medium heat, gently stirring the omelette with a fork, until the surface is just set and the underside is a golden brown colour.

5 When the omelette is set, slide it out of the pan, with the aid of a palette knife (spatula).

6 Cut the omelette into squares or slices to serve.

VARIATION

You could add extra flavour to the omelette by stirring in 3 tbsp finely chopped fresh coriander (cilantro) or 1 tsp sesame seeds with the chives in step 3.

COOK'S TIP

Add peas or other vegetables to the omelette and serve as a main course for 2 people.

Thai-Style Chicken Skewers

Serves 4

INGREDIENTS

4 chicken breasts, skinned and boned
1 onion, peeled and cut into wedges
1 large red (bell) pepper, deseeded
1 large yellow (bell) pepper deseeded
12 kaffir lime leaves
2 tbsp sunflower oil
2 tbsp lime juice
tomato halves, to serve

MARINADE:
1 tbsp Thai red curry paste
150 ml/5 fl oz/$^2/_3$ cup canned coconut milk

1 To make the marinade, place the red curry paste in a small saucepan over a medium heat and cook for 1 minute. Add half of the coconut milk to the saucepan and bring the mixture to the boil. Boil gently for 2–3 minutes until the liquid has reduced by about two-thirds.

2 Remove the saucepan from the heat and stir in the remaining coconut milk. Set the mixture aside to cool.

3 Cut the chicken into 2.5 cm/1 inch pieces. Stir the chicken into the cold marinade, cover and leave to chill for at least 2 hours.

4 Cut the onion into wedges and the (bell) peppers into 2.5 cm/1 inch pieces.

5 Remove the chicken pieces from the marinade and thread them on to skewers, alternating the chicken with the vegetables and lime leaves.

6 Combine the oil and lime juice in a small bowl and brush the mixture over the kebabs (kabobs). Barbecue (grill) the skewers over hot coals, turning and basting for 10–15 minutes until the chicken is cooked through. Barbecue (grill) the tomato halves and serve with the chicken skewers.

Sesame Chicken Brochettes with Cranberry Sauce

Makes 8

INGREDIENTS

4 chicken breasts, skinned and boned
4 tbsp dry white wine
1 tbsp light muscovado sugar
2 tbsp sunflower oil
100 g/3 1/2 oz sesame seeds

salt and pepper

TO SERVE:
boiled new potatoes
green salad leaves

SAUCE:
175 g/6 oz cranberries
150 ml/5 fl oz/2/3 cup cranberry juice drink
2 tbsp light muscovado sugar

1 Cut the chicken into 2.5 cm/1 inch pieces. Put the wine, sugar, oil and salt and pepper to taste in a large bowl, stirring to combine. Add the chicken pieces and toss to coat. Leave to marinate for at least 30 minutes, turning the chicken occasionally.

2 To make the sauce, place the ingredients in a small saucepan and bring slowly to the boil, stirring. Simmer gently for 5–10 minutes until the cranberries are soft and pulpy. Taste and add a little extra sugar if wished. Keep warm or leave to chill.

3 Remove the chicken pieces from the marinade with a perforated spoon. Thread the chicken pieces on to 8 skewers, spacing them slightly apart to ensure even cooking.

4 Barbecue (grill) on an oiled rack over hot coals for 4–5 minutes on each side until just cooked. Brush several times with the marinade.

5 Remove the chicken skewers from the rack and roll in the sesame seeds. Return to the barbecue (grill) and cook for about 1 minute on each side or until the sesame seeds are toasted. Serve with the cranberry sauce, new potatoes and green salad leaves.

Meat & Poultry

Meat is expensive in Far Eastern countries and is eaten in smaller proportions than in the Western world. However, meat is used to its full potential – it is marinated or spiced and combined with other delicious native flavourings to create a wide array of delicious dishes.

In Malaysia, a wide variety of spicy meats is offered, reflecting the many ethnic origins of the population. Chicken is the most frequently used poultry in Malaysia – it is marinated, grilled and stir-fried or cooked in the wok as delicious curries and stews.

In China, poultry, lamb, beef and pork are stir-fried or steamed in the wok and combined with sauces and seasonings such as soy, black bean and oyster sauce, and in Japan where a smaller amount of meat is consumed, it is generally marinated and quickly stir-fried in a wok or simmered in miso stock.

The use of meat in Thailand is similar, but it is leaner and has more flavour due to 'free-range' rearing. Meats differ slightly in that beef is probably taken from the buffalo, and lamb on the menu can often turn out to be goat!

Stir-Fried Ginger Chicken

Serves 4

INGREDIENTS

2 tbsp sunflower oil
1 onion, sliced
175 g/6 oz carrots, cut into thin sticks
1 clove garlic, crushed
350 g/12 oz boneless skinless chicken breasts
2 tbsp fresh ginger, peeled and grated
1 tsp ground ginger
4 tbsp sweet sherry
1 tbsp tomato purée
1 tbsp demerara sugar
100 ml/$3^1/_2$ fl oz/$^1/_3$ cup orange juice
1 tsp cornflour (cornstarch)
1 orange, peeled and segmented
fresh snipped chives, to garnish

1 Heat the oil in a large preheated wok. Add the onion, carrots and garlic and stir-fry over a high heat for 3 minutes or until the vegetables begin to soften.

2 Using a sharp knife, slice the chicken into thin strips. Add the chicken to the wok together with the fresh ginger and ground ginger. Stir-fry for a further 10 minutes, or until the chicken is well cooked through and golden in colour.

3 Mix together the sherry, tomato purée, sugar, orange juice and cornflour (cornstarch) in a bowl. Stir the mixture into the wok and heat through until the mixture bubbles and the juices start to thicken.

4 Add the orange segments and carefully toss to mix.

5 Transfer the stir-fried chicken to warm serving bowls and garnish with freshly snipped chives. Serve immediately.

COOK'S TIP

Make sure that you do not continue cooking the dish once the orange segments have been added in step 4, otherwise they will break up.

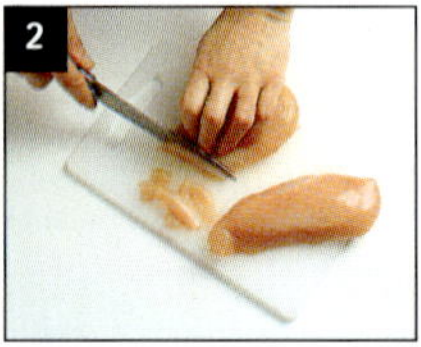

Chicken, Spring Green & Yellow Bean Stir-Fry

Serves 4

INGREDIENTS

2 tbsp sunflower oil
450 g/1 lb skinless, boneless chicken breasts
2 cloves garlic, crushed
1 green (bell) pepper
100 g/3½ oz/1½ cups mangetout (snow peas)
6 spring onions (scallions), sliced, plus extra to garnish
225 g/8 oz spring greens or cabbage, shredded
160 g/5¾ oz jar yellow bean sauce
50 g/1¾ oz/3 tbsp roasted cashew nuts

1 Heat the sunflower oil in a large preheated wok.

2 Using a sharp knife, slice the chicken into thin strips.

3 Add the chicken to the wok together with the garlic. Stir-fry for about 5 minutes or until the chicken is sealed on all sides and beginning to turn golden.

4 Using a sharp knife, deseed the green (bell) pepper and cut into thin strips.

5 Add the mangetout (snow peas), spring onions (scallions), green (bell) pepper strips and spring greens or cabbage to the wok. Stir-fry for a further 5 minutes or until the vegetables are just tender.

6 Stir in the yellow bean sauce and heat through for about 2 minutes or until the mixture starts to bubble.

7 Scatter with the roasted cashew nuts.

8 Transfer the chicken, spring green and yellow bean stir-fry to warm serving plates and garnish with extra spring onions (scallions), if desired. Serve the stir-fry immediately.

COOK'S TIP

Do not add salted cashew nuts to this dish otherwise, combined with the slightly salty sauce, the dish will be very salty indeed.

Chicken, (Bell) Pepper & Orange Stir-Fry

Serves 4

INGREDIENTS

3 tbsp sunflower oil
350 g/12 oz boneless chicken thighs, skinned and cut into thin strips
1 onion, sliced
1 clove garlic, crushed
1 red (bell) pepper, deseeded and sliced
75 g/2¾ oz/1¼ cups mangetout (snow peas)
4 tbsp light soy sauce
4 tbsp sherry
1 tbsp tomato purée
finely grated rind and juice of 1 orange
1 tsp cornflour (cornstarch)
2 oranges
100 g/3½ oz/1 cup beansprouts
cooked rice or noodles, to serve

1 Heat the sunflower oil in a large preheated wok.

2 Add the strips of chicken to the wok and stir-fry for 2–3 minutes or until sealed on all sides.

3 Add the sliced onion, garlic, (bell) pepper and mangetout (snow peas) to the wok. Stir-fry the mixture for a further 5 minutes, or until the vegetables are just becoming tender and the chicken is completely cooked through.

4 Mix together the soy sauce, sherry, tomato purée, orange rind and juice and the cornflour (cornstarch) in a measuring jug.

5 Add the mixture to the wok and cook, stirring, until the juices start to thicken.

6 Using a sharp knife, peel and segment the oranges.

7 Add the orange segments and bean-sprouts to the mixture in the wok and heat for a further 2 minutes.

8 Transfer the stir-fry to serving plates and serve at once with cooked rice or noodles.

COOK'S TIP

Beansprouts are sprouting mung beans and are a regular ingredient in Chinese cooking. They require very little cooking and may even be eaten raw, if wished.

2

4

6

Coconut Chicken Curry

Serves 4

INGREDIENTS

2 tbsp sunflower oil or 25 g/1 oz ghee
450 g/1 lb boneless, skinless chicken thighs or breasts
150 g/5½ oz/1 cup okra
1 large onion, sliced
2 cloves garlic, crushed
3 tbsp mild curry paste
300 ml/½ pint/2¼ cups chicken stock
1 tbsp fresh lemon juice
100 g/3½ oz/½ cup creamed coconut
175 g/6 oz/1¼ cups fresh or canned pineapple, cubed
150 ml/¼ pint/⅔ cup thick, natural yogurt
2 tbsp chopped fresh coriander (cilantro)
freshly boiled rice, to serve

TO GARNISH:
lemon wedges
fresh coriander (cilantro) sprigs

1 Heat the sunflower oil or ghee in a large preheated wok.

2 Using a sharp knife, cut the chicken into bite-sized pieces. Add the chicken to the wok and cook, stirring frequently, until evenly browned.

3 Using a sharp knife, trim the okra.

4 Add the onion, garlic and okra to the wok and cook for a further 2–3 minutes, stirring constantly.

5 Mix the curry paste with the chicken stock and lemon juice and pour over the mixture in the wok. Bring to the boil, cover and leave to simmer for 30 minutes.

6 Coarsley grate the creamed coconut, stir it into the curry and cook for about 5 minutes – the creamed coconut will help to thicken the juices.

7 Add the pineapple, yogurt and coriander (cilantro) and heat through for 2 minutes, stirring.

8 Garnish and serve hot with boiled rice.

COOK'S TIP

Score around the top of the okra with a knife before cooking to release the sticky glue-like substance which is bitter in taste.

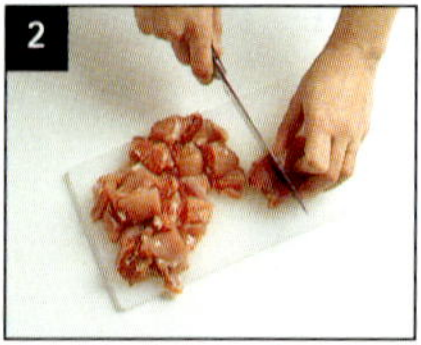

Sweet & Sour Chicken with Mango

Serves 4

INGREDIENTS

1 tbsp sunflower oil
6 skinless, boneless chicken thighs
1 ripe mango
2 cloves garlic, crushed
225 g/8 oz leeks, shredded
100 g/3½ oz/1 cup beansprouts
150 ml/¼ pint/⅔ cup mango juice
1 tbsp white wine vinegar
2 tbsp clear honey
2 tbsp tomato ketchup
1 tsp cornflour (cornstarch)

1 Heat the sunflower oil in a large preheated wok.

2 Using a sharp knife, cut the chicken into bite-sized cubes.

3 Add the chicken to the wok and stir-fry over a high heat for 10 minutes, tossing frequently until the chicken is cooked through and golden in colour.

4 Meanwhile, peel and slice the mango.

5 Add the garlic, leeks, mango and beansprouts to the wok and stir-fry for a further 2–3 minutes, or until softened.

6 Mix together the mango juice, white wine vinegar, clear honey and tomato ketchup with the cornflour (cornstarch) in a measuring jug.

7 Pour the mango juice and cornflour (cornstarch) mixture into the wok and stir-fry for a further 2 minutes, or until the juices start to thicken.

8 Transfer to a warmed serving dish and serve immediately.

COOK'S TIP

Mango juice is available in jars from most supermarkets and is quite thick and sweet. If unavailable, purée and sieve a ripe mango and add a little water to make up the required quantity.

Chicken Stir-Fry with Cumin Seeds & Trio of (Bell) Peppers

Serves 4

INGREDIENTS

450 g/1 lb boneless, skinless chicken breasts
2 tbsp sunflower oil
1 clove garlic, crushed
1 tbsp cumin seeds
1 tbsp grated fresh ginger root
1 red chilli, deseeded and sliced
1 red (bell) pepper, deseeded and sliced
1 green (bell) pepper, deseeded and sliced
1 yellow (bell) pepper, deseeded and sliced
100 g/3½ oz/1 cup beansprouts
350 g/12 oz pak choi or other green leaves
2 tbsp sweet chilli sauce
3 tbsp light soy sauce
deep-fried crispy ginger, to garnish (see Cook's Tip)

1 Using a sharp knife, slice the chicken breasts into thin strips.

2 Heat the oil in a large preheated wok.

3 Add the chicken to the wok and stir-fry for 5 minutes.

4 Add the garlic, cumin seeds, ginger and chilli to the wok, stirring to mix.

5 Add all of the (bell) peppers to the wok and stir-fry for a further 5 minutes.

6 Toss in the beansprouts and pak choi together with the sweet chilli sauce and soy sauce and continue to cook until the pak choi leaves start to wilt.

7 Transfer to warm serving bowls and garnish with deep-fried ginger (see Cook's Tip).

COOK'S TIP

To make the deep-fried ginger garnish, peel and thinly slice a large piece of root ginger, using a sharp knife. Carefully lower the slices of ginger into a wok or small pan of hot oil and cook for about 30 seconds. Remove the deep-fried ginger with a slotted spoon, transfer to sheets of absorbent kitchen paper and leave to drain thoroughly.

Stir-Fried Chicken with Lemon & Sesame Seeds

Serves 4

INGREDIENTS

4 boneless, skinless chicken breasts
1 egg white
25 g/1 oz/2 tbsp sesame seeds
2 tbsp vegetable oil
1 onion, sliced
1 tbsp demerara sugar
finely grated zest and juice of 1 lemon
3 tbsp lemon curd
200 g/7 oz can waterchestnuts
lemon zest, to garnish

1 Place the chicken breasts between 2 sheets of cling film (plastic wrap) and pound with a rolling pin to flatten. Slice the chicken into thin strips.

2 Whisk the egg white until light and foamy.

3 Dip the chicken strips into the egg white, then into the sesame seeds until coated evenly.

4 Heat the oil in a large preheated wok.

5 Add the onion to the wok and stir-fry for 2 minutes or until just softened.

6 Add the sesame-coated chicken to the wok and continue stir-frying for 5 minutes, or until the chicken turns golden.

7 Mix together the sugar, lemon zest, lemon juice and the lemon curd and add the mixture to the wok. Allow the lemon mixture to bubble slightly without stirring.

8 Drain the waterchestnuts and slice them thinly, using a sharp knife. Add the waterchestnuts to the wok and heat through for 2 minutes. Transfer to serving bowls, garnish with lemon zest and serve hot.

COOK'S TIP

Waterchestnuts are commonly added to Chinese recipes for their crunchy texture as they do not have a great deal of flavour.

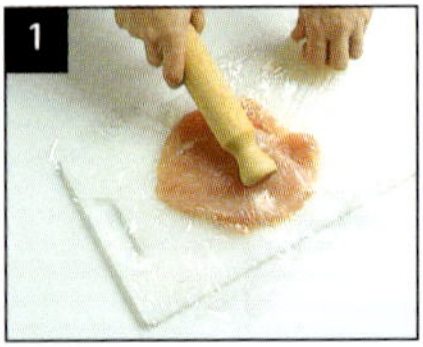
1

3

8

Thai Red Chicken with Cherry Tomatoes

Serves 4

INGREDIENTS

- 1 tbsp sunflower oil
- 450 g/1 lb boneless, skinless chicken
- 2 cloves garlic, crushed
- 2 tbsp Thai red curry paste
- 2 tbsp fresh grated galangal or root ginger
- 1 tbsp tamarind paste
- 4 lime leaves
- 225 g/8 oz sweet potato
- 600 ml/1 pint/2½ cups coconut milk
- 225 g/8 oz cherry tomatoes, halved
- 3 tbsp chopped fresh coriander (cilantro)
- cooked jasmine or Thai fragrant rice, to serve

1 Heat the sunflower oil in a large preheated wok.

2 Thinly slice the chicken. Add the chicken to the wok and stir-fry for 5 minutes.

3 Add the garlic, curry paste, galangal or root ginger, tamarind and lime leaves to the wok and stir-fry for 1 minute.

4 Using a sharp knife, peel and dice the sweet potato.

5 Add the coconut milk and sweet potato to the mixture in the wok and bring to the boil. Allow to bubble over a medium heat for 20 minutes, or until the juices start to thicken and reduce.

6 Add the cherry tomatoes and coriander (cilantro) to the curry and cook for a further 5 minutes, stirring occasionally. Transfer to serving plates and serve hot with cooked jasmine or Thai fragrant rice.

COOK'S TIP

Galangal is a spice very similar to ginger and is used to replace the latter in Thai cuisine. It can be bought fresh from Oriental food stores but is also available dried and as a powder. The fresh root, which is not as pungent as ginger, needs to be peeled before slicing.

Peppered Chicken Stir-Fried with Sugar Snap Peas

Serves 4

INGREDIENTS

2 tbsp tomato ketchup
2 tbsp soy sauce
450 g/1 lb boneless, skinless chicken breasts
2 tbsp crushed mixed peppercorns
2 tbsp sunflower oil
1 red (bell) pepper
1 green (bell) pepper
175 g/6 oz/2½ cups sugar snap peas
2 tbsp oyster sauce

1 Mix the tomato ketchup with the soy sauce in a bowl.

2 Using a sharp knife, slice the chicken into thin strips. Toss the chicken in the tomato ketchup and soy sauce mixture.

3 Sprinkle the crushed peppercorns on to a plate. Dip the coated chicken in the peppercorns until evenly coated.

4 Heat the sunflower oil in a preheated wok.

5 Add the chicken to the wok and stir-fry for 5 minutes.

6 Deseed and slice the (bell) peppers.

7 Add the (bell) peppers to the wok together with the sugar snap peas and stir-fry for a further 5 minutes.

8 Add the oyster sauce and allow to bubble for 2 minutes. Transfer to serving bowls and serve immediately.

VARIATION

Use mangetout (snow peas) instead of sugar snap peas, if you prefer.

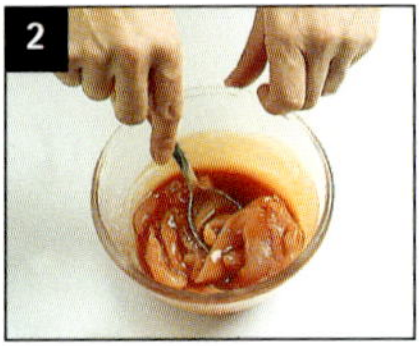

Honey & Soy Stir-Fried Chicken with Beansprouts

Serves 4

INGREDIENTS

2 tbsp clear honey
3 tbsp light soy sauce
1 tsp Chinese five-spice powder
1 tbsp sweet sherry
1 clove garlic, crushed
8 chicken thighs
1 tbsp sunflower oil
1 red chilli
100 g/3½ oz/1¼ cups baby corn cobs, halved
8 spring onions (scallions), sliced
150 g/5½ oz/1½ cups beansprouts

1 Mix together the honey, soy sauce, Chinese five-spice powder, sherry and garlic in a large bowl.

2 Using a sharp knife, make 3 slashes in the skin of each chicken thigh. Brush the honey and soy marinade over the chicken thighs, cover and leave to stand for at least 30 minutes.

3 Heat the oil in a large preheated wok.

4 Add the chicken to the wok and cook over a fairly high heat for 12–15 minutes, or until the chicken browns and the skin begins to crispen. Remove the chicken with a slotted spoon.

5 Using a sharp knife, deseed and very finely chop the chilli.

6 Add the chilli, corn cobs, spring onions (scallions) and beansprouts to the wok and stir-fry for 5 minutes.

7 Return the chicken to the wok and mix all of the ingredients together until completely heated through.

8 Transfer to serving plates and serve immediately.

COOK'S TIP

Chinese five-spice powder is found in most large supermarkets and is a blend of aromatic spices.

1

2

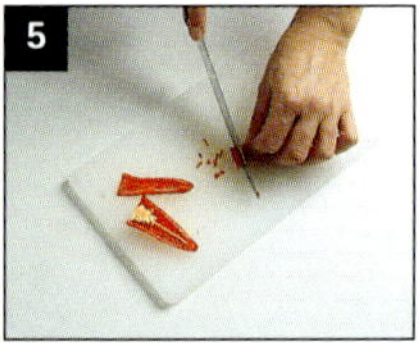
5

Stir-Fried Chicken with Cashew Nuts & Yellow Bean Sauce

Serves 4

INGREDIENTS

450 g/1 lb boneless chicken breasts
2 tbsp vegetable oil
1 red onion, sliced
175 g/6 oz/1½ cups flat mushrooms, sliced
100 g/3½ oz/⅓ cup cashew nuts
75 g/2¾ oz jar yellow bean sauce
fresh coriander (cilantro), to garnish
egg fried rice or plain boiled rice, to serve

1 Using a sharp knife, remove the excess skin from the chicken breasts if desired. Cut the chicken into small, bite-sized chunks.

2 Heat the vegetable oil in a preheated wok.

3 Add the chicken to the wok and stir-fry for 5 minutes.

4 Add the red onion and mushrooms to the wok and continue to stir-fry for a further 5 minutes.

5 Place the cashew nuts on a baking tray (cookie sheet) and toast under a preheated medium grill (broiler) until just browning – this brings out their flavour.

6 Toss the toasted cashew nuts into the wok together with the yellow bean sauce. Allow the sauce to bubble for 2–3 minutes.

7 Transfer to warm serving bowls and garnish with fresh coriander (cilantro). Serve hot with egg fried rice or plain boiled rice.

COOK'S TIP

Chicken thighs could be used instead of the chicken breasts for a more economical dish.

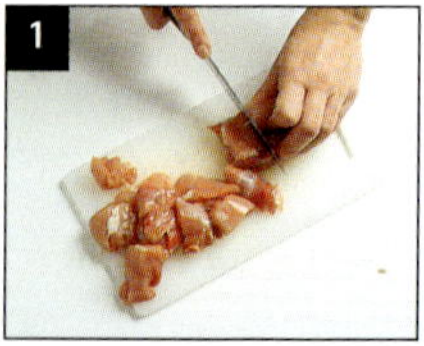

Stir-Fried Chicken with Chilli & Crispy Basil

Serves 4

INGREDIENTS

8 chicken drumsticks
2 tbsp soy sauce
1 tbsp sunflower oil
1 red chilli
100 g/3½ oz carrots, cut into thin sticks
6 celery stalks, cut into sticks
3 tbsp sweet chilli sauce
oil, for frying
about 50 fresh basil leaves

1 Remove the skin from the chicken drumsticks. Make 3 slashes in each drumstick. Brush the drumsticks with the soy sauce.

2 Heat the oil in a preheated wok and fry the drumsticks for 20 minutes, turning frequently, until they are cooked through.

3 Deseed and finely chop the chilli. Add the chilli, carrots and celery to the wok and cook for a further 5 minutes. Stir in the chilli sauce, cover and allow to bubble gently whilst preparing the basil leaves.

4 Heat a little oil in a heavy based pan. Carefully add the basil leaves – stand well away from the pan and protect your hand with a tea towel (dish cloth) as they may spit a little. Cook for about 30 seconds or until they begin to curl up but not brown. Transfer to kitchen paper to drain.

5 Arrange the cooked chicken, vegetables and pan juices on to a warm serving plate and garnish with the deep-fried crispy basil leaves.

COOK'S TIP

Basil has a very strong flavour which is perfect with chicken and Chinese flavourings. You could use baby spinach instead of the basil, if you prefer.

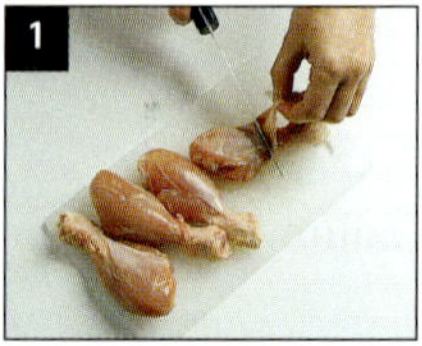

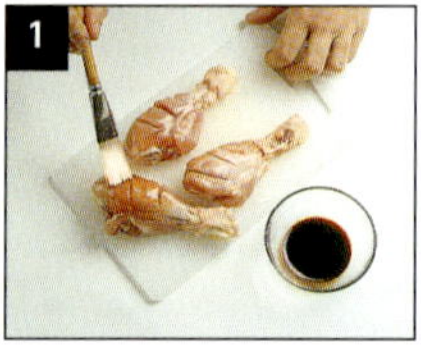

Stir-Fried Garlic Chicken with Coriander (Cilantro) & Lime

Serves 4

INGREDIENTS

4 large skinless, boneless chicken breasts
50 g/1$^{3}/_{4}$ oz/3 tbsp garlic butter, softened
3 tbsp chopped fresh coriander (cilantro)
1 tbsp sunflower oil
finely grated zest and juice of 2 limes
25 g/1 oz/4 tbsp palm sugar or demerara sugar
boiled rice, to serve

1 Place each chicken breast between 2 sheets of cling film (plastic wrap) and pound with a rolling pin until flattened to about 1 cm/½ inch thick.

2 Mix together the garlic butter and coriander (cilantro) and spread over each flattened chicken breast. Roll up like a Swiss roll and secure with a cocktail stick.

3 Heat the oil in a wok. Add the chicken rolls and cook, turning, for 15–20 minutes or until cooked through.

4 Remove the chicken from the wok and transfer to a board. Cut each chicken roll into slices.

5 Add the lime zest, juice and sugar to the wok and heat gently, stirring, until the sugar has dissolved. Raise the heat and allow to bubble for 2 minutes.

6 Arrange the chicken on warmed serving plates and spoon the pan juices over to serve.

7 Garnish with extra coriander (cilantro) if desired.

COOK'S TIP

Be sure to check that the chicken is cooked through before slicing and serving. Cook over a gentle heat so as not to overcook the outside, while the inside remains raw.

2

2

3

Stir-Fried Chicken with Cumin Seeds & Aubergine (Eggplant)

Serves 4

INGREDIENTS

5 tbsp sunflower oil
2 cloves garlic, crushed
1 tbsp cumin seeds
1 tbsp mild curry powder
1 tbsp paprika
450 g/1 lb boneless, skinless chicken breasts
1 large aubergine (eggplant), cubed
4 tomatoes, cut into quarters
100 ml/3½ fl oz/⅓ cup chicken stock
1 tbsp fresh lemon juice
½ tsp salt
150 ml/¼ pint/⅔ cup natural yogurt
1 tbsp chopped fresh mint

1 Heat 2 tablespoons of the sunflower oil in a large preheated wok.

2 Add the garlic, cumin seeds, curry powder and paprika to the wok and stir-fry for 1 minute.

3 Using a sharp knife, thinly slice the chicken breasts into sections.

4 Add the rest of the oil to the wok and stir-fry the chicken for 5 minutes.

5 Add the aubergine (eggplant) cubes, tomatoes and chicken stock and bring to the boil. Reduce the heat and leave to simmer for about 20 minutes.

6 Stir in the lemon juice, salt and yogurt and cook over a gentle heat for a further 5 minutes, stirring occasionally.

7 Scatter with chopped fresh mint and transfer to serving bowls. Serve immediately.

COOK'S TIP

Once the yogurt has been added, do not boil the sauce as the yogurt will curdle.

2

4

5

Speedy Peanut Pan-Fry

Serves 4

INGREDIENTS

300 g/10½ oz/2 cups courgettes (zucchini)
250 g/9 oz/1⅓ cups baby sweetcorn (baby corn)
300 g/10½ oz/3¾ cups button mushrooms
250 g/9 oz/3 cups thread egg noodles
2 tbsp corn oil
1 tbsp sesame oil
8 boneless chicken thighs or 4 breasts, sliced thinly
350 g/12 oz/1½ cups bean sprouts
4 tbsp smooth peanut butter
2 tbsp soy sauce
2 tbsp lime or lemon juice
60 g/2 oz/½ cup roasted peanuts
pepper
coriander (cilantro), to garnish

1 Using a sharp knife, trim and thinly slice the courgettes (zucchini), baby sweetcorn (baby corn) and button mushrooms.

2 Bring a large pan of lightly salted boiling water to the boil and cook the noodles for 3–4 minutes. Meanwhile, heat the corn oil and sesame oil in a large frying pan (skillet) or wok and fry the chicken over a fairly high heat for 1 minute.

3 Add the sliced courgettes (zucchini), corn (baby corn) and button mushrooms and stir-fry for 5 minutes.

4 Add the bean sprouts, peanut butter, soy sauce, lime or lemon juice and pepper, then cook for a further 2 minutes.

5 Drain the noodles, transfer to a serving dish and scatter with the peanuts. Serve with the stir-fried chicken and vegetables, garnished with a sprig of fresh coriander (cilantro).

COOK'S TIP

Try serving this stir-fry with rice sticks. These are broad, pale, translucent ribbon noodles made from ground rice.

1

3

4

Hoisin Duck with Leek & Stir-Fried Cabbage

Serves 4

INGREDIENTS

4 duck breasts
350 g/12 oz green cabbage, thinly shredded
225 g/8 oz leeks, sliced
finely grated zest of 1 orange
6 tbsp oyster sauce
1 tsp toasted sesame seeds, to serve

1 Heat a large wok and dry-fry the duck breasts, with the skin on, for 5 minutes on each side (you may need to do this in 2 batches).

2 Remove the duck breasts from the wok and transfer to a clean board. Using a sharp knife, cut the duck breasts into thin slices.

3 Remove all but 1 tablespoon of the fat from the duck left in the wok; discard the rest.

4 Using a sharp knife, thinly shred the green cabbage.

5 Add the leeks, green cabbage and orange zest to the wok and stir-fry for 5 minutes, or until the vegetables have softened.

6 Return the duck to the wok and heat through for 2–3 minutes.

7 Drizzle the oyster sauce over the top of the duck, toss well to combine and then heat through.

8 Scatter with toasted sesame seeds and serve hot.

VARIATION

Use Chinese leaves for a lighter, sweeter flavour instead of the green cabbage, if you prefer.

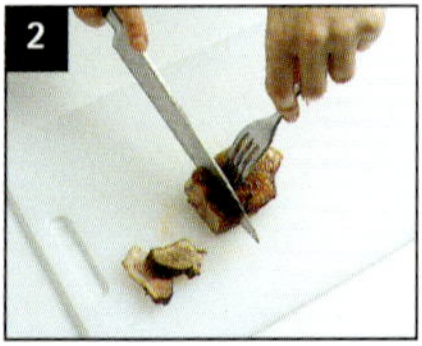

Duck with Baby Corn Cobs & Pineapple

Serves 4

INGREDIENTS

4 duck breasts
1 tsp Chinese five-spice powder
1 tbsp cornflour (cornstarch)
1 tbsp chilli oil
225 g/8 oz baby onions, peeled
2 cloves garlic, crushed
100 g/3½ oz/1 cup baby corn cobs
175 g/6 oz/1¼ cups canned pineapple chunks
6 spring onions (scallions), sliced
100 g/3½ oz/1 cup beansprouts
2 tbsp plum sauce

1 Remove any skin from the duck breasts. Cut the duck breasts into thin slices.

2 Mix together the five-spice powder and the cornflour (cornstarch) in a large bowl.

3 Toss the duck in the five-spice powder and cornflour (cornstarch) mixture until well coated.

4 Heat the oil in a preheated wok. Stir-fry the duck for 10 minutes, or until just begining to crispen around the edges.

5 Remove the duck from the wok and set aside until required.

6 Add the onions and garlic to the wok and stir-fry for 5 minutes, or until the onions have softened.

7 Add the baby corn cobs to the wok and stir-fry for a further 5 minutes.

8 Add the pineapple, spring onions (scallions) and beansprouts and stir-fry for 3–4 minutes. Stir in the plum sauce.

9 Return the cooked duck to the wok and toss until well mixed. Transfer to warm serving dishes and serve hot.

COOK'S TIP

Buy pineapple chunks in natural juice rather than syrup for a fresher flavour. If you can only obtain pineapple in syrup, rinse it in cold water and drain thoroughly before using.

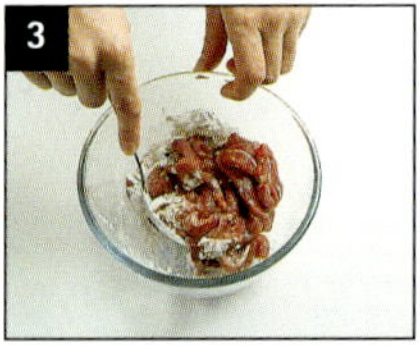

Stir-Fried Turkey with Cranberry Glaze

Serves 2–3

INGREDIENTS

1 turkey breast
2 tbsp sunflower oil
15 g/½ oz/2 tbsp stem ginger
50 g/1¾ oz/½ cup fresh or frozen cranberries
100 g/3½ oz/¼ cup canned chestnuts
4 tbsp cranberry sauce
3 tbsp light soy sauce
salt and pepper

1 Remove any skin from the turkey breast. Using a sharp knife, thinly slice the turkey breast.

2 Heat the oil in a large preheated wok.

3 Add the turkey to the wok and stir-fry for 5 minutes, or until cooked through.

4 Using a sharp knife, finely chop the stem ginger.

5 Add the ginger and the cranberries to the wok and stir-fry for 2–3 minutes or until the cranberries have softened.

6 Add the chestnuts, cranberry sauce and soy sauce, season to taste with salt and pepper and allow to bubble for 2–3 minutes.

7 Transfer to warm serving dishes and serve immediately.

COOK'S TIP

If you wish, use a turkey escalope instead of the breast for really tender, lean meat.

COOK'S TIP

It is very important that the wok is very hot before you stir-fry. Test by holding your hand flat about 7.5 cm/3 inches above the base of the interior – you should be able to feel the heat radiating from it.

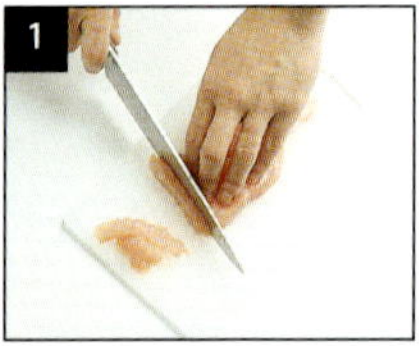

1

3

4

Stir-Fried Beef & Vegetables with Sherry & Soy Sauce

Serves 4

INGREDIENTS

2 tbsp sunflower oil
350 g/12 oz fillet of beef, sliced
1 red onion, sliced
175 g/6 oz courgettes (zucchini), sliced diagonally
175 g/6 oz carrots, thinly sliced
1 red (bell) pepper, deseeded and sliced
1 small head Chinese leaves, shredded
150 g/5½ oz/1½ cups beansprouts
225 g/8 oz can bamboo shoots, drained
150 g/5½ oz/½ cup cashew nuts, toasted

SAUCE:
3 tbsp medium sherry
3 tbsp light soy sauce
1 tsp ground ginger
1 clove garlic, crushed
1 tsp cornflour (cornstarch)
1 tbsp tomato purée

1 Heat the sunflower oil in a large preheated wok.

2 Add the beef and onion to the wok and stir-fry for 4–5 minutes or until the onion begins to soften and the meat is just browning.

3 Using a sharp knife, trim the courgette (zucchini) and slice diagonally.

4 Add the carrots, (bell) pepper, and courgettes (zucchini) and stir-fry for 5 minutes.

5 Toss in the Chinese leaves, beansprouts and bamboo shoots and heat through for 2–3 minutes, or until the leaves are just beginning to wilt.

6 Scatter the cashews nuts over the stir-fry.

7 To make the sauce, mix together the sherry, soy sauce, ground ginger, garlic, cornflour (cornstarch) and tomato purée. Pour the sauce over the stir-fry and toss until well combined. Allow the sauce to bubble for 2–3 minutes or until the juices start to thicken.

8 Transfer to warm serving dishes and serve at once.

2

3

4

Chilli Beef Stir-Fry

Serves 4

INGREDIENTS

450 g/1 lb lean rump steak
2 cloves garlic, crushed
1 tsp chilli powder
½ tsp salt
1 tsp ground coriander
1 ripe avocado
30 ml/2 tbsp sunflower oil
425 g/15 oz can red kidney beans, drained
175 g/6 oz cherry tomatoes, halved
1 large packet tortilla chips
shredded iceberg lettuce
chopped fresh coriander (cilantro), to serve

1 Using a sharp knife, slice the beef into thin strips.

2 Place the garlic, chilli powder, salt and ground coriander in a large bowl and mix until well combined.

3 Add the strips of beef to the marinade and toss well to coat all over.

4 Using a sharp knife, peel the avocado. Slice the avocado lengthways and then crossways to form small dice.

5 Heat the oil in a large preheated wok. Add the beef and stir-fry for 5 minutes, tossing frequently.

6 Add the kidney beans, tomatoes and avocado and heat through for 2 minutes.

7 Arrange a bed of tortilla chips and iceberg lettuce around the edge of a large serving plate and spoon the beef mixture into the centre. Alternatively, serve the tortilla chips and iceberg lettuce separately.

8 Garnish with chopped fresh coriander (cilantro) and serve immediately.

COOK'S TIP

Serve this dish immediately as avocado tends to discolour quickly. Once you have cut the avocado into dice, sprinkle it with a little lemon juice to prevent discolouration.

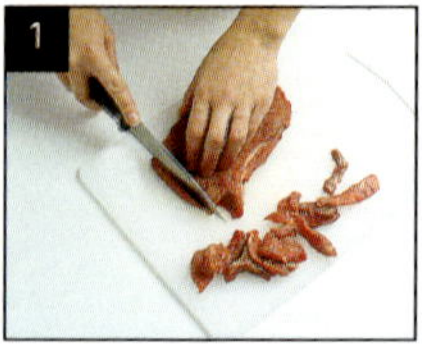

Marinated Beef Stir-Fry with Bamboo Shoots & Mangetout (Snow Peas)

Serves 4

INGREDIENTS

350 g/12 oz rump steak
3 tbsp dark soy sauce
1 tbsp tomato ketchup
2 cloves garlic, crushed
1 tbsp fresh lemon juice
1 tsp ground coriander
2 tbsp vegetable oil
175 g/6 oz/2¾ cups mangetout (snow peas)
200 g/7 oz can bamboo shoots
1 tsp sesame oil

1 Using a sharp knife, thinly slice the meat.

2 Place the meat in a non metallic dish together with the dark soy sauce, tomato ketchup, garlic, lemon juice and ground coriander. Mix well so that all of the meat is coated in the marinade, cover and leave for at least 1 hour.

3 Heat the vegetable oil in a preheated wok. Add the meat to the wok and stir-fry for 2–4 minutes (depending on how well cooked you like your meat) or until cooked through.

4 Add the mangetout (snow peas) and bamboo shoots to the mixture in the wok and stir-fry over a high heat, tossing frequently, for a further 5 minutes.

5 Drizzle with the sesame oil and toss well to combine.

6 Transfer to serving dishes and serve hot.

COOK'S TIP

Leave the meat to marinate for at least 1 hour in order for the flavour to penetrate and increase the tenderness of the meat. If possible, leave for a little longer for a fuller flavour to develop.

Stir-Fried Beef with Baby Onions & Palm Sugar

Serves 4

INGREDIENTS

450 g/1 lb fillet beef
2 tbsp soy sauce
1 tsp chilli oil
1 tbsp tamarind paste
2 tbsp palm sugar or demerara sugar
2 cloves garlic, crushed
2 tbsp sunflower oil
225 g/8 oz baby onions
2 tbsp chopped fresh coriander (cilantro)

1 Using a sharp knife, thinly slice the beef.

2 Place the slices of beef in a large, shallow non-metallic dish.

3 Mix together the soy sauce, chilli oil, tamarind paste, palm sugar and garlic.

4 Spoon the palm sugar mixture over the beef. Toss well to coat the beef in the mixture, cover and leave to marinate for at least 1 hour.

5 Heat the sunflower oil in a preheated wok.

6 Peel the onions and cut them in half. Add the onions to the wok and stir-fry for 2–3 minutes, or until just browning.

7 Add the beef and marinade juices to the wok and stir-fry over a high heat for about 5 minutes.

8 Scatter with chopped fresh coriander (cilantro) and serve at once.

COOK'S TIP

Use the chilli oil carefully as it is very hot and could easily spoil the dish if too much is added.

Sweet Potato Stir-Fry with Coconut Beef

Serves 4

INGREDIENTS

2 tbsp vegetable oil
350 g/12 oz rump steak
2 cloves garlic
1 onion, sliced
350 g/12 oz sweet potato
2 tbsp Thai red curry paste
300 ml/½ pint/1¼ cups coconut milk
3 limes leaves
cooked jasmine rice, to serve

1 Heat the vegetable oil in a large preheated wok.

2 Using a sharp knife, thinly slice the beef. Add the beef to the wok and stir-fry for about 2 minutes or until sealed on all sides.

3 Add the garlic and the onion to the wok and stir-fry for a further 2 minutes.

4 Using a sharp knife, peel and dice the sweet potato.

5 Add the sweet potato to the wok with the curry paste, coconut milk and lime leaves and bring to a rapid boil. Reduce the heat, cover and leave to simmer for about 15 minutes or until the potatoes are tender.

6 Remove the lime leaves and transfer the stir-fry to warm serving bowls. Serve hot with cooked jasmine rice.

COOK'S TIP

If you cannot obtain lime leaves, use grated lime zest instead.

COOK'S TIP

There are two basic curry pastes used in Thai cuisine – red and green, depending on whether they are made from red or green chillies.

Beef with Green Peas & Black Bean Sauce

Serves 4

INGREDIENTS

450 g/1 lb rump steak
2 tbsp sunflower oil
1 onion
2 cloves garlic, crushed
150 g/5½ oz/1 cup fresh or frozen peas
160 g/5¾ oz jar black bean sauce
150 g/5½ oz Chinese leaves, shredded

1 Using a sharp knife, trim away any fat from the beef. Cut the beef into thin slices.

2 Heat the sunflower oil in a large preheated wok.

3 Add the beef to the wok and stir-fry for 2 minutes.

4 Using a sharp knife, peel and slice the onion.

5 Add the onion, garlic and peas to the wok and stir-fry for a further 5 minutes.

6 Add the black bean sauce and Chinese leaves to the mixture in the wok and heat through for a further 2 minutes or until the Chinese leaves have wilted.

7 Transfer to warm serving bowls and serve immediately.

COOK'S TIP

Buy a chunky black bean sauce if you can for the best texture and flavour.

COOK'S TIP

Chinese leaves are now widely available. They look like a pale, elongated head of lettuce with light green, tightly packed crinkly leaves.

1
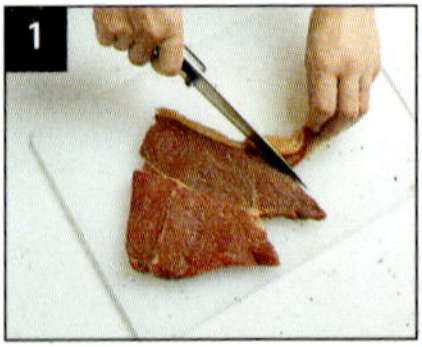

3

4
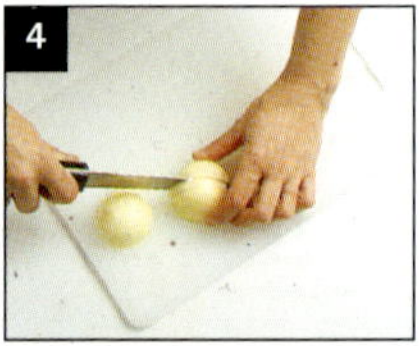

Stir-Fried Garlic Beef with Sesame Seeds & Soy Sauce

Serves 4

INGREDIENTS

25 g/1 oz/2 tbsp sesame seeds
450 g/1 lb beef fillet
2 tbsp vegetable oil
1 green (bell) pepper, deseeded and thinly sliced
4 cloves garlic, crushed
2 tbsp dry sherry
4 tbsp soy sauce
6 spring onions (scallions), sliced
noodles, to serve

1 Heat a large wok until it is very hot.

2 Add the sesame seeds to the wok and dry fry, stirring, for 1–2 minutes or until they just begin to brown. Remove the sesame seeds from the wok and set aside until required.

3 Using a sharp knife, thinly slice the beef.

4 Heat the oil in the wok. Add the beef and stir-fry for 2–3 minutes or until sealed on all sides.

5 Add the sliced (bell) pepper and crushed garlic to the wok and continue stir-frying for 2 minutes.

6 Add the sherry and soy sauce to the wok together with the spring onions (scallions) and allow to bubble, stirring occasionally, for about 1 minute.

7 Transfer the garlic beef stir-fry to warm serving bowls and scatter with the dry-fried sesame seeds. Serve hot with boiled noodles.

COOK'S TIP

You can spread the sesame seeds out on a baking tray (cookie sheet) and toast them under a preheated grill (broiler) until browned all over, if you prefer.

Beef Teriyaki

Serves 4

INGREDIENTS

450 g/1 lb extra thin beef steaks
8 spring onions (scallions), trimmed and cut into short lengths
1 yellow (bell) pepper, deseeded and cut into chunks
green salad, to serve

SAUCE:
1 tsp cornflour (cornstarch)
2 tbsp dry sherry
2 tbsp white wine vinegar
3 tbsp soy sauce
1 tbsp dark muscovado sugar
1 clove garlic, crushed
1/2 tsp ground cinnamon
1/2 tsp ground ginger

1 Place the meat in a shallow, non-metallic dish. To make the sauce, combine the cornflour (cornstarch) with the sherry, then stir in the remaining sauce ingredients. Pour the sauce over the meat and leave to marinate for at least 2 hours.

2 Remove the marinated meat from the sauce and set aside. Pour the sauce into a small saucepan.

3 Cut the meat into thin strips and thread these, concertina-style, on to pre-soaked wooden skewers, alternating each strip of meat with the prepared pieces of (bell) pepper and spring onion (scallion).

4 Gently heat the sauce until it is just simmering, stirring occasionally. Barbecue (grill) the kebabs (kabobs) over hot coals for 5–8 minutes, turning and basting the beef and vegetables occasionally with the reserved sauce.

5 Arrange the skewers on serving plates and pour the remaining sauce over the kebabs (kabobs). Serve with a green salad.

COOK'S TIP

If you are short of time, omit the marinating, but the flavour will not permeate the meat as well.

1

2

3

Pork Fillet Stir-Fry with Crunchy Satay Sauce

Serves 4

INGREDIENTS

150 g/5½ oz carrots
2 tbsp sunflower oil
350 g/12 oz pork neck fillet, thinly sliced
1 onion, sliced
2 cloves garlic, crushed
1 yellow (bell) pepper, deseeded and sliced
150 g/5½ oz/2⅓ cups mangetout (snow peas)
75 g/3 oz/1½ cups fine asparagus
chopped salted peanuts, to serve

SATAY SAUCE:
6 tbsp crunchy peanut butter
6 tbsp coconut milk
1 tsp chilli flakes
1 clove garlic, crushed
1 tsp tomato purée

1 Using a sharp knife, slice the carrots into thin sticks.

2 Heat the oil in a large wok. Add the pork, onion and garlic and stir-fry for 5 minutes or until the lamb is cooked through.

3 Add the carrots, (bell) pepper, mangetout (snow peas) and asparagus to the wok and stir-fry for 5 minutes.

4 To make the satay sauce, place the peanut butter, coconut milk, chilli flakes, garlic and tomato purée in a small pan and heat gently, stirring, until well combined.

5 Transfer the stir-fry to warm serving plates. Spoon the satay sauce over the stir-fry and scatter with chopped peanuts. Serve immediately.

COOK'S TIP

Cook the sauce just before serving as it tends to thicken very quickly and will not be spoonable if you cook it too far in advance.

Chinese Five-Spice Crispy Pork with Egg Fried Rice

Serves 4

INGREDIENTS

275 g/9½ oz/1¼ cups long-grain white rice
600 ml/1 pint/2½ cups cold water
350 g/12 oz pork tenderloin
2 tsp Chinese five-spice powder
25 g/1 oz/4 tbsp cornflour (cornstarch)
3 large eggs, beaten
25 g/1 oz/2 tbsp demerara sugar
2 tbsp sunflower oil
1 onion
2 cloves garlic, crushed
100 g/3½ oz carrots, diced
1 red (bell) pepper, deseeded and diced
100 g/3½ oz/¾ cup peas
15 g/1 oz/2 tbsp butter
salt and pepper

1 Rinse the rice under cold running water. Place the rice in a large saucepan, add the cold water and a pinch of salt. Bring to the boil, cover, then reduce the heat and leave to simmer for about 9 minutes, or until all of the liquid has been absorbed and the rice is tender.

2 Meanwhile, slice the pork tenderloin into very thin pieces, using a sharp knife. Set aside until required.

3 Whisk together the five-spice powder, cornflour (cornstarch), 1 egg and the demerara sugar. Toss the pork in the mixture until coated.

4 Heat the oil in a large wok. Add the pork and cook over a high heat until the pork is cooked through and crispy. Remove the pork from the wok with a slotted spoon and set aside.

5 Using a sharp knife, cut the onion into dice.

6 Add the onion, garlic, carrots, (bell) pepper and peas to the wok and stir-fry for 5 minutes.

7 Return the pork to the wok together with the cooked rice and stir-fry for 5 minutes.

8 Heat the butter in a frying pan (skillet). Add the remaining beaten eggs and cook until set. Turn out on to a clean board and slice thinly. Toss the strips of egg into the rice mixture and serve.

Spicy Pork Balls

Serves 4

INGREDIENTS

450 g/1 lb pork mince
2 shallots, finely chopped
2 cloves garlic, crushed
1 tsp cumin seeds
½ tsp chilli powder
25 g/1 oz/½ cup wholemeal breadcrumbs
1 egg, beaten
2 tbsp sunflower oil
400 g/14 oz can chopped tomatoes, flavoured with chilli
2 tbsp soy sauce
200 g/7 oz can water chestnuts, drained
3 tbsp chopped fresh coriander (cilantro)

1 Place the pork mince in a large mixing bowl. Add the shallots, garlic, cumin seeds, chilli powder, breadcrumbs and beaten egg and mix together well.

2 Take small pieces of the mixture and form into balls between the palms of your hands.

3 Heat the sunflower oil in a large preheated wok. Add the pork balls to the wok and stir-fry, in batches, over a high heat for about 5 minutes or until sealed on all sides.

4 Add the tomatoes, soy sauce and water chestnuts and bring to the boil. Return the pork balls to the wok, reduce the heat and leave to simmer for 15 minutes.

5 Scatter with chopped fresh coriander (cilantro) and serve hot.

COOK'S TIP

Add a few teaspoons of chilli sauce to a tin of chopped tomatoes, if you can't find the flavoured variety.

COOK'S TIP

Coriander (cilantro) is also known as Chinese parsley, but has a much stronger flavour and should be used with care. Parsley is not a viable alternative; use basil if coriander (cilantro) is not available.

Sweet & Sour Pork

Serves 4

INGREDIENTS

- 450 g/1 lb pork tenderloin
- 2 tbsp sunflower oil
- 225 g/8 oz courgettes (zucchini)
- 1 red onion, cut into thin wedges
- 2 cloves garlic, crushed
- 225 g/8 oz carrots, cut into thin sticks
- 1 red (bell) pepper, deseeded and sliced
- 100 g/3½ oz/1 cup baby corn corbs
- 100 g/3½ oz button mushrooms, halved
- 175 g/6 oz/1¼ cups fresh pineapple, cubed
- 100 g/3½ oz/1 cup beansprouts
- 150 ml/¼ pint/⅔ cup pineapple juice
- 1 tbsp cornflour (cornstarch)
- 2 tbsp soy sauce
- 3 tbsp tomato ketchup
- 1 tbsp white wine vinegar
- 1 tbsp clear honey

1 Using a sharp knife, thinly slice the pork tenderloin.

2 Heat the oil in a large preheated wok.

3 Add the pork to the wok and stir-fry for 10 minutes, or until the pork is completely cooked through and beginning to turn crispy at the edges.

4 Meanwhile, cut the courgettes (zucchini) into thin sticks.

5 Add the onion, garlic, carrots, courgettes (zucchini), (bell) pepper, corn cobs and mushrooms to the wok and stir-fry for a further 5 minutes.

6 Add the pineapple cubes and beansprouts to the wok and stir-fry for 2 minutes.

7 Mix together the pineapple juice, cornflour (cornstarch), soy sauce, ketchup, wine vinegar and honey.

8 Pour the sweet and sour mixture into the wok and cook over a high heat, tossing frequently, until the juices thicken. Transfer the sweet and sour pork to serving bowls and serve hot.

COOK'S TIP

If you prefer a crisper coating, toss the pork in a mixture of cornflour (cornstarch) and egg white and deep fry in the wok in step 3.

3

4

5

Twice-Cooked Pork with (Bell) Peppers

Serves 4

INGREDIENTS

15 g/½ oz Chinese dried mushrooms
450g/1 lb pork leg steaks
2 tbsp vegetable oil
1 onion, sliced
1 red (bell) pepper, deseeded and diced
1 green (bell) pepper, deseeded and diced
1 yellow (bell) pepper, deseeded and diced
4 tbsp oyster sauce

1 Place the mushrooms in a large bowl. Pour over enough boiling water to cover and leave to stand for 20 minutes.

2 Using a sharp knife, trim any excess fat from the pork steaks. Cut the pork into thin strips.

3 Bring a large saucepan of water to the boil. Add the pork to the boiling water and cook for 5 minutes.

4 Remove the pork from the pan with a slotted spoon and leave to drain thoroughly.

5 Heat the oil in a large preheated wok. Add the pork to the wok and stir-fry for about 5 minutes.

6 Remove the mushrooms from the water and leave to drain thoroughly. Roughly chop the mushrooms.

7 Add the mushrooms, onion and the (bell) peppers to the wok and stir-fry for 5 minutes.

8 Stir in the oyster sauce and cook for 2–3 minutes. Transfer to serving bowls and serve immediately.

VARIATION

Use open-cap mushrooms, sliced, instead of Chinese mushrooms, if you prefer.

Pork with Mooli (White Radish)

Serves 4

INGREDIENTS

4 tbsp vegetable oil
450 g/1 lb pork tenderloin
1 aubergine (eggplant)
225 g/8 oz mooli (white radish)
2 cloves garlic, crushed
3 tbsp soy sauce
2 tbsp sweet chilli sauce

1 Heat 2 tablespoons of the vegetable oil in a large preheated wok.

2 Using a sharp knife, thinly slice the pork.

3 Add the slices of pork to the wok and stir-fry for about 5 minutes.

4 Using a sharp knife, trim and dice the aubergine (eggplant). Peel and slice the mooli (white radish).

5 Add the remaining vegetable oil to the hot wok.

6 Add the diced aubergine (eggplant) to the wok together with the garlic and stir-fry for 5 minutes.

7 Add the mooli (white radish) to the wok and stir-fry for about 2 minutes.

8 Stir the soy sauce and sweet chilli sauce into the mixture in the wok and cook until heated through.

9 Transfer the pork and mooli (white radish) to warm serving bowls and serve immediately.

COOK'S TIP

Mooli (white radish) are long white vegetables common in Chinese cooking. They are generally available in most large supermarkets. They are usually grated and have a milder flavour than red radish.

2

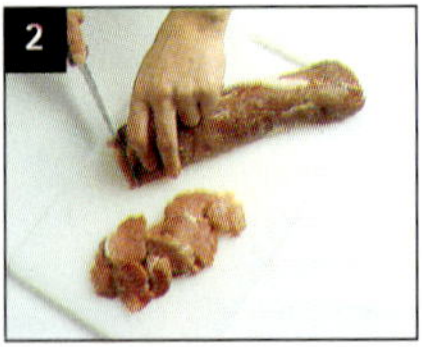

4

6

Lamb with Satay Sauce

Serves 4

INGREDIENTS

450 g/1 lb lamb loin fillet
1 tbsp mild curry paste
150 ml/5 fl oz/$^2/_3$ cup coconut milk
2 cloves garlic, crushed
$^1/_2$ tsp chilli powder
$^1/_2$ tsp cumin
1 tbsp corn oil
1 onion, diced
6 tbsp crunchy peanut butter
1 tsp tomato purée
1 tsp fresh lime juice
100 ml/3$^1/_2$ fl oz/1$^1/_3$ cup cold water

1 Using a sharp knife, thinly slice the lamb. Place the lamb in a large dish.

2 Mix together the curry paste, coconut milk, garlic, chilli powder and cumin in a bowl.

3 Pour the mixture over the lamb, toss well, cover and leave to marinate for 30 minutes.

4 Meanwhile, make the satay sauce. Heat the oil in a large wok. Add the onion and stir-fry for 5 minutes, then reduce the heat and cook for 5 minutes.

5 Add the peanut butter, tomato purée, lime juice and cold water to the wok, stirring well to combine.

6 Thread the lamb on to wooden skewers, reserving the marinade.

7 Grill (broil) the lamb skewers under a hot grill (broiler) for 6–8 minutes, turning once.

8 Add the reserved marinade to the wok, bring to the boil and cook for 5 minutes.Serve the lamb skewers with the satay sauce.

COOK'S TIP

Soak the wooden skewers in cold water for 30 minutes before grilling (broiling) to prevent the skewers from burning.

2

3

6

Stir-Fried Lamb with Black Bean Sauce & Mixed (Bell) Peppers

Serves 4

INGREDIENTS

450 g/1 lb lamb neck fillet or boneless leg of lamb chops
1 egg white, lightly beaten
25 g/1 oz/4 tbsp cornflour (cornstarch)
1 tsp Chinese five-spice powder
3 tbsp sunflower oil
1 red onion
1 red (bell) pepper, deseeded and sliced
1 green (bell) pepper, deseeded and sliced
1 yellow or orange (bell) pepper, deseeded and sliced
5 tbsp black bean sauce
boiled rice or noodles, to serve

1 Using a sharp knife, slice the lamb into very thin strips.

2 Mix the egg white, cornflour (cornstarch) and Chinese five-spice powder together in a large bowl. Toss the lamb strips in the mixture until evenly coated.

3 Heat the oil in a large preheated wok. Add the lamb and stir-fry over a high heat for 5 minutes or until the edges begin to crispen.

4 Using a sharp knife, slice the red onion. Add the onion and (bell) pepper slices to the wok and stir-fry for 5–6 minutes, or until the vegetables just begin to soften.

5 Stir the black bean sauce into the mixture in the wok and heat through.

6 Transfer the lamb and sauce to warm serving plates and serve hot with freshly boiled rice or noodles.

COOK'S TIP

Take care when frying the lamb as the cornflour (cornstarch) mixture may cause it to stick to the wok. Move the lamb around the wok constantly during stir-frying.

2

3

4

Spring Onion (Scallion) & Lamb Stir-Fry with Oyster Sauce

Serves 4

INGREDIENTS

450 g/1 lb lamb leg steaks
1 tsp ground Szechuan peppercorns
1 tbsp groundnut oil
2 cloves garlic, crushed
8 spring onions (scallions), sliced
2 tbsp dark soy sauce
6 tbsp oyster sauce
175 g/6 oz Chinese leaves
prawn (shrimp) crackers, to serve

1 Using a sharp knife, remove any excess fat from the lamb. Slice the lamb thinly.

2 Sprinkle the ground Szechuan peppercorns over the meat and toss together until well combined.

3 Heat the oil in a preheated wok. Add the lamb and stir-fry for 5 minutes.

4 Mix the garlic, spring onions (scallions) and soy sauce, add to the wok and stir-fry for 2 minutes.

5 Add the oyster sauce and Chinese leaves and stir-fry for a further 2 minutes, or until the leaves have wilted and the juices are bubbling.

6 Transfer the stir-fry to warm serving bowls and serve hot.

COOK'S TIP

Prawn (shrimp) crackers consist of compressed slivers of prawn (shrimp) and flour paste. They expand when deep-fried.

COOK'S TIP

Oyster sauce is made from oysters which are cooked in brine and soy sauce. Sold in bottles, it will keep in the refrigerator for months.

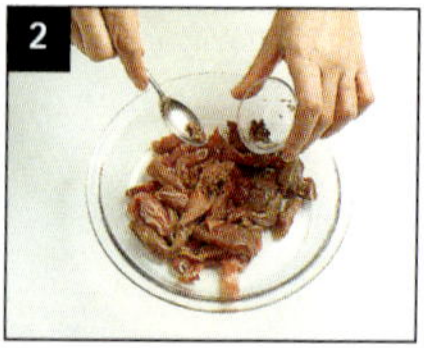

Curried Stir-Fried Lamb with Diced Potatoes

Serves 4

INGREDIENTS

450 g/1 lb potatoes, diced
450 g/1 lb lean lamb, cubed
2 tbsp medium hot curry paste
3 tbsp sunflower oil
1 onion, sliced
1 aubergine (eggplant), diced
2 cloves garlic, crushed
1 tbsp grated fresh root ginger
150 ml/5 fl oz/$^2/_3$ cup lamb or beef stock
2 tbsp chopped fresh coriander (cilantro)

1 Bring a large saucepan of lightly salted water to the boil. Add the potatoes and cook for 10 minutes. Remove the potatoes from the saucepan with a slotted spoon and drain thoroughly.

2 Meanwhile, place the lamb in a large mixing bowl. Add the curry paste and mix until well combined.

3 Heat the sunflower oil in a large preheated wok.

4 Add the onion, aubergine (eggplant), garlic and ginger to the wok and stir-fry for about 5 minutes.

5 Add the lamb to the wok and stir-fry for a further 5 minutes.

6 Add the stock and cooked potatoes to the wok, bring to the boil and leave to simmer for 30 minutes, or until the lamb is tender and completely cooked through.

7 Transfer the stir-fry to warm serving dishes and scatter with chopped fresh coriander (cilantro). Serve immediately.

COOK'S TIP

The wok is an ancient Chinese invention, the name coming from the Cantonese, meaning a 'cooking vessel'.

Garlic-Infused Lamb with Soy Sauce

Serves 4

INGREDIENTS

450 g/1 lb lamb loin fillet
2 cloves garlic
2 tbsp groundnut oil
3 tbsp dry sherry or rice wine
3 tbsp dark soy
1 tsp cornflour (cornstarch)
2 tbsp cold water
25 g/1 oz/2 tbsp butter

1 Using a sharp knife, make small slits in the flesh of the lamb.

2 Carefully peel the cloves of garlic and cut them into slices, using a sharp knife.

3 Push the slices of garlic into the slits in the lamb. Place the garlic-infused lamb in a shallow dish.

4 Drizzle 1 tablespoon each of the oil, sherry and soy sauce over the lamb, cover and leave to marinate for at least 1 hour, preferably overnight.

5 Using a sharp knife, thinly slice the marinated lamb.

6 Heat the remaining oil in a preheated wok. Add the lamb and stir-fry for 5 minutes.

7 Add the marinade juices and the remaining sherry and soy sauce to the wok and allow the juices to bubble for 5 minutes.

8 Mix the cornflour (cornstarch) with the cold water. Add the cornflour (cornstarch) mixture to the wok and cook, stirring occasionally, until the juices start to thicken.

9 Cut the butter into small pieces. Add the butter to the wok and stir until the butter melts. Transfer to serving dishes and serve immediately.

COOK'S TIP

Adding the butter at the end of the recipe gives a glossy, rich sauce which is ideal with the lamb.

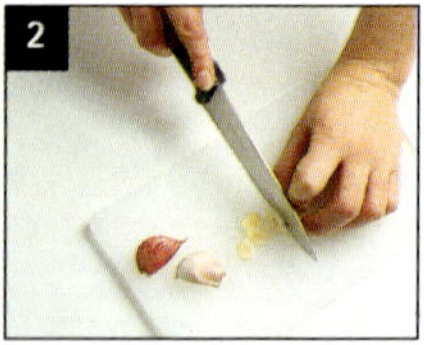

Thai-Style Lamb with Lime Leaves

Serves 4

INGREDIENTS

- 2 red Thai chillies
- 2 tbsp groundnut oil
- 2 cloves garlic, crushed
- 4 shallots, chopped
- 2 stalks lemon grass, sliced
- 6 lime leaves
- 1 tbsp tamarind paste
- 25 g/1 oz/2 tbsp palm sugar
- 450 g/1 lb lean lamb (leg or loin fillet)
- 600 ml/1 pint/2½ cups coconut milk
- 175 g/6 oz cherry tomatoes, halved
- 1 tbsp chopped fresh coriander (cilantro)
- fragrant rice, to serve

1 Using a sharp knife, deseed and very finely chop the Thai red chillies.

2 Heat the groundnut oil in a large preheated wok.

3 Add the garlic, shallots, lemon grass, lime leaves, tamarind paste, palm sugar and chillies to the wok and stir-fry for about 2 minutes.

4 Using a sharp knife, cut the lamb into thin strips or cubes.

5 Add the lamb to the wok and stir-fry for about 5 minutes, tossing well so that the lamb is evenly coated in the spice mixture.

6 Pour the coconut milk into the wok and bring to the boil. Reduce the heat and leave to simmer for 20 minutes.

7 Add the cherry tomatoes and chopped fresh coriander (cilantro) to the wok and leave to simmer for 5 minutes. Transfer to serving plates and serve hot with fragrant rice.

COOK'S TIP

Thai limes, also known as makut*, differ from the common lime in that the leaves are highly scented and the fruits resemble knobbly balls. Thai lime leaves are often used in cooking for flavour.*

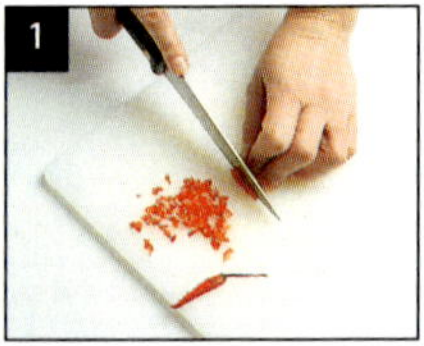

Stir-Fried Lamb with Orange

Serves 4

INGREDIENTS

450 g/1 lb minced lamb
2 cloves garlic, crushed
1 tsp cumin seeds
1 tsp ground coriander
1 red onion, sliced
finely grated zest and juice of 1 orange
2 tbsp soy sauce
1 orange, peeled and segmented
salt and pepper
snipped fresh chives, to garnish

1 Add the minced lamb to a preheated wok. Dry fry the minced lamb for 5 minutes, or until the mince is evenly browned. Drain away any excess fat from the wok.

2 Add the garlic, cumin seeds, coriander and red onion to the wok and stir-fry for a further 5 minutes.

3 Stir in the finely grated orange zest and juice and the soy sauce, cover, reduce the heat and leave to simmer, stirring occasionally, for 15 minutes.

4 Remove the lid, raise the heat, add the orange segments and salt and pepper to taste and heat through for a further 2–3 minutes.

5 Transfer to warm serving plates and garnish with snipped fresh chives. Serve immediately.

VARIATION

Use lime or lemon juice and zest instead of the orange, if you prefer.

COOK'S TIP

If you wish to serve wine with your meal, try light, dry white wines and lighter Burgundy-style red wines as they blend well with Oriental food.

Lamb's Liver with Green (Bell) Peppers & Sherry

Serves 4

INGREDIENTS

450 g/1 lb lamb's liver
2 tbsp cornflour (cornstarch)
2 tbsp groundnut oil
1 onion, sliced
2 cloves garlic, crushed
2 green (bell) peppers, deseeded and sliced
2 tbsp tomato purée
3 tbsp dry sherry
1 tbsp cornflour (cornstarch)
2 tbsp soy sauce

1 Using a sharp knife, trim any excess fat from the lamb's liver. Slice the lamb's liver into thin strips.

2 Place the cornflour (cornstarch) in a large bowl.

3 Add the strips of lamb's liver to the cornflour (cornstarch) and toss well until coated evenly all over.

4 Heat the groundnut oil in a large preheated wok.

5 Add the lamb's liver, onion, garlic and green (bell) pepper to the wok and stir-fry for 6–7 minutes, or until the lamb's liver is just cooked through and the vegetables are tender.

6 Mix together the tomato purée, sherry, cornflour (cornstarch) and soy sauce. Stir the mixture into the wok and cook for a further 2 minutes or until the juices have thickened. Transfer to warm serving bowls and serve immediately.

VARIATION

Use rice wine instead of the sherry for a really authentic Oriental flavour. Chinese rice wine is made from glutinous rice and is also known as 'yellow wine' because of its golden colour. The best variety, from south-east China, is called Shao Hsing *or* Shaoxing.

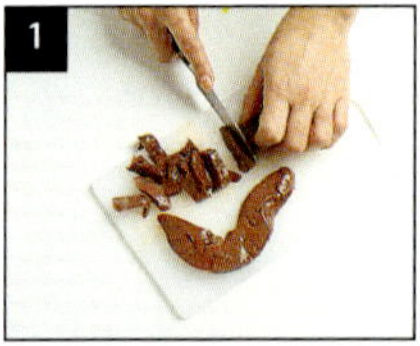
1

5

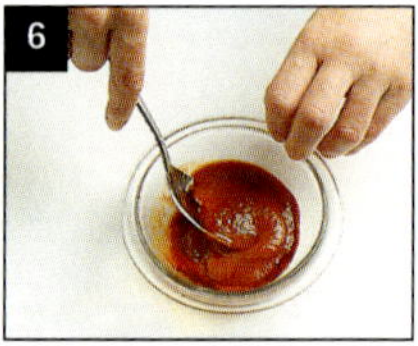
6

Chilli Chicken

Serves 4

INGREDIENTS

- 350 g/12 oz skinless, boneless lean chicken
- 1/2 tsp salt
- 1 egg white, lightly beaten
- 2 tbsp cornflour (cornstarch)
- 4 tbsp vegetable oil
- 2 garlic cloves, crushed
- 1-cm/1/2-inch piece fresh root ginger, grated
- 1 red (bell) pepper, seeded and diced
- 1 green (bell) pepper, seeded and diced
- 2 fresh red chillies, chopped
- 2 tbsp light soy sauce
- 1 tbsp dry sherry or Chinese rice wine
- 1 tbsp wine vinegar

1 Cut the chicken into cubes and place in a mixing bowl. Add the salt, egg white, cornflour (cornstarch) and 1 tbsp of the oil. Turn the chicken in the mixture to coat well.

2 Heat the remaining oil in a preheated wok. Add the garlic and ginger and stir-fry for 30 seconds.

3 Add the chicken pieces to the wok and stir-fry for 2–3 minutes, or until browned.

4 Stir in the (bell) peppers, chillies, soy sauce, sherry or Chinese rice wine and wine vinegar and cook for 2–3 minutes, until the chicken is cooked through. Transfer to a serving dish and serve.

VARIATION

This recipe works well if you use 350 g/12 oz lean steak, cut into thin strips or 450 g/1 lb raw prawns (shrimp) instead of the chicken.

COOK'S TIP

When preparing chillies, wear rubber gloves to prevent the juices from burning and irritating your hands. Be careful not to touch your face, especially your lips or eyes, until you have washed your hands.

Lemon Chicken

Serves 4

INGREDIENTS

vegetable oil, for deep-frying
650 g/1 1/2 lb skinless, boneless chicken, cut into strips
lemon slices and shredded spring onions (scallions), to garnish

SAUCE:
1 tbsp cornflour (cornstarch)
6 tbsp cold water
3 tbsp fresh lemon juice
2 tbsp sweet sherry
1/2 tsp caster (superfine) sugar

1 Heat the oil in a wok until almost smoking. Reduce the heat and stir-fry the chicken strips for 3–4 minutes, until cooked through. Remove the chicken with a slotted spoon, set aside and keep warm. Drain the oil from the wok.

2 To make the sauce, mix the cornflour with 2 tablespoons of the water to form a paste.

3 Pour the lemon juice and remaining water into the mixture in the wok. Add the sherry and sugar and bring to the boil, stirring until the sugar has completely dissolved.

4 Stir in the cornflour mixture and return to the boil. Reduce the heat and simmer, stirring constantly, for 2-3 minutes, until the sauce is thickened and clear.

5 Transfer the chicken to a warm serving plate and pour the sauce over the top. Garnish with the lemon slices and shredded spring onions (scallions) and serve immediately.

COOK'S TIP

If you would prefer to use chicken portions rather than strips, cook them in the oil, covered, over a low heat for about 30 minutes, or until cooked through.

Braised Chicken

Serves 4

INGREDIENTS

1.5 kg/3 lb 5 oz chicken
3 tbsp vegetable oil
1 tbsp peanut oil
2 tbsp dark brown sugar
5 tbsp dark soy sauce
150 ml/¼ pint/⅔ cup water
2 garlic cloves, crushed
1 small onion, chopped
1 fresh red chilli, chopped
celery leaves and chives, to garnish

1 Clean the chicken with damp kitchen paper (paper towels).

2 Put the oils in a wok, add the sugar and heat gently until the sugar caramelizes. Stir in the soy sauce. Add the chicken and turn it in the mixture to coat on all sides.

3 Add the water, garlic, onion and chilli. Cover and simmer, turning the chicken occasionally, for 1 hour, or until cooked through. Test by piercing a thigh with the point of a knife or a skewer – the juices will run clear when the chicken is cooked.

4 Remove the chicken from the wok and transfer to a serving plate. Increase the heat and reduce the sauce in the wok until thickened. Garnish the chicken and serve with the sauce.

COOK'S TIP

When caramelizing the sugar, do not turn the heat too high, or it may burn.

VARIATION

For a spicier sauce, add 1 tbsp finely chopped fresh root ginger and 1 tbsp ground Szechuan peppercorns with the chilli in step 3. If the flavour of dark soy sauce is too strong for your taste, substitute 2 tbsp dark soy sauce and 3 tbsp light soy sauce. This will result in a more delicate taste without sacrificing the attractive colour of the dish.

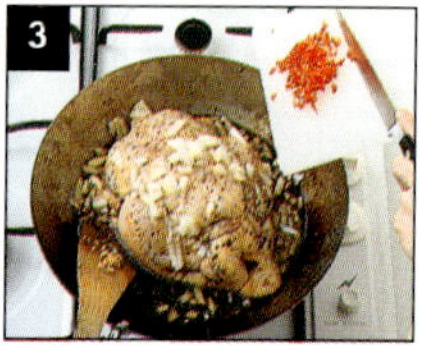

Chicken with Cashew Nuts & Vegetables

Serves 4

INGREDIENTS

300 g/10 1/2 oz boneless, skinless chicken breasts
1 tbsp cornflour (cornstarch)
1 tsp sesame oil
1 tbsp hoisin sauce
1 tsp light soy sauce
3 garlic cloves, crushed
2 tbsp vegetable oil
75 g/2 3/4 oz/3/4 cup unsalted cashew nuts
25 g/1 oz mangetout (snow peas)
1 celery stick, sliced
1 onion, cut into 8 pieces
60 g/2 oz beansprouts
1 red (bell) pepper, seeded and diced

SAUCE:
2 tsp cornflour (cornstarch)
2 tbsp hoisin sauce
200 ml/7 fl oz/7/8 cup chicken stock

1 Trim any fat from the chicken breasts and cut the meat into thin strips. Place the chicken in a large bowl. Sprinkle with the cornflour (cornstarch) and toss to coat the chicken strips in it, shaking off any excess. Mix together the sesame oil, hoisin sauce, soy sauce and 1 garlic clove. Pour this mixture over the chicken, turning to coat. Marinate for 20 minutes.

2 Heat half of the vegetable oil in a preheated wok. Add the cashew nuts and stir-fry for 1 minute, until browned. Add the mangetout (snow peas), celery, the remaining garlic, the onion, bean-sprouts and red (bell) pepper and cook, stirring occasionally, for 2–3 minutes. Remove the vegetables from the wok with a slotted spoon, set aside and keep warm.

3 Heat the remaining oil in the wok. Remove the chicken from the marinade and stir-fry for 3–4 minutes. Return the vegetables to the wok.

4 To make the sauce, mix the cornflour (cornstarch), hoisin sauce and chicken stock and pour into the wok. Bring to the boil, stirring until thickened and clear. Serve.

Chicken Chop Suey

Serves 4

INGREDIENTS

- 4 tbsp light soy sauce
- 2 tsp light brown sugar
- 500 g/1 1/4 lb skinless, boneless chicken breasts
- 3 tbsp vegetable oil
- 2 onions, quartered
- 2 garlic cloves, crushed
- 350 g/12 oz beansprouts
- 3 tsp sesame oil
- 1 tbsp cornflour (cornstarch)
- 3 tbsp water
- 425 ml/3/4 pint/2 cups chicken stock
- shredded leek, to garnish

1 Mix the soy sauce and sugar together, stirring until the sugar has dissolved.

2 Trim any fat from the chicken and cut the meat into thin strips. Place the chicken strips in a shallow glass dish and spoon the soy mixture over them, turning to coat. Leave to marinate in the refrigerator for 20 minutes.

3 Heat the oil in a preheated wok. Add the chicken and stir-fry for 2–3 minutes, until golden brown.

4 Add the onions and garlic and cook for a further 2 minutes. Add the beansprouts, cook for a further 4–5 minutes, then add the sesame oil.

5 Blend the cornflour (cornstarch) with the water to form a smooth paste. Pour the stock into the wok, together with the cornflour (cornstarch) paste and bring to the boil, stirring constantly until the sauce is thickened and clear. Transfer to a warm serving dish, garnish with shredded leek and serve immediately.

VARIATION

This recipe may be made with strips of lean steak, pork or with mixed vegetables. Change the type of stock accordingly.

2

3

4

Chicken with Yellow Bean Sauce

Serves 4

INGREDIENTS

450 g/1 lb skinless, boneless chicken breasts
1 egg white, beaten
1 tbsp cornflour (cornstarch)
1 tbsp rice wine vinegar
1 tbsp light soy sauce
1 tsp caster (superfine) sugar
3 tbsp vegetable oil
1 garlic clove, crushed
1-cm/½-inch piece fresh root ginger, grated
1 green (bell) pepper, seeded and diced
2 large mushrooms, sliced
3 tbsp yellow bean sauce
yellow or green (bell) pepper strips, to garnish

1 Trim any fat from the chicken. Cut the meat into 2.5-cm/1-inch cubes.

2 Mix the egg white and cornflour (cornstarch) in a shallow bowl. Add the chicken and turn in the mixture to coat. Set aside for 20 minutes.

3 Mix the vinegar, soy sauce and sugar in a bowl.

4 Remove the chicken from the egg white mixture.

5 Heat the oil in a preheated wok, add the chicken and stir-fry for 3–4 minutes, until golden brown. Remove the chicken from the wok with a slotted spoon, set aside and keep warm.

6 Add the garlic, ginger, (bell) pepper and mushrooms to the wok and stir-fry for 1–2 minutes.

7 Add the yellow bean sauce and cook for 1 minute. Stir in the vinegar mixture and return the chicken to the wok. Cook for 1–2 minutes and serve hot, garnished with (bell) pepper strips.

VARIATION

Black bean sauce would work equally well with this recipe. Although this would affect the appearance of the dish, as it is much darker in colour, the flavours would be compatible.

Crispy Chicken

Serves 4

INGREDIENTS

1.5 kg/3 lb 5 oz oven-ready chicken
2 tbsp clear honey
2 tsp Chinese five-spice powder
2 tbsp rice wine vinegar
850 ml/1 1/2 pints/3 3/4 cups vegetable oil, for frying
chilli sauce, to serve

1 Rinse the chicken inside and out under cold running water and pat dry with kitchen paper (paper towels).

2 Bring a large pan of water to the boil and remove from the heat. Place the chicken in the water, cover and set aside for 20 minutes. Remove the chicken from the water and pat dry with kitchen paper (paper towels). Cool and let chill overnight.

3 To make the glaze, mix the honey, Chinese five-spice powder and rice wine vinegar.

4 Brush some of the glaze all over the chicken and return to the refrigerator for 20 minutes. Repeat this process until all of the glaze has been used up. Return the chicken to the refrigerator for at least 2 hours after the final coating.

5 Using a cleaver or kitchen knife, open the chicken out by splitting it through the centre through the breast and then cut each half into 4 pieces.

6 Heat the oil for deep-frying in a wok until almost smoking. Reduce the heat and fry each piece of chicken for 5–7 minutes, until golden and cooked through. Remove from the oil with a slotted spoon and drain on absorbent kitchen paper (paper towels).

7 Transfer to a serving dish and serve hot with a little chilli sauce.

COOK'S TIP

If it is easier, use chicken portions instead of a whole chicken. You could also use chicken legs for this recipe, if you prefer.

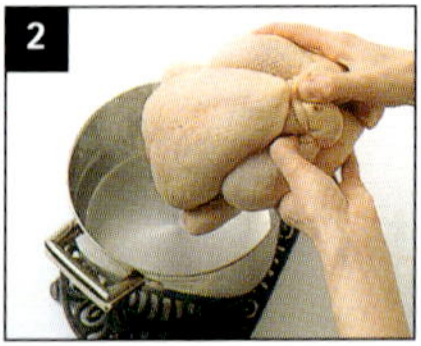

Spicy Peanut Chicken

Serves 4

INGREDIENTS

300 g/10 1/2 oz skinless, boneless chicken breast
2 tbsp peanut oil
125 g/4 1/2 oz/1 cup shelled peanuts
1 fresh red chilli, sliced
1 green (bell) pepper, seeded and cut into strips
1 tsp sesame oil
fried rice, to serve

SAUCE:
150 ml/1/4 pint/2/3 cup chicken stock
1 tbsp Chinese rice wine or dry sherry
1 tbsp light soy sauce
1 1/2 tsp light brown sugar
2 garlic cloves, crushed
1 tsp grated fresh root ginger
1 tsp rice wine vinegar

1 Trim any fat from the chicken and cut the meat into 2.5-cm/1-inch cubes. Set aside.

2 Heat the peanut oil in a preheated wok. Add the peanuts and stir-fry for 1 minute. Remove the peanuts with a slotted spoon and set aside.

3 Add the chicken to the wok and cook for 1–2 minutes. Stir in the chilli and (bell) pepper and cook for 1 minute. Remove from the wok with a slotted spoon.

4 Put half of the peanuts in a food processor and process until almost smooth. Alternatively, place them in a plastic bag and crush with a rolling pin.

5 To make the sauce, add the chicken stock, Chinese rice wine or dry sherry, soy sauce, sugar, garlic, ginger and rice wine vinegar to the wok.

6 Heat the sauce without boiling and stir in the peanut purée, remaining peanuts, chicken, chilli and (bell) pepper. Sprinkle with the sesame oil, stir and cook for 1 minute. Serve hot.

COOK'S TIP

If necessary, process the peanuts with a little of the stock in step 4 to form a softer paste.

Chinese Chicken Salad

Serves 4

INGREDIENTS

225 g/8 oz skinless, boneless chicken breasts
2 tsp light soy sauce
1 tsp sesame oil
1 tsp sesame seeds
2 tbsp vegetable oil
125 g/4 1/2 oz beansprouts
1 red (bell) pepper, seeded and thinly sliced
1 carrot, cut into matchsticks
3 baby corn cobs, sliced
snipped chives and carrot matchsticks, to garnish

SAUCE:
2 tsp rice wine vinegar
1 tbsp light soy sauce
dash of chilli oil

1 Place the chicken in a shallow glass dish.

2 Mix together the soy sauce and sesame oil and pour over the chicken. Sprinkle with sesame seeds and leave to stand for 20 minutes.

3 Remove the chicken from the marinade and cut the meat into slices.

4 Heat the oil in a preheated wok. Add the chicken and fry for 4-5 minutes, until cooked through and golden brown on both sides. Remove the chicken from the wok with a slotted spoon, set aside and leave to cool.

5 Add the beansprouts, (bell) pepper, carrot and baby corn cobs to the wok and stir-fry for 2–3 minutes. Remove from the wok with a slotted spoon, set aside and leave to cool.

6 To make the sauce, mix the rice wine vinegar, light soy sauce and chilli oil together.

7 Arrange the chicken and vegetables on a serving plate. Spoon the sauce over the salad, garnish and serve.

COOK'S TIP

If you have time, make the sauce and leave to stand for 30 minutes for the flavours to fully develop.

Peking Duck

Serves 4

INGREDIENTS

1.8 kg/4 lb duck
1.75 litres/3 pints/7 1/2 cups boiling water
4 tbsp clear honey
2 tsp dark soy sauce
2 tbsp sesame oil
125 ml/4 fl oz/1/2 cup hoisin sauce
125 g/4 1/2 oz/2/3 cup caster (superfine) sugar
125 ml/4 fl oz/1/2 cup water
carrot strips, to garnish
Chinese pancakes, cucumber matchsticks and spring onions (scallions), to serve

1 Place the duck on a rack set over a roasting tin (pan) and pour 1.2 litres/ 2 pints/5 cups of the boiling water over it. Remove the duck and rack and discard the water. Pat dry with paper towels, replace the duck and the rack and set aside for several hours.

2 Mix together the honey, remaining boiling water and soy sauce. Brush the mixture over the skin and inside the duck. Reserve the remaining glaze. Set the duck aside for 1 hour, until the glaze has dried.

3 Coat the duck with another layer of glaze. Let dry and repeat until all of the glaze is used.

4 Heat the oil and add the hoisin sauce, sugar and water. Simmer for 2–3 minutes, until thickened. Cool and refrigerate.

5 Cook the duck in a preheated oven, at 190°C/375°F/Gas Mark 5, for 30 minutes. Turn the duck over and cook for 20 minutes. Turn the duck again and cook for 20–30 minutes, or until cooked through and the skin is crisp.

6 Remove the duck from the oven and set aside for 10 minutes. Meanwhile, heat the pancakes in a steamer for 5–7 minutes. Cut the skin and duck meat into strips, garnish with the carrot strips and serve with the pancakes, sauce, cucumber and spring onions (scallions).

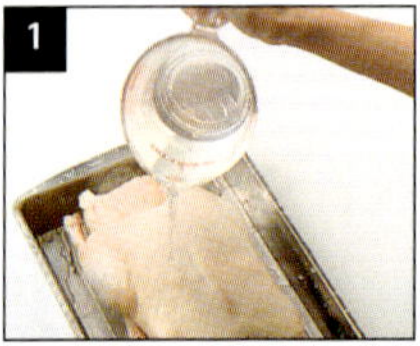

Duck in Spicy Sauce

Serves 4

INGREDIENTS

- 1 tbsp vegetable oil
- 1 tsp grated fresh root ginger
- 1 garlic clove, crushed
- 1 fresh red chilli, chopped
- 350 g/12 oz skinless, boneless duck meat, cut into strips
- 125 g/4 1/2 oz cauliflower, cut into florets
- 60 g/2 oz mangetout (snow peas)
- 60 g/2 oz baby corn cobs, halved lengthways
- 300 ml/1/2 pint/1 1/4 cups chicken stock
- 1 tsp Chinese five-spice powder
- 2 tsp Chinese rice wine or dry sherry
- 1 tsp cornflour (cornstarch)
- 2 tsp water
- 1 tsp sesame oil

1 Heat the vegetable oil in a preheated wok. Lower the heat slightly and add the ginger, garlic, chilli and duck and stir-fry for 2-3 minutes. Remove with a slotted spoon and set aside.

2 Add the cauliflower florets, mangetout (snow peas) and baby corn cobs to the wok and stir-fry for 2-3 minutes. Pour off any excess oil from the wok and push the vegetables to one side.

3 Return the duck to the wok and pour in the stock. Sprinkle the Chinese five-spice powder over the top, stir in the Chinese rice wine or sherry and cook over a low heat for about 15 minutes, or until the duck is tender.

4 Blend the cornflour (cornstarch) with the water to form a paste and stir into the wok, together with the sesame oil. Bring to the boil, stirring until the sauce has thickened and cleared.

5 Transfer the duck and spicy sauce to a warm serving dish and serve immediately.

COOK'S TIP

Omit the chilli for a milder dish, or deseed the chilli before adding it to remove some of the heat.

Honey-Glazed Duck

Serves 4

INGREDIENTS

1 tsp dark soy sauce
2 tbsp clear honey
1 tsp garlic vinegar
2 garlic cloves, crushed
1 tsp ground star anise
2 tsp cornflour (cornstarch)
2 tsp water
2 large boneless duck breasts, about 225g/8 oz each

TO GARNISH:
celery leaves
cucumber wedges
snipped chives

1 Mix the soy sauce, clear honey, garlic vinegar, garlic and star anise. Blend the cornflour (cornstarch) with the water to form a smooth paste and stir it into the mixture.

2 Place the duck breasts in a shallow ovenproof dish. Brush with the soy marinade, turning to coat them completely. Cover and leave to marinate in the refrigerator for at least 2 hours, or overnight.

3 Remove the duck from the marinade and cook in a preheated oven, at 220°C/425°F/Gas Mark 7, for 20–25 minutes, basting frequently with the glaze.

4 Remove the duck from the oven and transfer to a preheated grill (broiler). Grill (broil) for about 3–4 minutes to caramelize the top.

5 Remove the duck from the grill (broiler) pan and cut into thin slices. Arrange the duck slices in a warm serving dish, garnish with celery leaves, cucumber wedges and snipped chives and serve immediately.

COOK'S TIP

If the duck begins to burn slightly while it is cooking in the oven, cover with foil. Check that the duck breasts are cooked through by inserting the point of a sharp knife into the thickest part of the flesh – the juices should run clear.

Duck with Mangoes

Serves 4

INGREDIENTS

2 medium-size ripe mangoes
300 ml/$^{1}/_{2}$ pint/1 $^{1}/_{4}$ cups chicken stock
2 garlic cloves, crushed
1 tsp grated fresh root ginger
3 tbsp vegetable oil
2 large skinless duck breasts, about 225 g/8 oz each
1 tsp wine vinegar
1 tsp light soy sauce
1 leek, sliced
freshly chopped parsley, to garnish

1 Peel the mangoes and cut the flesh from each side of the stones (pits). Cut the flesh into strips.

2 Put half of the mango pieces and the stock in a food processor and process until smooth. Alternatively, press half of the mangoes through a sieve and mix with the stock.

3 Rub the garlic and ginger over the duck. Heat the oil in a wok and cook the duck breasts, turning, until sealed. Reserve the oil in the wok and remove the duck. Place the duck on a rack set over a roasting tin (pan) and cook in a preheated oven, at 220°C/425°F/Gas Mark 7, for 20 minutes, until cooked through.

4 Meanwhile, place the mango and stock mixture in a pan and add the vinegar and soy sauce. Bring to the boil and cook over a high heat, stirring, until reduced by half.

5 Heat the oil reserved in the wok and stir-fry the leek and remaining mango for about 1 minute. Remove from the wok, transfer to a serving dish and keep warm.

6 Slice the cooked duck breasts and arrange the slices on top of the leek and mango mixture. Pour the sauce over the duck slices, garnish and serve.

COOK'S TIP

Do not overcook the mango slices in the wok, or stir too vigorously, otherwise they will break up.

Stir-Fried Duck with Broccoli & (Bell) Peppers

Serves 4

INGREDIENTS

1 egg white
2 tbsp cornflour (cornstarch)
450 g/1 lb skinless, boneless duck meat
vegetable oil, for deep-frying
1 red (bell) pepper, seeded and diced
1 yellow (bell) pepper, seeded and diced
125 g/4½ oz small broccoli florets
1 garlic clove, crushed
2 tbsp light soy sauce
2 tsp Chinese rice wine or dry sherry
1 tsp light brown sugar
125 ml/4 fl oz/½ cup chicken stock
2 tsp sesame seeds

1 Beat the egg white and cornflour (cornstarch) together in a mixing bowl.

2 Cut the duck meat into cubes and stir into the egg white mixture. Let stand for 30 minutes.

3 Heat the oil for deep-frying in a wok until almost smoking. Remove the duck from the egg white mixture, add to the wok and fry in the oil for 4–5 minutes, until crisp. Remove the duck from the oil and drain on kitchen paper (paper towels).

4 Add the (bell) peppers and broccoli to the wok and fry for 2–3 minutes. Remove with a slotted spoon and drain on kitchen paper (paper towels).

5 Pour all but 2 tbsp of the oil from the wok and return to the heat. Add the garlic and stir-fry for 30 seconds. Stir in the soy sauce, Chinese rice wine or sherry, sugar and stock and bring to the boil.

6 Stir in the duck and reserved vegetables and cook for 1–2 minutes.

7 Carefully spoon the duck and vegetables on to a warmed serving dish and sprinkle with the sesame seeds. Serve.

2

3

6

Pork Fry with Vegetables

Serves 4

INGREDIENTS

350 g/12 oz lean pork fillet (tenderloin)
2 tbsp vegetable oil
2 garlic cloves, crushed
1-cm/$^{1}/_{2}$-inch piece fresh root ginger, cut into slivers
1 carrot, cut into thin strips
1 red (bell) pepper, seeded and diced
1 fennel bulb, sliced
25 g/1 oz water chestnuts, halved
75 g/2 $^{3}/_{4}$ oz beansprouts
2 tbsp Chinese rice wine
300 ml/$^{1}/_{2}$ pint/1 $^{1}/_{4}$ cups pork or chicken stock
pinch of dark brown sugar
1 tsp cornflour (cornstarch)
2 tsp water

1 Cut the pork into thin slices. Heat the oil in a preheated wok. Add the garlic, ginger and pork and stir-fry for 1–2 minutes, until the meat is sealed.

2 Add the carrot, (bell) pepper, fennel and water chestnuts to the wok and stir-fry for 2-3 minutes.

3 Add the beansprouts and stir-fry for 1 minute. Remove the pork and vegetables from the wok and keep warm.

4 Add the Chinese rice wine, pork or chicken stock and sugar to the wok. Blend the cornflour (cornstarch) to a smooth paste with the water and stir it into the sauce. Bring to the boil, stirring, until thickened and clear.

5 Return the meat and vegetables to the wok and cook for 1–2 minutes, until heated through and coated with the sauce. Transfer to a warm serving dish and serve immediately.

COOK'S TIP

Use dry sherry instead of the Chinese rice wine if you have difficulty obtaining it.

Pork with Plums

Serves 4

INGREDIENTS

450 g/1 lb pork fillet (tenderloin)
1 tbsp cornflour (cornstarch)
2 tbsp light soy sauce
2 tbsp Chinese rice wine
4 tsp light brown sugar
pinch of ground cinnamon
5 tsp vegetable oil
2 garlic cloves, crushed
2 spring onions (scallions), chopped
4 tbsp plum sauce
1 tbsp hoisin sauce
150 ml/$^1/_4$ pint/$^2/_3$ cup water
dash of chilli sauce
fried plum quarters and spring onions (scallions), to garnish

1 Cut the pork fillet (tenderloin) into slices.

2 Mix the cornflour (cornstarch), soy sauce, rice wine, sugar and cinnamon together.

3 Place the pork in a shallow dish and pour the cornflour (cornstarch) mixture over it. Cover and leave to marinate for at least 30 minutes.

4 Remove the pork from the dish, reserving the marinade.

5 Heat the oil in a preheated wok. Add the pork and stir-fry for 3–4 minutes, until lightly coloured.

6 Stir in the garlic, spring onions (scallions), plum sauce, hoisin sauce, water and chilli sauce. Bring the sauce to the boil. Reduce the heat, cover and simmer for 8–10 minutes, or until the pork is cooked through and tender.

7 Stir in the reserved marinade and cook, stirring, for 5 minutes. Transfer to a warm serving dish and garnish with fried plum quarters and spring onions (scallions). Serve immediately.

VARIATION

Strips of boneless duck meat may be used instead of the pork, if you prefer.

3

6

7

Deep-Fried Pork Fritters

Serves 4

INGREDIENTS

450 g/1 lb pork fillet (tenderloin)
2 tbsp peanut oil
200 g/7 oz/1$^{3}/_{4}$ cups plain (all-purpose) flour
2 tsp baking powder
1 egg, beaten
225 ml/8 fl oz/1 cup milk
pinch of chilli powder
vegetable oil, for deep-frying

SAUCE:
2 tbsp dark soy sauce
3 tbsp clear honey
1 tbsp wine vinegar
1 tbsp chopped chives
1 tbsp tomato purée (paste)
chives, to garnish

1 Cut the pork into 2.5-cm/1-inch cubes.

2 Heat the peanut oil in a preheated wok. Add the pork and stir-fry for 2-3 minutes, until sealed. Remove the pork with a slotted spoon and set aside until required.

3 Sift the flour into a bowl and make a well in the centre. Gradually beat in the baking powder, egg, milk and chilli powder to make a thick batter.

4 Heat the oil for deep-frying in a wok until almost smoking, then reduce the heat slightly.

5 Toss the pork pieces in the batter to coat. Add the pork to the wok and deep-fry until golden and cooked through. Remove with a slotted spoon and drain on absorbent kitchen paper (paper towels).

6 To make the sauce, mix the soy sauce, honey, wine vinegar, chives and tomato purée (paste) and spoon into a small bowl.

7 Transfer the fritters to serving dishes, garnish and serve with the sauce.

COOK'S TIP

Be careful when heating the oil for deep-frying. It must be heated so that it is almost smoking, then the heat must be reduced immediately. Place the pork in the oil carefully.

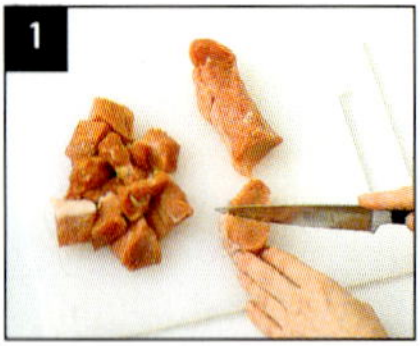

Beef & Broccoli Stir-Fry

Serves 4

INGREDIENTS

225 g/8 oz lean steak, trimmed
2 garlic cloves, crushed
dash of chilli oil
1-cm/½-inch piece fresh root ginger, grated
½ tsp Chinese five-spice powder
2 tbsp dark soy sauce
2 tbsp vegetable oil
150 g/5 oz broccoli florets
1 tbsp light soy sauce
150 ml/¼ pint/⅔ cup beef stock
2 tsp cornflour (cornstarch)
4 tsp water
carrot strips, to garnish

1 Cut the steak into thin strips and place in a shallow glass dish. Mix together the garlic, chilli oil, ginger, Chinese five-spice powder and soy sauce in a small bowl and pour over the beef, tossing to coat the strips. Leave to marinate in the refrigerator.

2 Heat 1 tbsp of the vegetable oil in a wok. Add the broccoli and stir-fry over a medium heat for 4–5 minutes. Remove from the wok with a slotted spoon and set aside.

3 Heat the remaining oil in the wok. Add the steak together with the marinade, and stir-fry for 2-3 minutes, until the steak is browned and sealed.

4 Return the broccoli to the wok and stir in the soy sauce and stock.

5 Blend the cornflour (cornstarch) with the water to form a smooth paste and stir it into the wok. Bring to the boil, stirring, until thickened and clear. Cook for 1 minute.

6 Transfer the beef and broccoli stir-fry to a warm serving dish, arrange the carrot strips in a lattice on top and serve.

COOK'S TIP

Leave the steak to marinate for several hours for a fuller flavour. Cover and leave to marinate in the refrigerator if preparing in advance.

Marinated Beef with Oyster Sauce

Serves 4

INGREDIENTS

225 g/8 oz lean steak, cut into 2.5-cm/1-inch cubes
1 tbsp light soy sauce
1 tsp sesame oil
2 tsp Chinese rice wine or dry sherry
1 tsp caster (superfine) sugar
2 tsp hoisin sauce
1 garlic clove, crushed
1/2 tsp cornflour (cornstarch)
green (bell) pepper slices, to garnish
rice or noodles, to serve

SAUCE:
2 tbsp dark soy sauce
1 tsp caster (superfine) sugar
1/2 tsp cornflour (cornstarch)
3 tbsp oyster sauce
8 tbsp water
2 tbsp vegetable oil
3 garlic cloves, crushed
1-cm/1/2-inch piece fresh root ginger, grated
8 baby corn cobs, halved lengthways
1/2 green (bell) pepper, seeded and thinly sliced
25 g/1 oz bamboo shoots, drained and rinsed

1 Place the steak in a shallow dish. Mix together the soy sauce, sesame oil, Chinese rice wine or sherry, sugar, hoisin sauce, garlic and cornflour (cornstarch) and pour over the steak, turning it to coat. Cover and marinate for at least 1 hour.

2 To make the sauce, mix the dark soy sauce with the sugar, cornflour (cornstarch), oyster sauce and water. Heat the oil in a wok. Add the steak and the marinade and stir-fry for 2–3 minutes, until sealed and lightly browned.

3 Add the garlic, ginger, baby corn cobs, (bell) pepper and bamboo shoots. Stir in the oyster sauce mixture and bring to the boil. Reduce the heat and cook for 2–3 minutes. Transfer to a warm serving dish, garnish with green (bell) pepper slices and serve immediately.

COOK'S TIP

For a fuller flavour, marinate the beef in the refrigerator overnight.

萬
疆

Spicy Beef

Serves 4

INGREDIENTS

225 g/8 oz fillet steak
2 garlic cloves, crushed
1 tsp powdered star anise
1 tbsp dark soy sauce
spring onion (scallion) tassels, to garnish

SAUCE:
2 tbsp vegetable oil
1 bunch spring onions (scallions), halved lengthways
1 tbsp dark soy sauce
1 tbsp dry sherry
$^{1}/_{4}$ tsp chilli sauce
150 ml/$^{1}/_{4}$ pint/$^{2}/_{3}$ cup water
2 tsp cornflour (cornstarch)
4 tsp water

1 Cut the steak into thin strips and place in a shallow dish.

2 Mix together the garlic, star anise and dark soy sauce in a bowl and pour over the steak strips, turning them to coat thoroughly. Cover and leave to marinate in the refrigerator for at least 1 hour.

3 To make the sauce, heat the oil in a preheated wok. Reduce the heat, add the halved spring onions (scallions) and stir-fry for 1-2 minutes. Remove from the wok with a slotted spoon and set aside.

4 Add the beef to the wok, together with the marinade, and stir-fry for 3–4 minutes. Return the halved spring onions (scallions) to the wok and add the soy sauce, sherry, chilli sauce and two thirds of the water.

5 Blend the cornflour (cornstarch) with the remaining water and stir into the wok. Bring to the boil, stirring until the sauce thickens and clears.

6 Transfer to a warm serving dish, garnish with spring onion (scallion) tassels and serve immediately.

COOK'S TIP

Omit the chilli sauce for a milder dish.

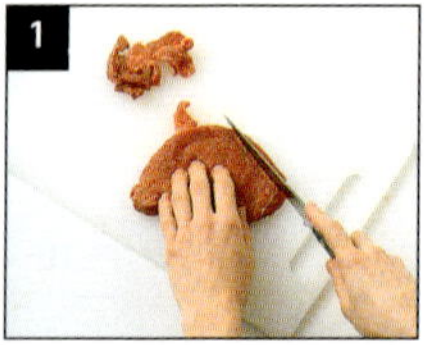

Beef & Beans

Serves 4

INGREDIENTS

450 g/1 lb rump or fillet steak, cut into 2.5-cm/1-inch pieces

MARINADE:
- 2 tsp cornflour (cornstarch)
- 2 tbsp dark soy sauce
- 2 tsp peanut oil

SAUCE:
- 2 tbsp vegetable oil
- 3 garlic cloves, crushed
- 1 small onion, cut into 8
- 225 g/8 oz thin green beans, halved
- 25 g/1 oz/¼ cup unsalted cashews
- 25 g/1 oz canned bamboo shoots, drained and rinsed
- 2 tsp dark soy sauce
- 2 tsp Chinese rice wine or dry sherry
- 125 ml/4 fl oz/½ cup beef stock
- 2 tsp cornflour (cornstarch)
- 4 tsp water
- salt and pepper

1 To make the marinade, mix together the cornflour (cornstarch), soy sauce and peanut oil.

2 Place the steak in a shallow glass bowl. Pour the marinade over the steak, turn to coat, cover and marinate in the refrigerator for 30 minutes.

3 To make the sauce, heat the oil in a preheated wok. Add the garlic, onion, beans, cashews and bamboo shoots and stir-fry for 2–3 minutes.

4 Remove the steak from the marinade, drain, add to the wok and stir-fry for 3–4 minutes.

5 Mix the soy sauce, Chinese rice wine or sherry and beef stock together. Blend the cornflour (cornstarch) with the water and add to the soy sauce mixture, mixing to combine.

6 Stir the mixture into the wok and bring the sauce to the boil, stirring until thickened and clear. Reduce the heat and leave to simmer for 2–3 minutes. Season to taste and serve immediately.

Lamb Meatballs

Serves 4

INGREDIENTS

450 g/1 lb minced (ground) lamb
3 garlic cloves, crushed
2 spring onions (scallions), finely chopped
$^1/_2$ tsp chilli powder
1 tsp Chinese curry powder
1 tbsp chopped fresh parsley
25 g/1 oz/$^1/_2$ cup fresh white breadcrumbs
1 egg, beaten
3 tbsp vegetable oil
125 g/4$^1/_2$ oz Chinese cabbage, shredded
1 leek, sliced
1 tbsp cornflour (cornstarch)
2 tbsp water
300 ml/$^1/_2$ pint/1$^1/_4$ cups lamb stock
1 tbsp dark soy sauce
shredded leek, to garnish

1 Mix the lamb, garlic, spring onions (scallions), chilli powder, Chinese curry powder, parsley and breadcrumbs together in a bowl. Work the egg into the mixture, bringing it together to form a firm mixture. Roll into 16 even-sized balls.

2 Heat the oil in a wok. Add the cabbage and leek and stir-fry for 1 minute. Remove from the wok with a slotted spoon and set aside.

3 Add the meatballs to the wok and fry in batches, turning gently, for 3-4 minutes, until golden.

4 Mix the cornflour (cornstarch) and water together to form a smooth paste and set aside. Pour the lamb stock and soy sauce into the wok and cook for 2–3 minutes. Stir in the cornflour (cornstarch) paste. Bring to the boil and cook, stirring constantly, until the sauce is thickened and clear.

5 Return the cabbage and leek to the wok and cook for 1 minute, until heated through. Arrange the cabbage and leek on a warm serving dish, top with the meatballs, garnish with shredded leek and serve immediately.

VARIATION

Use minced (ground) pork or beef instead of the lamb as an alternative.

Lamb with Mushroom Sauce

Serves 4

INGREDIENTS

- 350 g/12 oz lean boneless lamb, such as fillet or loin
- 2 tbsp vegetable oil
- 3 garlic cloves, crushed
- 1 leek, sliced
- 1 tsp cornflour (cornstarch)
- 4 tbsp light soy sauce
- 3 tbsp Chinese rice wine or dry sherry
- 3 tbsp water
- 1/2 tsp chilli sauce
- 175 g/6 oz large mushrooms, sliced
- 1/2 tsp sesame oil
- fresh red chillies, to garnish

1 Cut the lamb into thin strips.

2 Heat the oil in a preheated wok. Add the lamb strips, garlic and leek and stir-fry for about 2-3 minutes.

3 Mix together the cornflour (cornstarch), soy sauce, Chinese rice wine or dry sherry, water and chilli sauce in a bowl and set aside.

4 Add the mushrooms to the wok and stir-fry for 1 minute.

5 Stir in the sauce and cook for 2–3 minutes, or until the lamb is cooked through and tender. Sprinkle the sesame oil over the top and transfer to a warm serving dish. Garnish with red chillies and serve immediately.

COOK'S TIP

Use rehydrated dried Chinese mushrooms obtainable from specialist shops or Chinese supermarkets for a really authentic flavour.

VARIATION

The lamb can be replaced with lean steak or pork fillet (tenderloin) in this classic recipe from Beijing. You could also use 2–3 spring onions (scallions), 1 shallot or 1 small onion instead of the leek, if you prefer.

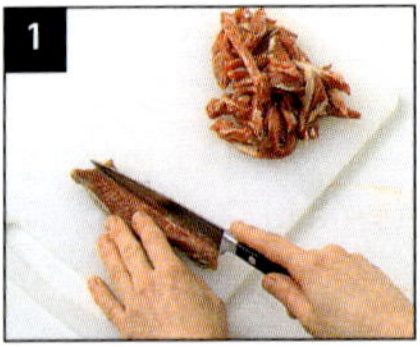

Lamb with Garlic Sauce

Serves 4

INGREDIENTS

450 g/1 lb lamb fillet or loin
2 tbsp dark soy sauce
2 tsp sesame oil
2 tbsp Chinese rice wine or dry sherry
1/2 tsp Szechuan pepper
4 tbsp vegetable oil
4 garlic cloves, crushed
60 g/2 oz water chestnuts, quartered
1 green (bell) pepper, seeded and sliced
1 tbsp wine vinegar
1 tbsp sesame oil
rice or noodles, to serve

1 Cut the lamb into 2.5-cm/1-inch pieces and place in a shallow dish.

2 Mix together 1 tbsp of the soy sauce, the sesame oil, Chinese rice wine or sherry and Szechuan pepper. Pour the mixture over the lamb, turning to coat, and leave to marinate for 30 minutes.

3 Heat the vegetable oil in a preheated wok. Remove the lamb from the marinade and add to the wok with the garlic. Stir-fry for 2–3 minutes.

4 Add the water chestnuts and (bell) pepper to the wok and stir-fry for 1 minute.

5 Add the remaining soy sauce and the wine vinegar, mixing well.

6 Add the sesame oil and cook, stirring, for 1–2 minutes, or until the lamb is cooked through.

7 Transfer the lamb and garlic sauce to a warm serving dish and serve at once with rice or noodles.

COOK'S TIP

Sesame oil is used as a flavouring, rather than for frying, as it burns readily, hence it is added at the end of cooking.

VARIATION

Chinese chives, also known as garlic chives, would make an appropriate garnish for this dish.

Hot Lamb

Serves 4

INGREDIENTS

450 g/1 lb lean, boneless lamb
2 tbsp hoisin sauce
1 tbsp dark soy sauce
1 garlic clove, crushed
2 tsp grated fresh root ginger
2 tbsp vegetable oil
2 onions, sliced
1 fennel bulb, sliced
4 tbsp water

SAUCE:
1 large fresh red chilli, cut into thin strips
1 fresh green chilli, cut into thin strips
2 tbsp rice wine vinegar
2 tsp light brown sugar
2 tbsp peanut oil
1 tsp sesame oil

1 Cut the lamb into 2.5-cm/1-inch cubes and place in a shallow glass dish.

2 Mix together the hoisin sauce, soy sauce, garlic and ginger in a bowl and pour over the lamb, turning to coat well. Leave to marinate in the refrigerator for 20 minutes.

3 Heat the vegetable oil in a preheated wok. Add the lamb and stir-fry for 1–2 minutes.

4 Add the onions and fennel to the wok and cook for a further 2 minutes, or until they are just beginning to brown.

5 Stir in the water, cover and cook for 2–3 minutes.

6 To make the sauce, place the chillies, rice wine vinegar, sugar, peanut oil and sesame oil in a saucepan and cook over a low heat for 3-4 minutes, stirring to combine.

7 Transfer the lamb and onions to a warm serving dish, pour the sauce on top, toss lightly and serve immediately.

VARIATION

Use beef, pork or duck instead of the lamb and vary the vegetables, using leeks or celery instead of the onion and fennel.

Sesame Lamb Stir-Fry

Serves 4

INGREDIENTS

450 g/1 lb boneless lean lamb
2 tbsp peanut oil
2 leeks, sliced
1 carrot, cut into matchsticks
2 garlic cloves, crushed
3 fl oz/85 ml/$^1/_3$ cup lamb or vegetable stock
2 tsp light brown sugar
1 tbsp dark soy sauce
4$^1/_2$ tsp sesame seeds

1 Cut the lamb into thin strips. Heat the peanut oil in a preheated wok. Add the lamb and stir-fry for 2–3 minutes. Remove the lamb from the wok with a slotted spoon and set aside.

2 Add the leek, carrot and garlic to the wok and stir-fry in the remaining oil for 1–2 minutes. Remove from the wok with a slotted spoon and set aside. Drain any oil from the wok.

3 Place the stock, sugar and soy sauce in the wok and add the lamb. Cook, stirring constantly to coat the lamb, for 2–3 minutes. Sprinkle the sesame seeds over the top, turning the lamb to coat.

4 Spoon the leek mixture on to a warm serving dish and top with the lamb. Serve immediately.

COOK'S TIP

Be careful not to burn the sugar in the wok when heating and coating the meat, otherwise the flavour of the dish will be spoiled.

VARIATION

This recipe would be equally delicious made with strips of skinless chicken or turkey breast or with prawns (shrimp). The cooking times remain the same.

Fish & Seafood

Throughout the Far Eastern countries, fish and seafood play a major role in the diet, as they are both plentiful and healthy. There are many different ways of cooking fish and seafood in a wok – they may be steamed, deep-fried or stir-fried with a range of delicious spices and sauces.

Japan is famed for its sashimi *or raw fish, but this is just one of the wide range of fish dishes served. Fish and seafood are offered at every meal in Japan, many of them cooked in a wok. Many unusual and tasty dishes are offered in this chapter, combining fish and seafood with aromatic herbs and spices, pastes and sauces.*

When buying fish and seafood for the recipes in this chapter, freshness is imperative to flavour, so be sure to buy and use it as soon as possible, preferably on the same day.

Teriyaki Stir-Fried Salmon with Crispy Leeks

Serves 4

INGREDIENTS

450 g/1 lb salmon fillet, skinned
2 tbsp sweet soy sauce
2 tbsp tomato ketchup
1 tsp rice wine vinegar
1 tbsp demerara sugar
1 clove garlic, crushed
4 tbsp corn oil
450 g/1 lb leeks, thinly shredded
finely chopped red chillies, to garnish

1 Using a sharp knife, cut the salmon into slices. Place the slices of salmon in a shallow non-metallic dish.

2 Mix together the soy sauce, tomato ketchup, rice wine vinegar, sugar and garlic.

3 Pour the mixture over the salmon, toss well and leave to marinate for about 30 minutes.

4 Meanwhile, heat 3 tablespoons of the corn oil in a large preheated wok.

5 Add the leeks to the wok and stir-fry over a medium high heat for about 10 minutes, or until the leeks become crispy and tender.

6 Using a slotted spoon, carefully remove the leeks from the wok and transfer to warm serving plates.

7 Add the remaining oil to the wok. Add the salmon and the marinade to the wok and cook for 2 minutes. Spoon over the leeks, garnish and serve immediately.

VARIATION

You can use a fillet of beef instead of the salmon, if you prefer.

Stir-Fried Salmon with Pineapple

Serves 4

INGREDIENTS

100 g/3¾ oz/1 cup baby corn cobs, halved
2 tbsp sunflower oil
1 red onion, sliced
1 orange (bell) pepper, deseeded and sliced
1 green (bell) pepper, deseeded and sliced
450 g/1 lb salmon fillet, skin removed
1 tbsp paprika
225 g/8 oz can cubed pineapple, drained
100 g/3½ oz/1 cup beansprouts
2 tbsp tomato ketchup
2 tbsp soy sauce
2 tbsp medium sherry
1 tsp cornflour (cornstarch)

1 Using a sharp knife, cut the baby corn cobs in half.

2 Heat the sunflower oil in a large preheated wok. Add the onion, (bell) peppers and baby corn cobs to the wok and stir-fry for 5 minutes.

3 Rinse the salmon fillet under cold running water and pat dry with absorbent kitchen paper.

4 Cut the salmon flesh into thin strips and place in a large bowl. Sprinkle with the paprika and toss until well coated.

5 Add the salmon to the wok together with the pineapple and stir-fry for a further 2–3 minutes or until the fish is tender.

6 Add the beansprouts to the wok and toss well.

7 Mix together the tomato ketchup, soy sauce, sherry and cornflour (cornstarch). Add the mixture to the wok and cook until the juices start to thicken. Transfer to warm serving plates and serve immediately.

VARIATION

You can use trout fillets instead of the salmon as an alternative, if you prefer.

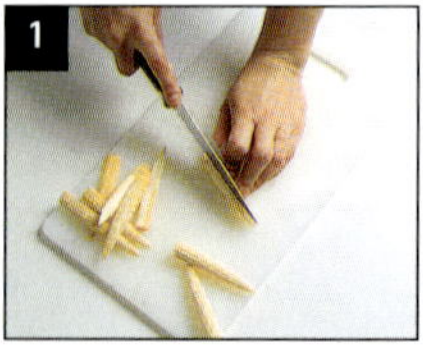

Tuna & Vegetable Stir-Fry

Serves 4

INGREDIENTS

225 g/8 oz carrots
2 tbsp corn oil
1 onion, sliced
175 g/6 oz/2½ cups mangetout (snow peas)
175 g/6 oz/1¾ cups baby corn cobs, halved
450 g/1 lb fresh tuna
2 tbsp fish sauce
15 g/½ oz/1 tbsp palm sugar
finely grated zest and juice of 1 orange
2 tbsp sherry
1 tsp cornflour (cornstarch)
rice or noodles, to serve

1 Using a sharp knife, cut the carrots into thin sticks.

2 Heat the corn oil in a large preheated wok.

3 Add the onion, carrots, mangetout (snow peas) and baby corn cobs to the wok and stir-fry for 5 minutes.

4 Using a sharp knife, thinly slice the tuna.

5 Add the tuna to the wok and stir-fry for 2–3 minutes, or until the tuna turns opaque.

6 Mix together the fish sauce, palm sugar, orange zest and juice, sherry and cornflour (cornstarch).

7 Pour the mixture over the tuna and vegetables and cook for 2 minutes, or until the juices thicken. Serve with rice or noodles.

VARIATION

Try using swordfish steaks instead of the tuna. Swordfish steaks are now widely available and are similar in texture to tuna.

COOK'S TIP

Palm sugar is a thick, coarse brown sugar that has a slightly caramel taste. It is sold in round cakes or in small, round, flat containers.

1

3

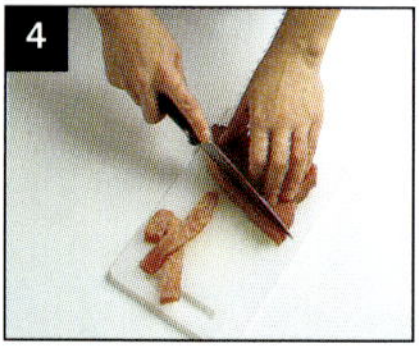
4

Stir-Fried Cod with Mango

Serves 4

INGREDIENTS

175 g/6 oz carrots
2 tbsp vegetable oil
1 red onion, sliced
1 red (bell) pepper, deseeded and sliced
1 green (bell) pepper, deseeded and sliced
450 g/1 lb skinless cod fillet
1 ripe mango
1 tsp cornflour (cornstarch)
1 tbsp soy sauce
100 ml/3½ fl oz/1⅓ cup tropical fruit juice
1 tbsp lime juice
1 tbsp chopped coriander (cilantro)

1 Using a sharp knife, slice the carrots into thin sticks.

2 Heat the vegetable oil in a preheated wok.

3 Add the onions, carrots and (bell) peppers to the wok and stir-fry for 5 minutes.

4 Using a sharp knife, cut the cod into small cubes.

5 Peel the mango, then carefully remove the flesh from the centre stone. Cut the flesh into thin slices.

6 Add the cod and mango to the wok and stir-fry for a further 4–5 minutes, or until the fish is cooked through. Do not stir the mixture too much or you may break the fish up.

7 Mix the cornflour (cornstarch), soy sauce, fruit juice and lime juice in a small bowl.

8 Pour the cornflour (cornstarch) mixture over the stir-fry and allow the mixture to bubble and the juices to thicken. Scatter with coriander (cilantro) and serve immediately.

VARIATION

You can use paw-paw (papaya) as an alternative to the mango, if you prefer.

1

5

7

Stir-Fried Gingered Monkfish

Serves 4

INGREDIENTS

450 g/1 lb monkfish
1 tbsp freshly grated root ginger
2 tbsp sweet chilli sauce
1 tbsp corn oil
100 g/3½ oz/1 cup fine asparagus
3 spring onions (scallions), sliced
1 tsp sesame oil

1. Using a sharp knife, slice the monkfish into thin flat rounds.

2. Mix the ginger with the chilli sauce in a small bowl.

3. Brush the ginger and chilli sauce mixture over the monkfish pieces.

4. Heat the corn oil in a large preheated wok.

5. Add the monkfish, asparagus and spring onions (scallions) to the wok and stir-fry for about 5 minutes.

6. Remove the wok from the heat, drizzle the sesame oil over the stir-fry and toss well to combine.

7. Transfer to warm serving plates and serve immediately.

VARIATION

Monkfish is quite expensive, but it is well worth using it as it has a wonderful flavour and texture. At a push you could use cubes of chunky cod fillet instead.

COOK'S TIP

Some recipes specify to grate ginger before it is cooked with other ingredients. To do this, just peel the flesh and rub it at a 45° angle up and down on the fine section of a metal grater, or use a special wooden or ceramic ginger grater.

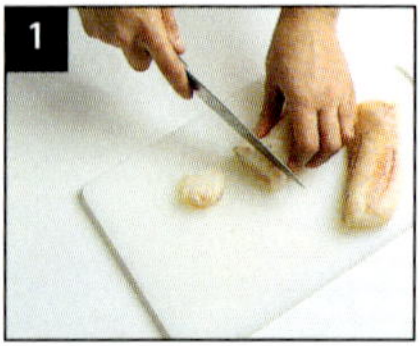
1

3

5

Braised Fish Fillets

Serves 4

INGREDIENTS

3–4 small Chinese dried mushrooms
300–350 g/10½–12 oz fish fillets
1 tsp salt
½ egg white, lightly beaten
1 tsp cornflour (cornstarch) paste
600 ml/1 pint/2½ cups vegetable oil
1 tsp finely chopped ginger root
2 spring onions (scallions), finely chopped
1 garlic clove, finely chopped
½ small green (bell) pepper, deseeded and cut into small cubes
½ small carrot, thinly sliced
60 g/2 oz/½ cup canned sliced bamboo shoots, rinsed and drained
½ tsp sugar
1 tbsp light soy sauce
1 tsp rice wine or dry sherry
1 tbsp chilli bean sauce
2–3 tbsp Chinese stock or water
a few drops of sesame oil

1 Soak the dried mushrooms in a bowl of warm water for 30 minutes. Drain the mushrooms thoroughly on paper towels, reserving the soaking water for stock or soup. Squeeze the mushrooms to extract all of the moisture, cut off and discard any hard stems and slice thinly.

2 Cut the fish into bite-sized pieces, then place in a shallow dish and mix with a pinch of salt, the egg white and cornflour (cornstarch) paste, turning the fish to coat well.

3 Heat the oil in a preheated wok. Add the fish pieces to the wok and deep-fry for about 1 minute. Remove the fish pieces with a slotted spoon and leave to drain on paper towels.

4 Pour off the excess oil, leaving about 1 tablespoon in the wok. Add the ginger, spring onions (scallions) and garlic to flavour the oil for a few seconds, then add the (bell) pepper, carrots and bamboo shoots and stir-fry for about 1 minute.

5 Add the sugar, soy sauce, wine, chilli bean sauce, stock or water, and the remaining salt and bring to the boil. Add the fish pieces, stir to coat well with the sauce, and braise for 1 minute.

6 Sprinkle with sesame oil and serve immediately.

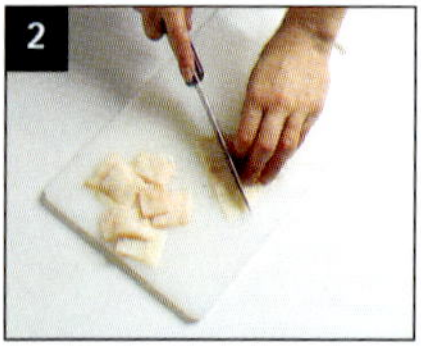
2

2

4

Fried Fish with Coconut & Basil

Serves 4

INGREDIENTS

2 tbsp vegetable oil
450 g/1 lb skinless cod fillet
25 g/1 oz/1/4 cup seasoned flour
1 clove garlic, crushed
2 tbsp red Thai curry paste
1 tbsp fish sauce
300 ml/1/2 pint/1 1/4 cups coconut milk
175 g/6 oz cherry tomatoes, halved
20 fresh basil leaves
fragrant rice, to serve

1 Heat the vegetable oil in a large preheated wok.

2 Using a sharp knife, cut the fish into large cubes, taking care to remove any bones with a pair of tweezers.

3 Place the seasoned flour in a bowl. Add the cubes of fish and mix until well coated.

4 Add the coated fish to the wok and stir-fry over a high heat for 3–4 minutes, or until the fish just begins to brown at the edges.

5 Mix together the garlic, curry paste, fish sauce and coconut milk in a bowl. Pour the mixture over the fish and bring to the boil.

6 Add the tomatoes to the mixture in the wok and leave to simmer for 5 minutes.

7 Roughly chop or tear the fresh basil leaves. Add the basil to the wok, stir carefully to combine, taking care not to break up the cubes of fish.

8 Transfer to serving plates and serve hot with fragrant rice.

COOK'S TIP

Take care not to overcook the dish once the tomatoes are added, otherwise they will break down and the skins will come away.

Coconut Prawns (Shrimp)

Serves 4

INGREDIENTS

50 g/1¾ oz/½ cup desiccated (shredded) coconut
25 g/1 oz/½ cup fresh white breadcrumbs
1 tsp Chinese five-spice powder
½ tsp salt
finely grated zest of 1 lime
1 egg white
450 g/1 lb fan-tail prawns (shrimp)
sunflower or corn oil, for frying
lemon wedges, to garnish

1 Mix together the dessicated (shredded) coconut, white breadcrumbs, Chinese five-spice powder, salt and finely grated lime zest in a bowl.

2 Lightly whisk the egg white in a separate bowl.

3 Rinse the prawns (shrimp) under cold running water and pat dry with absorbent kitchen paper.

4 Dip the prawns (shrimp) into the egg white then into the coconut crumb mixture, so that they are evenly coated.

5 Heat about 5 cm/2 inches of sunflower or corn oil in a large preheated wok.

6 Add the prawns (shrimp) to the wok and stir-fry for about 5 minutes or until golden and crispy.

7 Remove the prawns (shrimp) with a slotted spoon, transfer to absorbent kitchen paper and leave to drain thoroughly.

8 Transfer the coconut prawns (shrimp) to warm serving dishes and garnish with lemon wedges. Serve immediately.

COOK'S TIP

Serve the prawns (shrimp) with a soy sauce or chilli sauce, if you wish.

Prawn (Shrimp) Omelette

Serves 4

INGREDIENTS

2 tbsp sunflower oil
4 spring onions (scallions), sliced
350 g/12 oz peeled prawns (shrimp)
100 g/3½ oz/1 cup beansprouts
1 tsp cornflour (cornstarch)
1 tbsp light soy sauce
6 eggs

1 Heat the sunflower oil in a large preheated wok.

2 Using a sharp knife, trim the spring onions (scallions) and cut into slices.

3 Add the prawns (shrimp), spring onions (scallions) and beansprouts to the wok and stir-fry for 2 minutes.

4 Mix together the cornflour (cornstarch) and soy sauce in a small bowl.

5 Beat the eggs with 3 tablespoons of cold water and then blend with the cornflour (cornstarch) and soy mixture.

6 Add the egg mixture to the wok and cook for 5–6 minutes, or until the mixture sets.

7 Transfer the omelette to a serving plate and cut into quarters to serve.

COOK'S TIP

It is important to use fresh beansprouts for this dish as the canned ones don't have the crunchy texture necessary.

VARIATION

Add any other vegetables of your choice, such as grated carrot or cooked peas, to the omelette in step 3, if you wish.

Prawns (Shrimp) with Spicy Tomatoes

Serves 4

INGREDIENTS

2 tbsp corn oil
1 onion
2 cloves garlic, crushed
1 tsp cumin seeds
1 tbsp demerara sugar
400 g/14 oz can chopped tomatoes
1 tbsp sundried tomato purée
1 tbsp chopped fresh basil
450 g/1 lb peeled king prawns (shrimp)
salt and pepper

1 Heat the corn oil in a large preheated wok.

2 Using a sharp knife, finely chop the onion.

3 Add the onion and garlic to the wok and stir-fry for 2–3 minutes, or until softened.

4 Stir in the cumin seeds and stir-fry for 1 minute.

5 Add the sugar, chopped tomatoes and sundried tomato purée to the wok. Bring the mixture to the boil, then reduce the heat and leave the sauce to simmer for 10 minutes.

6 Add the basil, prawns (shrimp) and salt and pepper to taste to the mixture in the wok. Increase the heat and cook for a further 2–3 minutes or until the prawns (shrimp) are completely cooked through.

COOK'S TIP

Always heat your wok before you add oil or other ingredients. This will prevent anything from sticking to it.

COOK'S TIP

Sundried tomato purée has a much more intense flavour than that of normal tomato purée. It adds a distinctive intensity to any tomato-based dish.

Prawns (Shrimp) with Crispy Ginger

Serves 4

INGREDIENTS

5 cm/2 inch piece fresh root ginger
oil, for frying
1 onion, diced
225 g/8 oz carrots, diced
100 g/3½ oz/½ cup frozen peas
100 g/3½ oz/1 cup beansprouts
450 g/1 lb peeled king prawns (shrimp)
1 tsp Chinese five-spice powder
1 tbsp tomato purée
1 tbsp soy sauce

1 Using a sharp knife, peel the ginger and slice it into very thin sticks.

2 Heat about 2.5 cm/1 inch of oil in a large preheated wok.

3 Add the ginger to the wok and stir-fry for 1 minute or until the ginger is crispy. Remove the ginger with a slotted spoon and leave to drain on absorbent kitchen paper. Set aside.

4 Drain all of the oil from the wok except for about 2 tablespoons.

5 Add the onions and carrots to the wok and stir-fry for 5 minutes.

6 Add the peas and beansprouts to the wok and stir-fry for 2 minutes.

7 Rinse the prawns (shrimp) under cold running water and pat dry thoroughly with absorbent kitchen paper.

8 Mix together the five-spice powder, tomato purée and soy sauce. Brush the mixture over the prawns (shrimp).

9 Add the prawns (shrimp) to the wok and stir-fry for a further 2 minutes, or until the prawns (shrimp) are completely cooked through. Transfer the prawn (shrimp) mixture to a warm serving bowl and top with the reserved crispy ginger. Serve immediately.

VARIATION

Use slices of white fish instead of the prawns (shrimp) as an alternative, if you wish.

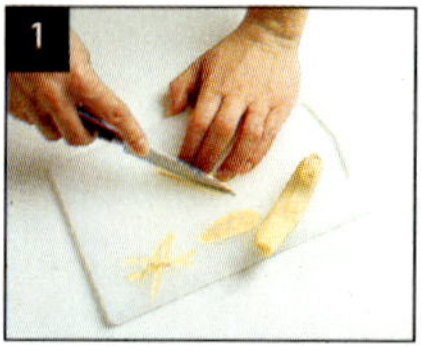

Vegetables with Prawns (Shrimp) & Egg

Serves 4

INGREDIENTS

225 g/8 oz courgettes (zucchini)
3 tbsp vegetable oil
2 eggs
225 g/8 oz carrots, grated
1 onion, sliced
150 g/5½ oz/1½ cups beansprouts
225 g/8 oz peeled prawns (shrimp)
2 tbsp soy sauce
pinch of five-spice Chinese powder
25 g/1 oz/¼ cup peanuts, chopped
2 tbsp fresh chopped coriander (cilantro)

1 Finely grate the courgettes (zucchini).

2 Heat 1 tablespoon of the oil in a large preheated wok.

3 Beat the eggs with 2 tablespoons of cold water. Pour the mixture into the wok and cook for 2–3 minutes or until the egg sets.

4 Remove the omelette from the wok and transfer to a clean board. Fold the omelette, cut it into thin strips and set aside until required.

5 Add the remaining oil to the wok. Add the carrots, onion and courgettes (zucchini) and stir-fry for 5 minutes.

6 Add the beansprouts and prawns (shrimp) to the wok and cook for a further 2 minutes, or until the prawns (shrimp) are heated through.

7 Add the soy sauce, five-spice powder and peanuts to the wok together with the strips of omelette and heat through. Garnish with chopped fresh coriander (cilantro) and serve.

COOK'S TIP

The water is mixed with the egg in step 3 for a lighter, less rubbery omelette.

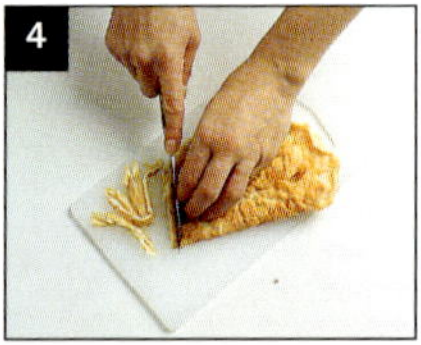

Stir-Fried Crab Claws with Chilli

Serves 4

INGREDIENTS

700 g/1 lb 9 oz crab claws
1 tbsp corn oil
2 cloves garlic, crushed
1 tbsp grated fresh root ginger
3 red chillies, deseeded and finely chopped
2 tbsp sweet chilli sauce
3 tbsp tomato ketchup
300 ml/½ pint/1¼ cups cooled fish stock
1 tbsp cornflour (cornstarch)
salt and pepper
1 tbsp fresh chives, snipped

1 Gently crack the crab claws with a nut cracker. This process will allow the flavours of the chilli, garlic and ginger to fully penetrate the crab meat.

2 Heat the corn oil in a large preheated wok.

3 Add the crab claws to the wok and stir-fry for about 5 minutes.

4 Add the garlic, ginger and chillies to the wok and stir-fry for 1 minute, tossing the crab claws to coat all over.

5 Mix together the chilli sauce, tomato ketchup, fish stock and cornflour (cornstarch) in a small bowl.

6 Add the chilli and cornflour (cornstarch) mixture to the wok and cook, stirring occasionally, until the sauce starts to thicken. Season with salt and pepper to taste.

7 Transfer the crab claws and chilli sauce to warm serving dishes and garnish with plenty of snipped fresh chives. Serve immediately.

COOK'S TIP

If crab claws are not easily available, use a whole crab, cut into eight pieces, instead.

Chinese Leaves with Shiitake Mushrooms & Crab Meat

Serves 4

INGREDIENTS

225 g/8 oz shiitake mushrooms
2 tbsp vegetable oil
2 cloves garlic, crushed
6 spring onions (scallions), sliced
1 head Chinese leaves, shredded
1 tbsp mild curry paste
6 tbsp coconut milk
200 g/7 oz can white crab meat, drained
1 tsp chilli flakes

1 Using a sharp knife, cut the the mushrooms into slices.

2 Heat the vegetable oil in a large preheated wok.

3 Add the mushrooms and garlic to the wok and stir-fry for 3 minutes or until the mushrooms have softened.

4 Add the spring onions (scallions) and shredded Chinese leaves to the wok and stir-fry until the leaves have wilted.

5 Mix together the mild curry paste and coconut milk in a small bowl.

6 Add the curry paste and coconut milk mixture to the wok together with the crab meat and chilli flakes. Mix together until well combined and heat through until the juices start to bubble.

7 Transfer to warm serving bowls and then serve immediately.

COOK'S TIP

Shiitake mushrooms are now readily available in the fresh vegetable section of most large supermarkets.

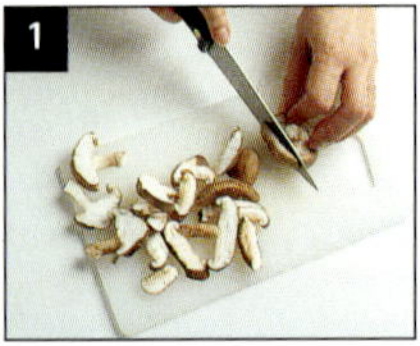

Stir-Fried Lettuce with Mussels & Lemon Grass

Serves 4

INGREDIENTS

1 kg/2 lb 4oz mussels in their shells, scrubbed
2 stalks lemon grass, thinly sliced
2 tbsp lemon juice
100 ml/3½ fl oz/⅓ cup water
25 g/1 oz/2 tbsp butter
1 Iceberg lettuce
finely grated zest of 1 lemon
2 tbsp oyster sauce

1 Place the mussels in a large saucepan.

2 Add the lemon grass, lemon juice and water to the pan of mussels, cover with a tight-fitting lid and cook for 5 minutes or until the mussels have opened. Discard any mussels that do not open.

3 Carefully remove the cooked mussels from their shells, using a fork.

4 Heat the butter in a large preheated wok.

5 Add the lettuce and lemon zest to the wok and stir-fry for 2 minutes, or until the lettuce begins to wilt.

6 Add the oyster sauce to the mixture in the wok, stir and heat through. Serve immediately.

COOK'S TIP

Lemon grass with its citrus fragrance and lemon flavour looks like a fibrous spring onion (scallion) and is often used in Thai cooking.

COOK'S TIP

When using fresh mussels, be sure to discard any opened mussels before scrubbing and any unopened mussels after cooking.

Mussels in Black Bean Sauce with Spinach

Serves 4

INGREDIENTS

350 g/12 oz leeks
350 g/12 oz cooked green-lipped mussels (shelled)
1 tsp cumin seeds
2 tbsp vegetable oil
2 cloves garlic, crushed
1 red (bell) pepper, deseeded and sliced
50 g/1¾ oz/¾ cup canned bamboo shoots, drained
175 g/6 oz baby spinach
160 g/5¾ oz jar black bean sauce

1 Using a sharp knife, trim the leeks and shred them.

2 Place the mussels in a large bowl, sprinkle with the cumin seeds and toss well to coat all over.

3 Heat the vegetable oil in a large preheated wok.

4 Add the leeks, garlic and red (bell) pepper to the wok and stir-fry for 5 minutes, or until the vegetables are tender.

5 Add the bamboo shoots, baby spinach leaves and cooked green-lipped mussels to the wok and stir-fry for about 2 minutes.

6 Pour the black bean sauce over the ingredients in the wok, toss well to coat all over and leave to simmer for a few seconds, stirring occasionally.

7 Transfer the stir-fry to warm serving bowls and serve immediately.

COOK'S TIP

If the green-lipped mussels are not available they can be bought shelled in cans and jars from most large supermarkets.

Scallop Pancakes

Serves 4

INGREDIENTS

100 g/3½ oz fine green beans
1 red chilli
450 g/1 lb scallops, without roe
1 egg
3 spring onions (scallions), sliced
50 g/1¾ oz/½ cup rice flour
1 tbsp fish sauce
oil, for frying
sweet chilli dip, to serve

1 Using a sharp knife, trim the green beans and slice them very thinly.

2 Using a sharp knife, deseed and very finely chop the red chilli.

3 Bring a small saucepan of lightly salted water to the boil. Add the green beans to the pan and cook for 3–4 minutes or until just softened.

4 Roughly chop the scallops and place them in a large bowl. Add the cooked beans to the scallops.

5 Mix the egg with the spring onions (scallions), rice flour, fish sauce and chilli until well combined. Add to the scallops and mix well.

6 Heat about 2.5 cm/1 inch of oil in a large preheated wok. Add a ladleful of the mixture to the wok and cook for 5 minutes until golden and set. Remove the pancake from the wok and leave to drain on absorbent kitchen paper. Repeat with the remaining pancake mixture.

7 Serve the pancakes hot with a sweet chilli dip.

VARIATION

You could use prawns (shrimp) or shelled clams instead of the scallops, if you prefer.

Seared Scallops with Butter Sauce

Serves 4

INGREDIENTS

450 g/1 lb scallops, without roe
6 spring onions (scallions)
2 tbsp vegetable oil
1 green chilli, deseeded and sliced
3 tbsp sweet soy sauce
50 g/1¾ oz/1½ tbsp butter, cubed

1 Rinse the scallops under cold running water, then pat the scallops dry with absorbent kitchen paper.

2 Using a sharp knife, slice each scallop in half horizontally.

3 Using a sharp knife, trim and slice the spring onions (scallions).

4 Heat the vegetable oil in a large preheated wok.

5 Add the chilli, spring onions (scallions) and scallops to the wok and stir-fry over a high heat for 4–5 minutes, or until the scallops are just cooked through.

6 Add the soy sauce and butter to the scallop stir-fry and heat through until the butter melts.

7 Transfer to warm serving bowls and serve hot.

COOK'S TIP

If you buy scallops on the shell, slide a knife underneath the membrane to loosen and cut off the tough muscle that holds the scallop to the shell. Discard the black stomach sac and intestinal vein.

COOK'S TIP

Use frozen scallops if preferred, but make sure they are completely defrosted before cooking. In addition, do not overcook them as they will easily disintegrate.

Stir-Fried Oysters with Tofu (Bean Curd), Lemon & Coriander (Cilantro)

Serves 4

INGREDIENTS

225 g/8 oz leeks
350 g/12 oz tofu (bean curd)
2 tbsp sunflower oil
350 g/12 oz shelled oysters
2 tbsp fresh lemon juice
1 tsp cornflour (cornstarch)
2 tbsp light soy sauce
100 ml/3½ fl oz/⅓ cup fish stock
2 tbsp chopped fresh coriander (cilantro)
1 tsp finely grated lemon zest

1 Using a sharp knife, trim and slice the leeks.

2 Cut the tofu (bean curd) into bite-sized pieces.

3 Heat the sunflower oil in a large preheated wok.

4 Add the leeks to the wok and stir-fry for about 2 minutes.

5 Add the tofu (bean curd) and oysters to the wok and stir-fry for 1–2 minutes.

6 Mix together the lemon juice, cornflour (cornstarch), light soy sauce and fish stock in a small bowl.

7 Pour the cornflour (cornstarch) mixture into the wok and cook, stirring occasionally, until the juices start to thicken.

8 Transfer to serving bowls and scatter the coriander (cilantro) and lemon zest on top. Serve immediately.

VARIATION

Shelled clams or mussels could be used instead of the oysters, if you prefer.

1

2

6

Crispy Fried Squid with Salt & Pepper

Serves 4

INGREDIENTS

450 g/1 lb squid, cleaned
25 g/1 oz/4 tbsp cornflour (cornstarch)
1 tsp salt
1 tsp freshly ground black pepper
1 tsp chilli flakes
groundnut oil, for frying
dipping sauce, to serve

1 Using a sharp knife, remove the tentacles from the squid and trim. Slice the bodies down one side and open out to give a flat piece.

2 Score the flat pieces with a criss-cross pattern then cut each piece into 4.

3 Mix together the cornflour (cornstarch), salt, pepper and chilli flakes.

4 Place the salt and pepper mixture in a large polythene bag. Add the squid pieces and shake the bag thoroughly to coat the squid in the flour mixture.

5 Heat about 5 cm/2 inches of groundnut oil in a large preheated wok.

6 Add the squid pieces to the wok and stir-fry, in batches, for about 2 minutes, or until the squid pieces start to curl up. Do not overcook or the squid will become tough.

7 Remove the squid pieces with a slotted spoon, transfer to absorbent kitchen paper and leave to drain thoroughly.

8 Transfer to serving plates and serve immediately with a dipping sauce.

COOK'S TIP

Squid tubes may be purchased frozen if they are not available fresh. They are usually ready-cleaned and are easy to use. Ensure that they are completely defrosted before cooking.

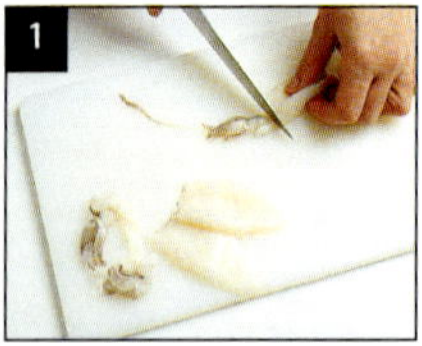

Stir-Fried Squid with Green (Bell) Peppers & Black Bean Sauce

Serves 4

INGREDIENTS

450 g/1 lb squid rings
2 tbsp plain (all-purpose) flour
½ tsp salt
1 green (bell) pepper
2 tbsp groundnut oil
1 red onion, sliced
160 g/5¾ oz jar black bean sauce

1 Rinse the squid rings under cold running water and pat dry with absorbent kitchen paper.

2 Place the plain (all-purpose) flour and salt in a bowl and mix together. Add the squid rings and toss until they are finely coated.

3 Using a sharp knife, deseed the (bell) pepper. Slice the (bell) pepper into thin strips.

4 Heat the groundnut oil in a large preheated wok.

5 Add the (bell) pepper and red onion to the wok and stir-fry for about 2 minutes, or until the vegetables are just beginning to soften.

6 Add the squid rings to the wok and cook for a further 5 minutes, or until the squid is cooked through.

7 Add the black bean sauce to the wok and heat through until the juices are bubbling. Transfer to warm serving bowls and serve immediately.

COOK'S TIP

Serve this recipe with fried rice or noodles tossed in soy sauce, if you wish.

Steamed Fish with Black Bean Sauce

Serves 4

INGREDIENTS

900 g/2 lb whole snapper, cleaned and scaled
3 garlic cloves, crushed
2 tbsp black bean sauce
1 tsp cornflour (cornstarch)
2 tsp sesame oil
2 tbsp light soy sauce
2 tsp caster (superfine) sugar
2 tbsp dry sherry
1 small leek, shredded
1 small red (bell) pepper, seeded and cut into thin strips
shredded leek and lemon wedges, to garnish
boiled rice or noodles, to serve

1 Rinse the fish inside and out with cold running water and pat dry with kitchen paper (paper towels). Make 2-3 diagonal slashes in the flesh on each side of the fish, using a sharp knife. Rub the garlic into the fish.

2 Thoroughly mix the black bean sauce, cornflour (cornstarch), sesame oil, light soy sauce, sugar and dry sherry together in a bowl. Place the fish in a shallow heatproof dish and pour the sauce mixture over the top of the fish.

3 Sprinkle the leek and (bell) pepper strips on top of the sauce. Place the dish in the top of a steamer, cover and steam for 10 minutes, or until the fish is cooked through.

4 Transfer to a serving dish, garnish with shredded leek and lemon wedges and serve with boiled rice or noodles.

VARIATION

Whole sea bream or sea bass may be used in this recipe instead of snapper, if you prefer.

COOK'S TIP

Insert the point of a sharp knife into the fish to test if it is cooked. The fish is cooked through if the knife goes into the flesh easily.

Steamed Snapper with Fruit & Ginger Stuffing

Serves 4

INGREDIENTS

1.4 kg/3 lb whole snapper, cleaned and scaled
175 g/6 oz spinach
orange slices and shredded spring onions (scallions), to garnish

STUFFING:
60 g/2 oz/2 cups cooked long-grain rice
1 tsp grated fresh root ginger
2 spring onions (scallions), finely chopped
2 tsp light soy sauce
1 tsp sesame oil
1/2 tsp ground star anise
1 orange, segmented and chopped

1 Rinse the fish inside and out under cold running water and pat dry with kitchen paper (paper towels). Blanch the spinach for 40 seconds, rinse in cold water and drain well, pressing out as much moisture as possible. Arrange the spinach on a heatproof plate and place the fish on top.

2 To make the stuffing, mix together the cooked rice, grated ginger, spring onion (scallion), soy sauce, sesame oil, star anise and orange in a bowl.

3 Spoon the stuffing into the body cavity of the fish, pressing it in well with a spoon.

4 Cover the plate and cook in a steamer for 10 minutes, or until the fish is cooked through. Transfer the fish to a warmed serving dish, garnish with orange slices and shredded spring onion (scallion) and serve immediately.

COOK'S TIP

The name snapper covers a family of tropical and subtropical fish that vary in colour. They may be red, orange, pink, red, grey or blue-green. Some are striped or spotted and they range in size from about 15 cm/6 inches to 90 cm/3 ft.

Trout with Pineapple

Serves 4

INGREDIENTS

4 trout fillets, skinned
2 tbsp vegetable oil
2 garlic cloves, cut into slivers
4 slices fresh pineapple, peeled and diced
1 celery stick, sliced
1 tbsp light soy sauce
50 ml/2 fl oz/¼ cup fresh or unsweetened pineapple juice
150 ml/¼ pint/⅔ cup fish stock
1 tsp cornflour (cornstarch)
2 tsp water
shredded celery leaves and fresh red chilli strips, to garnish

1 Cut the trout fillets into strips. Heat 1 tbsp of the oil in a preheated wok until almost smoking. Reduce the heat slightly, add the fish and sauté for 2 minutes. Remove from the wok and set aside.

2 Add the remaining oil to the wok, reduce the heat and add the garlic, pineapple and celery. Stir-fry for 1–2 minutes.

3 Add the soy sauce, pineapple juice and fish stock to the wok. Bring to the boil and cook, stirring, for 2–3 minutes, or until the sauce has reduced.

4 Blend the cornflour (cornstarch) with the water to form a paste and stir it into the wok. Bring the sauce to the boil and cook, stirring constantly, until the sauce thickens and clears.

5 Return the fish to the wok, and cook, stirring gently, until heated through. Transfer to a warmed serving dish and serve, garnished with shredded celery leaves and red chilli strips.

COOK'S TIP

Use canned pineapple instead of fresh pineapple if you wish, choosing slices in unsweetened, natural juice in preference to a syrup.

1

2

3

Mullet with Ginger

Serves 4

INGREDIENTS

1 whole mullet, cleaned and scaled
2 spring onions (scallions), chopped
1 tsp grated fresh root ginger
125 ml/4 fl oz/½ cup garlic wine vinegar
125 ml/4 fl oz/½ cup light soy sauce
3 tsp caster (superfine) sugar
dash of chilli sauce
125 ml/4 fl oz/½ cup fish stock
1 green (bell) pepper, seeded and thinly sliced
1 large tomato, skinned, seeded and cut into thin strips
salt and pepper
sliced tomato, to garnish

1 Rinse the fish inside and out and pat dry with kitchen paper (paper towels).

2 Make 3 diagonal slits in the flesh on each side of the fish. Season with salt and pepper inside and out.

3 Place the fish on a heatproof plate and scatter the spring onions (scallions) and ginger over the top. Cover and steam for 10 minutes, or until the fish is cooked through.

4 Place the vinegar, soy sauce, sugar, chilli sauce, fish stock, (bell) pepper and tomato in a saucepan and bring to the boil, stirring occasionally. Cook over a high heat until the sauce has slightly reduced and thickened.

5 Remove the fish from the steamer and transfer to a warm serving dish. Pour the sauce over the fish, garnish with tomato slices and serve immediately.

COOK'S TIP

Use fillets of fish for this recipe if preferred, and reduce the cooking time to 5–7 minutes.

Szechuan White Fish

Serves 4

INGREDIENTS

350 g/12 oz white fish fillets
1 small egg, beaten
3 tbsp plain (all-purpose) flour
4 tbsp dry white wine
3 tbsp light soy sauce
vegetable oil, for frying
1 garlic clove, cut into slivers
1-cm/$^1/_2$-inch piece fresh root ginger, finely chopped
1 onion, finely chopped
1 celery stick, chopped
1 fresh red chilli, chopped
3 spring onions (scallions), chopped
1 tsp rice wine vinegar
$^1/_2$ tsp ground Szechuan pepper
175 ml/6 fl oz/$^3/_4$ cup fish stock
1 tsp caster (superfine) sugar
1 tsp cornflour (cornstarch)
2 tsp water
chilli flowers and celery leaves, to garnish (optional)

1 Cut the fish into 4-cm/1$^1/_2$-inch cubes.

2 In a bowl, beat the egg, flour, wine and 1 tbsp of soy sauce to make a batter.

3 Dip the cubes of fish into the batter to coat.

4 Heat the oil in a preheated wok until it is almost smoking. Reduce the heat slightly and cook the fish, in batches, for 2–3 minutes, until golden. Drain on kitchen paper (paper towels) and set aside.

5 Pour all but 1 tbsp of oil from the wok and return to the heat. Add the garlic, ginger, onion, celery, chilli and spring onions (scallions) and stir-fry for 1–2 minutes.

6 Stir in the remaining soy sauce and the vinegar.

7 Add the Szechuan pepper, fish stock and sugar to the wok. Blend the cornflour (cornstarch) with the water to form a smooth paste and stir it into the stock. Bring to the boil and cook, stirring, for 1 minute, until the sauce thickens and clears.

8 Return the fish to the wok and cook for 1–2 minutes, until hot. Transfer to a serving dish.

Crispy Fish

Serves 4

INGREDIENTS

450 g/1 lb white fish fillets

BATTER:
60 g/2 oz/$^1/_2$ cup plain (all-purpose) flour
1 egg, separated
1 tbsp peanut oil
4 tbsp milk
vegetable oil, for deep-frying

SAUCE:
1 fresh red chilli, chopped
2 garlic cloves, crushed
pinch of chilli powder
3 tbsp tomato purée (paste)
1 tbsp rice wine vinegar
2 tbsp dark soy sauce
2 tbsp Chinese rice wine
2 tbsp water
pinch of caster (superfine) sugar

1 Cut the fish into 2.5-cm/1-inch cubes and set aside. To make the batter, sift the flour into a bowl and make a well in the centre. Add the egg yolk and oil to the bowl and stir in the milk, incorporating the flour to form a smooth batter. Let stand for 20 minutes.

2 Whisk the egg white until it forms peaks and fold it into the batter. Heat the oil in a preheated wok. Dip the fish into the batter and fry, in batches, for 8–10 minutes, until cooked through. Remove the fish from the wok with a slotted spoon, set aside and keep warm.

3 Pour off all but 1 tbsp of oil from the wok and return to the heat. To make the sauce, add the chilli, garlic, chilli powder, tomato purée (paste), rice wine vinegar, soy sauce, Chinese rice wine, water and sugar and cook, stirring, for 3–4 minutes.

4 Return the fish to the wok and stir gently to coat it in the sauce. Cook for 2-3 minutes, until hot. Transfer the fish and sauce to a serving dish and serve immediately.

COOK'S TIP

Take care when pouring hot oil from the wok and ensure that you transfer it to a suitable bowl until cool.

Seafood Medley

Serves 4

INGREDIENTS

2 tbsp dry white wine
1 egg white, lightly beaten
$^1/_2$ tsp Chinese five-spice powder
1 tsp cornflour (cornstarch)
300 g/10$^1/_2$ oz raw prawns (shrimp), peeled and deveined
125 g/4$^1/_2$ oz prepared squid, cut into rings
125 g/4$^1/_2$ oz white fish fillets, cut into strips
vegetable oil, for deep-frying
1 green (bell) pepper, seeded and cut into thin strips
1 carrot, cut into thin strips
4 baby corn cobs, halved lengthways

1 Mix together the wine, egg white, Chinese five-spice powder and cornflour (cornstarch) in a large bowl. Add the prawns (shrimp), squid rings and fish fillets and stir to coat evenly. Remove the fish and seafood with a slotted spoon, reserving any leftover cornflour (cornstarch) mixture.

2 Heat the oil in a preheated wok and deep-fry the prawns (shrimp), squid and fish for 2–3 minutes. Remove the seafood mixture from the wok with a slotted spoon and set aside.

3 Pour off all but 1 tablespoon of oil from the wok and return to the heat. Add the (bell) pepper, carrot and corn cobs and stir-fry for 4–5 minutes.

4 Return the seafood mixture to the wok and add any remaining cornflour mixture. Cook, stirring and tossing well, to heat through. Transfer to a serving plate and serve immediately.

COOK'S TIP

Open up the squid rings and using a sharp knife, score a lattice pattern on the flesh to make them look more attractive.

Fried Prawns (Shrimp) with Cashews

Serves 4

INGREDIENTS

2 garlic cloves, crushed
1 tbsp cornflour (cornstarch)
pinch of caster (superfine) sugar
450 g/1 lb raw tiger prawns (jumbo shrimp)
4 tbsp vegetable oil
1 leek, sliced
125 g/4 $^{1}/_{2}$ oz broccoli florets
1 orange (bell) pepper, seeded and diced
75 g/2 $^{3}/_{4}$ oz/$^{3}/_{4}$ cup unsalted cashew nuts

SAUCE:
175 ml/6 fl oz/$^{3}/_{4}$ cup fish stock
1 tbsp cornflour (cornstarch)
dash of chilli sauce
2 tsp sesame oil
1 tbsp Chinese rice wine

1 Mix together the garlic, cornflour (cornstarch) and sugar in a bowl. Peel and devein the prawns (shrimp). Stir the prawns (shrimp) into the mixture to coat.

2 Heat the oil in a preheated wok and add the prawn (shrimp) mixture. Stir-fry over a high heat for 20–30 seconds until the prawns (shrimp) turn pink. Remove the prawns (shrimp) from the wok with a slotted spoon and set aside.

3 Add the leek, broccoli and (bell) pepper to the wok and stir-fry for 2 minutes.

4 To make the sauce, mix together the fish stock, cornflour (cornstarch), chilli sauce to taste, the sesame oil and Chinese rice wine. Add the mixture to the wok, together with the cashew nuts. Return the prawns (shrimp) to the wok and cook for 1 minute to heat through. Transfer to a warm serving dish and serve immediately.

VARIATION

This recipe also works well with chicken, pork or beef strips instead of the prawns (shrimp). Use 225 g/8 oz meat instead of 450 g/1 lb prawns (shrimp).

1

3

4

Prawn (Shrimp) Fu Yong

Serves 4

INGREDIENTS

2 tbsp vegetable oil
1 carrot, grated
5 eggs, beaten
225 g/8 oz raw (small) shrimp, peeled
1 tbsp light soy sauce
pinch of Chinese five-spice powder
2 spring onions (scallions), chopped
2 tsp sesame seeds
1 tsp sesame oil

1 Heat the vegetable oil in a preheated wok.

2 Add the carrot and stir-fry for 1–2 minutes.

3 Push the carrot to one side of the wok and add the eggs. Cook, stirring gently, for 1–2 minutes.

4 Stir the (small) shrimp, soy sauce and five-spice powder into the mixture in the wok. Stir-fry the mixture for 2–3 minutes, or until the (small) shrimps change colour and the mixture is almost dry.

5 Turn the (small) shrimp fu yong out on to a warm plate and sprinkle the spring onions (scallions), sesame seeds and sesame oil on top. Serve immediately.

VARIATION

For a more substantial dish, you could add 225 g/8 oz/ 1 cup cooked long-grain rice with the (small) shrimp in step 4. Taste and adjust the quantities of soy sauce, Chinese five-spice powder and sesame oil if necessary.

COOK'S TIP

If only cooked prawns (shrimp) are available, add them just before the end of cooking, but make sure that they are fully incorporated into the fu yong. They require only heating through – overcooking will make them chewy and tasteless.

Cantonese Prawns (Shrimp)

Serves 4

INGREDIENTS

5 tbsp vegetable oil
4 garlic cloves, crushed
675 g/1 1/2 lb raw prawns (shrimp), shelled and deveined
5-cm/2-inch piece fresh root ginger, chopped
175 g/6 oz lean pork, diced
1 leek, sliced
3 eggs, beaten
shredded leek and red (bell) pepper matchsticks, to garnish

SAUCE:
2 tbsp dry sherry
2 tbsp light soy sauce
2 tsp caster (superfine) sugar
150 ml/1/4 pint/2/3 cup fish stock
4 1/2 tsp cornflour (cornstarch)
3 tbsp water

1 Heat 2 tablespoons of the oil in a preheated wok. Add the garlic and stir-fry for 30 seconds. Add the prawns (shrimp) and stir-fry for 5 minutes, or until they change colour. Remove the prawns (shrimp) from the wok with a slotted spoon, set aside and keep warm.

2 Add the remaining oil to the wok and heat. Add the ginger, diced pork and leek and stir-fry over a medium heat for 4-5 minutes, or until the pork is lightly coloured.

3 Add the sherry, soy, sugar and fish stock to the wok. Blend the cornflour (cornstarch) with the water to form a smooth paste and stir it into the wok. Cook, stirring, until the sauce thickens and clears.

4 Return the prawns (shrimp) to the wok and add the beaten eggs. Cook for 5–6 minutes, gently stirring occasionally, until the eggs set. Transfer to a warm serving dish, garnish with shredded leek and pepper matchsticks and serve at once.

COOK'S TIP

If possible, use Chinese rice wine instead of the sherry.

Squid with Oyster Sauce

Serves 4

INGREDIENTS

450 g/1 lb squid
150 ml/1/4 pint/2/3 cup vegetable oil
1-cm/1/2-inch piece fresh root ginger, grated
60 g/2 oz mangetout (snow peas)
5 tbsp hot fish stock
red (bell) pepper triangles, to garnish

SAUCE:
1 tbsp oyster sauce
1 tbsp light soy sauce
pinch of caster (superfine) sugar
1 garlic clove, crushed

1 To prepare the squid, cut down the centre of the body lengthways. Flatten the squid out, inside uppermost, and score a lattice design deep into the flesh, using a sharp knife.

2 To make the sauce, combine the oyster sauce, soy sauce, sugar and garlic in a small bowl. Stir to dissolve the sugar and set aside until required.

3 Heat the oil in a preheated wok until almost smoking. Lower the heat slightly, add the squid and stir-fry until they curl up. Remove with a slotted spoon and drain thoroughly on kitchen paper (paper towels).

4 Pour off all but 2 tablespoons of the oil and return the wok to the heat. Add the ginger and mangetout (snow peas) and stir-fry for 1 minute.

5 Return the squid to the wok and pour in the sauce and hot fish stock. Leave the mixture to simmer for 3 minutes, or until thickened.

6 Transfer to a warm serving dish, garnish with (bell) pepper triangles and serve immediately.

COOK'S TIP

Take care not to overcook the squid, otherwise it will be rubbery and unappetizing.

Scallops in Ginger Sauce

Serves 4

INGREDIENTS

2 tbsp vegetable oil
450 g/1 lb scallops, cleaned and halved
2.5-cm/1-inch piece fresh root ginger, finely chopped
3 garlic cloves, crushed
2 leeks, shredded
75 g/2 3/4 oz/3/4 cup shelled peas
125 g/4 1/2 oz canned bamboo shoots, drained and rinsed
2 tbsp light soy sauce
2 tbsp unsweetened orange juice
1 tsp caster (superfine) sugar
orange zest, to garnish

1 Heat the oil in a wok. Add the scallops and stir-fry for 1–2 minutes. Remove the scallops from the wok with a slotted spoon and set aside.

2 Add the ginger and garlic to the wok and stir-fry for 30 seconds. Stir in the leeks and peas and cook, stirring, for 2 minutes.

3 Add the bamboo shoots and return the scallops to the wok. Stir gently to mix without breaking up the scallops.

4 Stir in the soy sauce, orange juice and sugar and cook for 1–2 minutes. Transfer to a serving dish, garnish and serve.

COOK'S TIP

The edible parts of a scallop are the round white muscle and the orange and white coral or roe. The frilly skirt surrounding the muscle – the gills and mantle – may be used for making shellfish stock. All other parts should be discarded.

COOK'S TIP

Frozen scallops may be thawed and used in this recipe, adding them at the end of cooking to prevent them from breaking up. If you are buying scallops already shelled, check whether they are fresh or frozen. Fresh scallops are cream coloured and more translucent, while frozen scallops tend to be pure white.

Crab in Ginger Sauce

Serves 4

INGREDIENTS

2 small cooked crabs
2 tbsp vegetable oil
9-cm/3-inch piece fresh root ginger, grated
2 garlic cloves, thinly sliced
1 green (bell) pepper, seeded and cut into thin strips
6 spring onions (scallions), cut into 2.5-cm/1-inch lengths
2 tbsp dry sherry
$^1/_2$ tsp sesame oil
150 ml/$^1/_4$ pint/$^2/_3$ cup fish stock
1 tsp light brown sugar
2 tsp cornflour (cornstarch)
150 ml/$^1/_4$ pint/$^2/_3$ cup water

1 Rinse the crabs and gently loosen around the shell at the top. Using a sharp knife, cut away the grey tissue and discard. Rinse the crabs again.

2 Twist off the legs and claws from the crabs. Using a pair of crab claw crackers or a cleaver, crack the claws to break through the shell to expose the flesh. Remove and discard any loose pieces of shell.

3 Separate the body and discard the inedible lungs and sac. Cut down the centre of each crab to separate the body into two pieces and then cut each of these in half again.

4 Heat the oil in a preheated wok. Add the ginger and garlic and stir-fry for 1 minute. Add the crab pieces and stir-fry for 1 minute.

5 Stir in the (bell) pepper, spring onions (scallions), sherry, sesame oil, stock and sugar. Bring to the boil, reduce the heat, cover and simmer for 3–4 minutes.

6 Blend the cornflour (cornstarch) with the remaining water and stir it into the wok. Bring to the boil, stirring, until the sauce is thickened and clear. Serve.

COOK'S TIP

If preferred, remove the crabmeat from the shells prior to stir-frying and add to the wok with the (bell) pepper.

Indonesian-Style Spicy Cod

Serves 4

INGREDIENTS

4 cod steaks
1 stalk lemon grass
1 small red onion, chopped
3 cloves garlic, chopped
2 fresh red chillies, deseeded and chopped
1 tsp grated root (fresh) ginger
1/4 tsp turmeric
2 tbsp butter, cut into small cubes
8 tbsp canned coconut milk
2 tbsp lemon juice
salt and pepper
red chillies, to garnish (optional)

1 Rinse the cod steaks and pat them thoroughly dry on absorbent kitchen paper.

2 Remove and discard the outer leaves from the lemon grass and thinly slice the inner section.

3 Place the lemon grass, onion, garlic, chilli, ginger and turmeric in a food processor and blend until the ingredients are finely chopped. Season with salt and pepper to taste.

4 With the processor running, add the butter, coconut milk and lemon juice and process until well blended.

5 Place the fish in a shallow, non-metallic dish. Pour over the coconut mixture and turn the fish until well coated.

6 If you have one, place the fish steaks in a hinged basket, which will make them easier to turn. Barbecue (grill) over hot coals for 15 minutes or until the fish is cooked through, turning once. Serve garnished with red chillies, if wished.

COOK'S TIP

If you prefer a milder flavour omit the chillies altogether. For a hotter flavour do not remove the seeds from the chillies.

Salmon Yakitori

Serves 4

INGREDIENTS

350 g/12 oz chunky salmon fillet
8 baby leeks

YAKITORI SAUCE:
5 tbsp light soy sauce
5 tbsp fish stock
2 tbsp caster (superfine) sugar
5 tbsp dry white wine
3 tbsp sweet sherry
1 clove garlic, crushed

1 Skin the salmon and cut the flesh into 5 cm/2 inch chunks. Trim the leeks and cut them into 5 cm/2 inch lengths.

2 Thread the salmon and leeks alternately on to 8 pre-soaked wooden skewers. Leave to chill in the refrigerator until required.

3 To make the sauce, place all of the ingredients in a small pan and heat gently, stirring, until the sugar dissolves. Bring to the boil, then reduce the heat and simmer for 2 minutes. Strain the sauce and leave to cool.

4 Pour about one-third of the sauce into a small dish and set aside to serve with the kebabs (kabobs).

5 Brush plenty of the remaining sauce over the skewers and cook directly on the rack or, if preferred, place a sheet of oiled kitchen foil on the rack and cook the salmon on that. Barbecue (grill) the skewers over hot coals for about 10 minutes, turning once. Baste frequently during cooking with the remaining sauce to prevent the fish and vegetables from drying out. Serve the kebebs (kabobs) with the reserved sauce for dipping.

COOK'S TIP

Soak the wooden skewers in cold water for at least 30 minutes to prevent them from burning during cooking. You can make the kebabs (kabobs) and sauce several hours before required and refrigerate.

3

4

5

Japanese-Style Chargrilled (Broiled) Flounder

Serves 4

INGREDIENTS

4 small plaice
6 tbsp soy sauce
2 tbsp sake or dry white wine
2 tbsp sesame oil
1 tbsp lemon juice
2 tbsp light muscovado sugar
1 tsp root (fresh) ginger, grated
1 clove garlic, crushed

TO GARNISH:
1 small carrot
4 spring onions (scallions)

1 Rinse the fish and pat them dry on absorbent kitchen paper. Cut a few slashes into both sides of each fish.

2 Mix together the soy sauce, sake or wine, oil, lemon juice, sugar, ginger and garlic in a large, shallow dish.

3 Place the fish in the marinade and turn so that they are coated on both sides. Chill in the refrigerator for 1–6 hours.

4 Meanwhile, prepare the garnish. Cut the carrot into evenly-sized thin sticks and clean and shred the spring onions (scallions).

5 Barbecue (grill) the fish over hot coals for about 10 minutes, turning the fish once.

6 Scatter the spring onions (scallions) and carrot over the fish and transfer the fish to a serving dish. Serve immediately.

VARIATION

Use sole instead of the plaice (flounders) and scatter over some toasted sesame seeds instead of the carrot and spring onions (scallions), if you prefer.

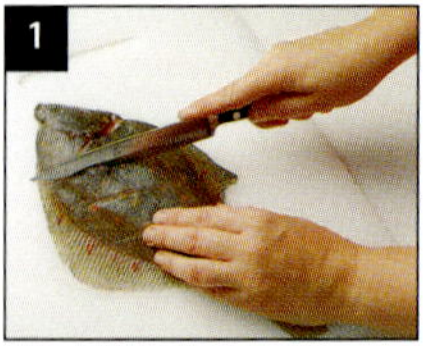

Vegetables, Rice & Noodles

As vegetables are so plentiful and diverse in the Far East, they play a major role in the diet. Other ingredients, such as tofu (bean curd), are added to the vegetarian diet, which is both a healthy and economical choice. Tofu (bean curd) is produced from the soya bean, which is grown in abundance in these countries. Tofu (bean curd) is frequently used in stir-frying for texture and it is perfect for absorbing all the component flavours of the dish.

The wok is perfect for cooking vegetables as it cooks them very quickly, which helps to retain nutrients and crispness, and produces a range of colourful and flavourful recipes. Some of the dishes contained in this chapter are ideal accompaniments to main dishes, whilst others, such as vegetable curries, are combined with spices to produce more substantial main meals.

The following chapter shows the wonderful versatility of vegetables and contains something for everyone, which should delight vegetarians and meat-eaters alike.

Stir-Fried Japanese Mushroom Noodles

Serves 4

INGREDIENTS

250 g/9 oz Japanese egg noodles
2 tbsp sunflower oil
1 red onion, sliced
1 clove garlic, crushed
450 g/1 lb mixed mushrooms (shiitake, oyster, brown cap)
350 g/12 oz pak choi (or Chinese leaves)
2 tbsp sweet sherry
6 tbsp soy sauce
4 spring onions (scallions), sliced
1 tbsp toasted sesame seeds

1 Place the Japanese egg noodles in a large bowl. Pour over enough boiling water to cover and leave to soak for 10 minutes.

2 Heat the sunflower oil in a large preheated wok.

3 Add the red onion and garlic to the wok and stir-fry for 2–3 minutes, or until softened.

4 Add the mushrooms to the wok and stir-fry for about 5 minutes, or until the mushrooms have softened.

5 Drain the egg noodles thoroughly.

6 Add the the pak choi (or Chinese leaves), noodles, sweet sherry and soy sauce to the wok. Toss all of the ingredients together and stir-fry for 2–3 minutes or until the liquid is just bubbling.

7 Transfer the mushroom noodles to warm serving bowls and scatter with sliced spring onions (scallions) and toasted sesame seeds. Serve immediately.

COOK'S TIP

The variety of mushrooms in supermarkets has greatly improved and a good mixture should be easily obtainable. If not, use the more common button and flat mushrooms.

Stir-Fried Vegetables with Sherry & Soy Sauce

Serves 4

INGREDIENTS

2 tbsp sunflower oil
1 red onion, sliced
175 g/6 oz carrots, thinly sliced
175 g/6 oz courgettes (zucchini), sliced diagonally
1 red (bell) pepper, deseeded and sliced
1 small head Chinese leaves, shredded
150 g/5½ oz/3 cups beansprouts
225 g/8 oz can bamboo shoots, drained
150 g/5½ oz/¼ cup cashew nuts, toasted

SAUCE:
3 tbsp medium sherry
3 tbsp light soy sauce
1 tsp ground ginger
1 clove garlic, crushed
1 tsp cornflour (cornstarch)
1 tbsp tomato purée

1 Heat the sunflower oil in a large preheated wok.

2 Add the red onion slices to the wok and stir-fry for 2–3 minutes, or until just beginning to soften.

3 Add the carrots, courgettes (zucchini) and (bell) pepper slices to the wok and stir-fry for a further 5 minutes.

4 Add the Chinese leaves, beansprouts and bamboo shoots to the wok and heat through for 2–3 minutes, or until the leaves just begin to wilt.

5 Scatter the cashew nuts over the top of the vegetables.

6 Mix together the sherry, soy sauce, ginger, garlic, cornflour (cornstarch) and tomato purée.

7 Pour the mixture over the vegetables and toss well. Leave to simmer for 2–3 minutes or until the juices start to thicken. Serve immediately.

COOK'S TIP

Use any mixture of fresh vegetables that you have to hand in this very versatile dish.

Stir-Fried Pak Choi with Red Onion & Cashew Nuts

Serves 4

INGREDIENTS

2 tbsp groundnut oil
2 red onions, cut into thin wedges
175 g/6 oz red cabbage, thinly shredded
225 g/8 oz pak choi
2 tbsp plum sauce
100 g/3½ oz/⅓ cup roasted cashew nuts

1 Heat the groundnut oil in a large preheated wok.

2 Add the onion wedges to the wok and stir-fry for about 5 minutes or until the onions are just beginning to brown.

3 Add the red cabbage to the wok and stir-fry for a further 2–3 minutes.

4 Add the pak choi to the wok and stir-fry for about 5 minutes, or until the leaves have wilted.

5 Drizzle the plum sauce over the vegetables, toss together until well combined and heat until the liquid is bubbling.

6 Scatter with the roasted cashew nuts and transfer to warm serving bowls. Serve immediately.

COOK'S TIP

Plum sauce has a unique, fruity flavour – a sweet and sour with a difference.

VARIATION

Use unsalted peanuts instead of the cashew nuts, if you prefer.

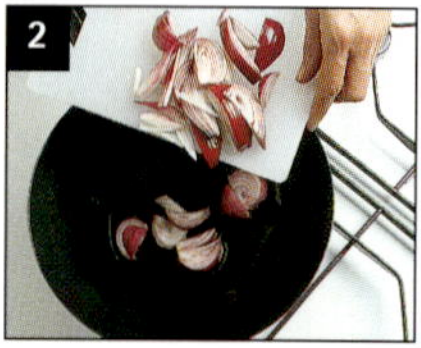

Tofu (Bean Curd) with Soy Sauce, Green (Bell) Peppers & Crispy Onions

Serves 4

INGREDIENTS

350 g/12 oz tofu (bean curd)
2 cloves garlic, crushed
4 tbsp soy sauce
1 tbsp sweet chilli sauce
6 tbsp sunflower oil
1 onion, sliced
1 green (bell) pepper, deseeded and diced
1 tbsp sesame oil

1 Using a sharp knife, cut the tofu (bean curd) into bite-sized pieces. Place the tofu (bean curd) pieces in a shallow non-metallic dish.

2 Mix together the garlic, soy sauce and sweet chilli sauce and drizzle over the tofu (bean curd). Toss well to coat each piece and leave to marinate for about 20 minutes.

3 Meanwhile, heat the sunflower oil in a large preheated wok.

4 Add the onion slices to the wok and stir-fry over a high heat until they brown and become crispy. Remove the onion slices with a slotted spoon and leave to drain on absorbent kitchen paper.

5 Add the tofu (bean curd) to the hot oil and stir-fry for about 5 minutes.

6 Remove all but 1 tablespoon of the oil from the wok. Add the (bell) pepper to the wok and stir-fry for 2–3 minutes, or until softened.

7 Return the tofu (bean curd) and onions to the wok and heat through, stirring occasionally. Drizzle with the sesame oil.

8 Transfer to serving plates and serve immediately.

COOK'S TIP

If you are in a real hurry, buy ready-marinated tofu (bean curd) from your supermarket.

Stir-Fried Green Beans with Lettuce & Black Bean Sauce

Serves 4

INGREDIENTS

1 tsp chilli oil
25 g/1 oz/2 tbsp butter
225 g/8 oz fine green beans, sliced
4 shallots, sliced
1 clove garlic, crushed
100 g/3½ oz shiitake mushrooms, thinly sliced
1 Iceberg lettuce, shredded
4 tbsp black bean sauce

1 Heat the chilli oil and butter in a large preheated wok.

2 Add the green beans, shallots, garlic and mushrooms to the wok and stir-fry for 2–3 minutes.

3 Add the shredded lettuce to the wok and stir-fry until the leaves have wilted.

4 Stir the black bean sauce into the mixture in the wok and heat through, tossing to mix, until the sauce is bubbling. Serve.

COOK'S TIP

To make your own black bean sauce, soak 60 g/2 oz/⅓ cup of dried black beans overnight in cold water. Drain and place in a pan of cold water, boil for 10 minutes, then drain. Return the beans to the pan with 450 ml/¾ pint/2 cups vegetable stock and boil. Blend 1 tbsp each of malt vinegar, soy sauce, sugar, 1½ tsp cornflour (cornstarch), 1 chopped red chilli and ½ inch ginger root. Add to the pan and simmer for 40 minutes.

COOK'S TIP

If possible, use Chinese green beans which are tender and can be eaten whole. They are available from specialist Chinese stores.

Deep-Fried Courgettes (Zucchini)

Serves 4

INGREDIENTS

450 g/1 lb courgettes (zucchini)
1 egg white
50 g/1¾ oz/⅓ cup cornflour (cornstarch)
1 tsp salt
1 tsp Chinese five-spice powder
oil, for deep-frying

1 Using a sharp knife, slice the courgettes (zucchini) into rings or chunky sticks.

2 Place the egg white in a small mixing bowl. Lightly whip the egg white until foamy, using a fork.

3 Mix the cornflour (cornstarch), salt and five-spice powder and sprinkle on to a large plate.

4 Heat the oil for deep-frying in a large preheated wok.

5 Dip each piece of courgette (zucchini) into the beaten egg white then coat in the cornflour (cornstarch) mixture.

6 Deep-fry the courgettes (zucchini), in batches, for about 5 minutes or until pale golden and crispy. Repeat with the remaining courgettes (zucchini).

7 Remove the courgettes (zucchini) with a slotted spoon and leave to drain on absorbent kitchen paper while you deep-fry the remainder.

8 Transfer the courgettes (zucchini) to serving plates and serve immediately.

VARIATION

Alter the seasoning by using chilli powder or curry powder instead of the Chinese five-spice powder, if you prefer.

Deep-Fried Chilli Corn Balls

Serves 4

INGREDIENTS

6 spring onions (scallions), sliced
3 tbsp fresh coriander (cilantro), chopped
225 g/8 oz canned sweetcorn
5 ml/1 tsp mild chilli powder
1 tbsp sweet chilli sauce
25 g /1 oz/¼ cup desiccated (shredded) coconut
1 egg
75 g/2¾ oz/⅓ cup polenta (cornmeal)
oil, for deep-frying
extra sweet chilli sauce, to serve

1 In a large mixing bowl, mix together the spring onions (scallions), coriander (cilantro), sweetcorn, chilli powder, chilli sauce, coconut, egg and polenta (cornmeal). Cover and leave to stand for about 10 minutes.

2 Heat the oil for deep-frying in a large preheated wok.

3 Carefully drop spoonfuls of the chilli and polenta (cornmeal) mixture into the hot oil. Deep-fry the chill corn balls, in batches, for 4–5 minutes or until crispy and a deep golden brown colour.

4 Remove the chilli corn balls with a slotted spoon, transfer to kitchen towels and leave to drain thoroughly.

5 Transfer to serving plates and serve with an extra sweet chilli sauce for dipping.

COOK'S TIP

Polenta (cornmeal) is a type of meal ground from sweetcorn or maize. It is available in most large supermarkets or in health food shops.

COOK'S TIP

For safe deep-frying in a round-bottomed wok, place it on a wok rack so that it rests securely. Only half-fill the wok with oil. Never leave the wok unattended over a high heat.

1

3

4

Aspagarus & Red (Bell) Pepper Parcels

Serves 4

INGREDIENTS

100 g/3½ oz fine tip asparagus
1 red (bell) pepper, deseeded and thinly sliced
50 g/1¾ oz/½ cup beansprouts
2 tbsp plum sauce
8 sheets filo pastry
1 egg yolk, beaten
oil, for deep-frying

1 Place the asparagus, (bell) pepper and beansprouts in a large mixing bowl.

2 Add the plum sauce to the vegetables and mix until well combined.

3 Lay the sheets of filo pastry out on to a clean work surface (counter).

4 Place a little of the asparagus and red (bell) pepper filling at the top end of each filo pastry sheet. Brush the edges of the filo pastry with a little of the beaten egg yolk.

5 Roll up the filo pastry, tucking in the ends and enclosing the filling like a spring roll.

6 Heat the oil for deep-frying in a large preheated wok.

7 Carefully cook the parcels, 2 at a time, in the hot oil for 4–5 minutes or until crispy.

8 Remove the parcels with a slotted spoon and leave to drain on absorbent kitchen paper.

9 Transfer the parcels to warm serving plates and serve immediately.

COOK'S TIP

Be sure to use fine-tipped asparagus as it is more tender than the larger stems.

Carrot & Orange Stir-Fry

Serves 4

INGREDIENTS

2 tbsp sunflower oil
450 g/1 lb carrots, grated
225 g/8 oz leeks, shredded
2 oranges, peeled and segmented
2 tbsp tomato ketchup
1 tbsp demerara sugar
2 tbsp light soy
100 g/3½ oz/½ cup chopped peanuts

1 Heat the sunflower oil in a large preheated wok.

2 Add the grated carrot and leeks to the wok and stir-fry for 2–3 minutes, or until the vegetables have just softened.

3 Add the orange segments to the wok and heat through gently, ensuring that you do not break up the orange segments as you stir the mixture.

4 Mix the tomato ketchup, demerara sugar and soy sauce together in a small bowl.

5 Add the tomato and sugar mixture to the wok and stir-fry for a further 2 minutes.

6 Transfer the stir-fry to warm serving bowls and scatter with the chopped peanuts. Serve immediately.

VARIATION

Scatter with toasted sesame seeds instead of the peanuts, if you prefer.

VARIATION

You could use pineapple instead of orange. If using canned pineapple, make sure that it is in natural juice not syrup as it will spoil the fresh taste of this dish.

Spinach Stir-Fry with Shiitake & Honey

Serves 4

INGREDIENTS

3 tbsp groundnut oil
350 g/12 oz shiitake mushrooms, sliced
2 cloves garlic, crushed
350 g/12 oz baby leaf spinach
2 tbsp dry sherry
2 tbsp clear honey
4 spring onions (scallions), sliced

1 Heat the groundnut oil in a large preheated wok.

2 Add the shiitake mushrooms to the wok and stir-fry for about 5 minutes, or until the mushrooms have softened.

3 Add the crushed garlic and baby leaf spinach to the mushrooms in the wok and stir-fry for a further 2–3 minutes, or until the spinach leaves have just wilted.

4 Mix together the dry sherry and clear honey in a small bowl until well combined.

5 Drizzle the sherry and honey mixture over the spinach and heat through.

6 Transfer the stir-fry to warm serving dishes and scatter with spring onions (scallion) slices. Serve immediately.

COOK'S TIP

Nutmeg complements the flavour of spinach and it is a classic combination. Add a pinch of nutmeg to the dish in step 3, if you wish.

COOK'S TIP

A good quality, dry pale sherry should be used in this recipe. Cream or sweet sherry should not be substituted. Rice wine is often used in Oriental cooking, but sherry can be used instead.

Chinese Vegetable Rice

Serves 4

INGREDIENTS

350 g/12 oz/1¾ cups long-grain white rice
1 tsp turmeric
2 tbsp sunflower oil
225 g/8 oz courgettes (zucchini), sliced
1 red (bell) pepper, deseeded and sliced
1 green (bell) pepper, deseeded and sliced
1 green chilli, deseeded and finely chopped
1 medium carrot, coarsley grated
150 g/5½ oz/1½ cups beansprouts
6 spring onions (scallions), sliced, plus extra to garnish
2 tbsp soy sauce

1 Place the rice and turmeric in a saucepan of lightly salted water and bring to the boil. Reduce the heat and leave to simmer until the rice is just tender. Drain the rice thoroughly and press out any excess water with a sheet of double thickness kitchen paper.

2 Heat the sunflower oil in a large preheated wok.

3 Add the courgettes (zucchini) to the wok and stir-fry for about 2 minutes.

4 Add the (bell) peppers and chilli to the wok and stir-fry for 2–3 minutes.

5 Add the cooked rice to the mixture in the wok, a little at a time, tossing well after each addition.

6 Add the carrots, beansprouts and spring onions (scallions) to the wok and stir-fry for a further 2 minutes. Drizzle with soy sauce and serve at once, garnished with extra spring onions (scallions), if desired.

VARIATION

For real luxury, add a few saffron strands infused in boiling water instead of the turmeric.

Vegetable Stir-Fry with Hoisin Sauce

Serves 4

INGREDIENTS

- 2 tbsp sunflower oil
- 1 red onion, sliced
- 100 g/3½ oz carrots, sliced
- 1 yellow (bell) pepper, deseeded and diced
- 50 g/1¾ oz/1 cup cooked brown rice
- 175 g/6 oz mangetout (snow peas)
- 175 g/6 oz/1½ cups beansprouts
- 4 tbsp hoisin sauce
- 1 tbsp snipped fresh chives

1 Heat the sunflower oil in a large preheated wok.

2 Add the red onion slices, carrots and yellow (bell) pepper to the wok and stir-fry for about 3 minutes.

3 Add the cooked brown rice, mangetout (snow peas) and beansprouts to the mixture in the wok and stir-fry for a further 2 minutes.

4 Stir the hoisin sauce into the vegetables and mix until well combined and completely heated through.

5 Transfer to warm serving dishes and scatter with the snipped fresh chives. Serve immediately.

COOK'S TIP

Hoisin sauce is a dark brown, reddish sauce made from soy beans, garlic, chilli and various other spices, and is commonly used in Chinese cookery. It may also be used as a dipping sauce.

VARIATION

Almost any vegetables could be used in this dish: other good choices would be broccoli florets, baby corn cobs, green peas, Chinese leaves and young spinach leaves. Either white or black (oyster) mushrooms can also be used to give a greater diversity of textures. In addition, make sure that there is a good variety of colour in this dish.

Sweet & Sour Cauliflower & Coriander (Cilantro) Stir-Fry

Serves 4

INGREDIENTS

450 g/1 lb cauliflower florets
2 tbsp sunflower oil
1 onion, sliced
225 g/8 oz carrots, sliced
100 g/3½ oz mangetout (snow peas)
1 ripe mango, sliced
100 g/3½ oz/1 cup beansprouts
3 tbsp chopped fresh coriander (cilantro)
3 tbsp fresh lime juice
1 tbsp clear honey
6 tbsp coconut milk

1 Bring a large saucepan of water to the boil. Add the cauliflower to the pan and cook for 2 minutes. Drain the cauliflower thoroughly.

2 Heat the sunflower oil in a large preheated wok.

3 Add the onion and carrots to the wok and stir-fry for about 5 minutes.

4 Add the drained cauliflower and mangetout (snow peas) to the wok and stir-fry for 2–3 minutes.

5 Add the mango and bean-sprouts to the wok and stir-fry for about 2 minutes.

6 Mix together the coriander (cilantro), lime juice, honey and coconut milk in a bowl.

7 Add the coriander (cilantro) mixture to the wok and stir-fry for about 2 minutes or until the juices are bubbling.

8 Transfer the stir-fry to serving dishes and serve.

VARIATION

Use broccoli instead of the cauliflower as an alternative, if you prefer.

1

4

6

Broccoli & Chinese Leaves with Black Bean Sauce

Serves 4

INGREDIENTS

450 g/1 lb broccoli florets
2 tbsp sunflower oil
1 onion, sliced
2 cloves garlic, thinly sliced
25 g/1 oz/¼ cup flaked (slivered) almonds
1 head Chinese leaves, shredded
4 tbsp black bean sauce

1 Bring a large saucepan of water to the boil. Add the broccoli florets to the pan and cook for 1 minute. Drain the broccoli thoroughly.

2 Meanwhile, heat the sunflower oil in a large preheated wok.

3 Add the onion and garlic to the wok and stir-fry until just beginning to brown.

4 Add the drained broccoli florets and the flaked almonds to the mixture in the wok and stir-fry for a further 2–3 minutes.

5 Add the Chinese leaves to the wok and stir-fry for a further 2 minutes.

6 Stir the black bean sauce into the vegetables in the wok, tossing to mix, and cook until the juices are just beginning to bubble.

7 Transfer the vegetables to warm serving bowls and serve immediately.

VARIATION

Use unsalted cashew nuts instead of the almonds, if preferred.

Chinese Mushrooms with Deep-Fried Tofu (Bean Curd)

Serves 4

INGREDIENTS

25 g/1 oz dried Chinese mushrooms
450 g/1 lb tofu (bean curd)
25 g/1 oz/4 tbsp cornflour (cornstarch)
oil, for deep-frying
2 cloves garlic, finely chopped
2.5 cm/1 inch piece of root ginger, grated
100 g/3½ oz/¾ cup frozen or fresh peas

1 Place the Chinese mushrooms in a large bowl. Pour in enough boiling water to cover and leave to stand for about 10 minutes.

2 Meanwhile, cut the tofu (bean curd) into bite-sized cubes, using a sharp knife.

3 Place the cornflour (cornstarch) in a bowl.

4 Toss the tofu (bean curd) in the cornflour (cornstarch) until evenly coated.

5 Heat the oil for deep-frying in a large preheated wok.

6 Add the cubes of tofu (bean curd) to the wok and deep-fry, in batches, for 2–3 minutes or until golden and crispy. Remove the tofu (bean curd) with a slotted spoon and leave to drain on absorbent kitchen paper.

7 Drain off all but 2 tablespoons of oil from the wok. Add the garlic, ginger and Chinese mushrooms to the wok and stir-fry for 2–3 minutes.

8 Return the cooked tofu (bean curd) to the wok and add the peas. Heat through for 1 minute then serve hot.

COOK'S TIP

Use marinated tofu (bean curd) for extra flavour.

Stir-Fried Butternut Squash with Cashew Nuts & Coriander (Cilantro)

Serves 4

INGREDIENTS

1 kg/2 lb 4oz butternut squash, peeled
3 tbsp groundnut oil
1 onion, sliced
2 cloves garlic, crushed
1 tsp coriander (cilantro) seeds
1 tsp cumin seeds
2 tbsp chopped coriander (cilantro)
150 ml/$^{1}/_{4}$ pint/$^{2}/_{3}$ cup coconut milk
100 ml/3$^{1}/_{2}$ fl oz/$^{1}/_{2}$ cup water
100 g/3$^{1}/_{2}$ oz/$^{1}/_{3}$ cup salted cashew nuts

TO GARNISH:
freshly grated lime zest
fresh coriander (cilantro)
lime wedges

1 Using a sharp knife, slice the butternut squash into small, bite-sized cubes.

2 Heat the groundnut oil in a large preheated wok.

3 Add the squash, onion and garlic to the wok and stir-fry for 5 minutes.

4 Stir in the coriander (cilantro) seeds, cumin and fresh coriander (cilantro) and stir-fry for 1 minute.

5 Add the coconut milk and water to the wok and bring to the boil. Cover the wok and leave to simmer for 10–15 minutes, or until the squash is tender.

6 Add the cashew nuts and stir to combine.

7 Transfer to warm serving dishes and garnish with freshly grated lime zest, fresh coriander (cilantro) and lime wedges. Serve hot.

COOK'S TIP

If you do not have coconut milk, grate some creamed coconut into the dish with the water in step 5.

Quorn with Ginger & Mixed Vegetables

Serves 4

INGREDIENTS

1 tbsp grated fresh root ginger
1 tsp ground ginger
1 tbsp tomato purée
2 tbsp sunflower oil
1 clove garlic, crushed
2 tbsp soy sauce
350 g/12 oz Quorn or soya cubes
225 g/8 oz carrots, sliced
100 g/3½ oz green beans, sliced
4 stalks celery, sliced
1 red (bell) pepper, deseeded and sliced
boiled rice, to serve

1 Place the grated fresh ginger, ground ginger, tomato purée, 1 tablespoon of the sunflower oil, garlic, soy sauce and Quorn or soya cubes in a large bowl. Mix well to combine, stirring carefully so that you don't break up the Quorn or soya cubes. Cover and leave to marinate for 20 minutes.

2 Heat the remaining sunflower oil in a large preheated wok.

3 Add the marinated Quorn mixture to the wok and stir-fry for about 2 minutes.

4 Add the carrots, green beans, celery and red (bell) pepper to the wok and stir-fry for a further 5 minutes.

5 Transfer the stir-fry to warm serving dishes and serve immediately with freshly cooked boiled rice.

VARIATION

Use tofu (bean curd) instead of the Quorn, if you prefer.

COOK'S TIP

Ginger root will keep for several weeks in a cool, dry place. Ginger root can also be kept frozen – break off lumps as needed.

1

3

4

Leeks with Baby Corn Cobs & Yellow Bean Sauce

Serves 4

INGREDIENTS

3 tbsp groundnut oil	225 g/8 oz Chinese leaves, shredded	6 spring onions (scallions), sliced
450 g/1 lb leeks, sliced	175 g/6 oz baby corn cobs, halved	4 tbsp yellow bean sauce

1 Heat the groundnut oil in a large preheated wok.

2 Add the leeks, shredded Chinese leaves and baby corn cobs to the wok and stir-fry over a high heat for about 5 minutes or until the edges of the vegetables are slightly brown.

3 Add the spring onions (scallions) to the wok, stirring to combine.

4 Add the yellow bean sauce to the mixture in the wok and stir-fry for a further 2 minutes, or until heated through.

5 Transfer to warm serving dishes and serve immediately.

COOK'S TIP

Yellow bean sauce adds an authentic Chinese flavour to stir-fries. It is made from crushed salted soya beans mixed with flour and spices to make a thick paste. It is mild in flavour and is excellent with a range of vegetables.

COOK'S TIP

Baby corn cobs are sweeter and have a more delicate flavour than the larger corn cobs and are therefore perfect for stir-frying.

Vegetable Stir-Fry

Serves 4

INGREDIENTS

3 tbsp olive oil
8 baby onions, halved
1 aubergine (eggplant), cubed
225 g/8 oz courgettes (zucchini), sliced
225 g/8 oz open-cap mushrooms, halved
2 cloves garlic, crushed
400 g/14 oz can chopped tomatoes
2 tbsp sundried tomato purée
freshly ground black pepper
fresh basil leaves, to garnish

1 Heat the olive oil in a large preheated wok.

2 Add the baby onions and aubergine (eggplant) to the wok and stir-fry for 5 minutes, or until the vegetables are golden and just beginning to soften.

3 Add the courgettes (zucchini), mushrooms, garlic, tomatoes and tomato purée to the wok and stir-fry for about 5 minutes. Reduce the heat and leave to simmer for 10 minutes, or until the vegetables are tender.

4 Season with freshly ground black pepper and scatter with fresh basil leaves. Serve immediately.

VARIATION

If you want to serve this as a vegetarian main meal, add cubed tofu (bean curd) in step 3.

COOK'S TIP

Wok cooking is an excellent means of cooking for vegetarians as it is a quick and easy way of serving up delicious dishes of crisp, tasty vegetables. All ingredients should be cut into uniform sizes with as many cut surfaces exposed as possible for quick cooking.

Stir-Fried (Bell) Pepper Trio with Chestnuts & Garlic

Serves 4

INGREDIENTS

225 g/8 oz leeks
oil, for deep-frying
3 tbsp groundnut oil
1 yellow (bell) pepper, deseeded and diced
1 green (bell) pepper, deseeded and diced
1 red (bell) pepper, deseeded and diced
200 g/7 oz can water chestnuts, drained and sliced
2 cloves garlic, crushed
3 tbsp light soy sauce

1 To make the garnish, finely slice the leeks into thin strips, using a sharp knife.

2 Heat the oil for deep-frying in a wok and cook the leeks for 2–3 minute, or until crispy. Set the crispy leeks aside until required.

3 Heat the 3 tablespoons of groundnut oil in the wok.

4 Add the (bell) peppers to the wok and stir-fry over a high heat for about 5 minutes, or until they are just beginning to brown at the edges and to soften.

5 Add the sliced water chestnuts, garlic and light soy sauce to the wok and stir-fry all of the vegetables for a further 2–3 minutes.

6 Spoon the (bell) pepper stir-fry on to warm serving plates.

7 Garnish the stir-fry with the crispy leeks.

VARIATION

Add 1 tbsp of hoisin sauce with the soy sauce in step 5 for extra flavour and spice.

Spiced Aubergine (Eggplant) Stir-Fry

Serves 4

INGREDIENTS

3 tbsp groundnut oil
2 onions, sliced
2 cloves garlic, chopped
2 aubergines (eggplants), diced
2 red chillies, deseeded and very finely chopped
2 tbsp demerara sugar
6 spring onions (scallions), sliced
3 tbsp mango chutney
oil, for deep-frying
2 cloves garlic, sliced, to garnish

1 Heat the groundnut oil in a large preheated wok.

2 Add the onions and chopped garlic to the wok, stirring well.

3 Add the aubergine (eggplant) and chillies to the wok and stir-fry for 5 minutes.

4 Add the sugar, spring onions (scallions) and mango chutney to the wok, stirring well. Reduce the heat, cover and leave to simmer, stirring from time to time, for 15 minutes or until the aubergine (eggplant) is tender.

5 Transfer the stir-fry to serving bowls and keep warm. Heat the oil for deep-frying in the wok and quickly stir-fry the slices of garlic. Garnish the stir-fry with the deep-fried garlic and serve immediately.

COOK'S TIP

Keep the vegetables moving around the wok as the aubergines (eggplant) will soak up the oil very quickly and may begin to burn if left unattended.

COOK'S TIP

The 'hotness' of chillies varies enormously so always use with caution, but as a general guide the smaller they are the hotter they will be. The seeds are the hottest part and so are usually discarded.

Stir-Fried Vegetables with Peanuts & Eggs

Serves 4

INGREDIENTS

2 eggs
225 g/8 oz carrots
350 g/12 oz white cabbage
2 tbsp vegetable oil
1 red (bell) pepper, deseeded and thinly sliced
150 g/5½ oz/1½ cups beansprouts
1 tbsp tomato ketchup
2 tbsp soy sauce
75 g/2¾ oz/⅓ cup salted peanuts, chopped

1 Bring a small saucepan of water to the boil. Add the eggs to the pan and cook for about 7 minutes. Remove the eggs from the pan and leave to cool under cold running water for 1 minute.

2 Peel the shell from the eggs and then cut the eggs into quarters.

3 Peel and coarsely grate the carrots.

4 Using a sharp knife, thinly shred the white cabbage.

5 Heat the vegetable oil in a large preheated wok.

6 Add the carrots, white cabbage and (bell) pepper to the wok and stir-fry for 3 minutes.

7 Add the beansprouts to the wok and stir-fry for 2 minutes.

8 Add the tomato ketchup, soy sauce and peanuts to the wok and stir-fry for 1 minute.

9 Transfer the stir-fry to warm serving plates and garnish with the hard-boiled (hard-cooked) egg quarters. Serve immediately.

COOK'S TIP

The eggs are cooled in cold water immediately after cooking in order to prevent the egg yolk blackening around the edges.

2

3

4

Spicy Aubergines (Eggplants)

Serves 4

INGREDIENTS

- 450 g/1 lb aubergines (eggplants), rinsed
- 2 tsp salt
- 3 tbsp vegetable oil
- 2 garlic cloves, crushed
- 2.5-cm/1-inch piece fresh root ginger, chopped
- 1 onion, halved and sliced
- 1 fresh red chilli, sliced
- 2 tbsp dark soy sauce
- 1 tbsp hoisin sauce
- 1/2 tsp chilli sauce
- 1 tbsp dark brown sugar
- 1 tbsp wine vinegar
- 1 tsp ground Szechuan pepper
- 300 ml/1/2 pint/1 1/4 cups vegetable stock

1 Cut the aubergines (eggplants) into cubes if you are using the larger variety, or cut the smaller type in half. Place the aubergines (eggplants) in a colander and sprinkle with the salt. Let stand for 30 minutes. Rinse the aubergines (eggplants) under cold running water and pat dry with kitchen paper (paper towels).

2 Heat the oil in a preheated wok and add the garlic, ginger, onion and fresh chilli. Stir-fry for 30 seconds and add the aubergines (eggplants). Continue to cook for 1–2 minutes.

3 Add the soy sauce, hoisin sauce, chilli sauce, sugar, wine vinegar, Szechuan pepper and vegetable stock to the wok, reduce the heat and leave to simmer, uncovered, for 10 minutes, or until the aubergines (eggplants) are cooked. Increase the heat and boil to reduce the sauce until thickened enough to coat the aubergines (eggplants). Serve immediately.

COOK'S TIP

Sprinkling the aubergines (eggplants) with salt and letting them stand removes the bitter juices, which would otherwise taint the flavour of the dish.

Fried Tofu (Bean Curd) & Vegetables

Serves 4

INGREDIENTS

450 g/1 lb tofu (bean curd)
150 ml/¼ pint/⅔ cup vegetable oil
1 leek, sliced
4 baby corn cobs, halved lengthways
60 g/2 oz mangetout (snow peas)
1 red (bell) pepper, seeded and diced
60 g/2 oz canned bamboo shoots, drained and rinsed
rice or noodles, to serve

SAUCE:
1 tbsp Chinese rice wine or dry sherry
4 tbsp oyster sauce
3 tsp light soy sauce
2 tsp caster (superfine) sugar
pinch of salt
50 ml/2 fl oz/¼ cup vegetable stock
1 tsp cornflour (cornstarch)
2 tsp water

1 Rinse the tofu (bean curd) in cold water and pat dry with kitchen paper (paper towels). Cut the tofu (bean curd) into 2.5-cm/1-inch cubes.

2 Heat the oil in a preheated wok until almost smoking. Reduce the heat, add the tofu (bean curd) and stir-fry until golden brown. Remove from the wok with a slotted spoon and drain on absorbent kitchen paper (paper towels).

3 Pour all but 2 tbsp of the oil from the wok and return to the heat. Add the leek, corn cobs, mangetout (snow peas), (bell) pepper and bamboo shoots and stir-fry for 2–3 minutes.

4 Add the Chinese rice wine or sherry, oyster sauce, soy sauce, sugar, salt and vegetable stock to the wok and bring to the boil. Blend the cornflour (cornstarch) with the water to form a smooth paste and stir it into the sauce. Bring the sauce to the boil and cook, stirring constantly, until thickened and clear.

5 Stir the tofu (bean curd) into the mixture in the wok and cook for about 1 minute until hot. Serve with rice or noodles.

Tofu (Bean Curd) Casserole

Serves 4

INGREDIENTS

450 g/1 lb tofu (bean curd)
2 tbsp peanut oil
8 spring onions (scallions), cut into batons
2 celery sticks, sliced
125 g/4$^{1}/_{2}$ oz broccoli florets
125 g/4$^{1}/_{2}$ oz courgettes (zucchini), sliced
2 garlic cloves, thinly sliced
450 g/1 lb baby spinach
rice, to serve

SAUCE:
425 ml/$^{3}/_{4}$ pint/2 cups vegetable stock
2 tbsp light soy sauce
3 tbsp hoisin sauce
$^{1}/_{2}$ tsp chilli powder
1 tbsp sesame oil

1 Cut the tofu (bean curd) into 2.5-cm/1-inch cubes and set aside.

2 Heat the oil in a preheated wok. Add the spring onions (scallions), celery, broccoli, courgettes (zucchini), garlic, spinach and tofu (bean curd) and stir-fry for 3–4 minutes.

3 To make the sauce, mix together the vegetable stock, soy sauce, hoisin sauce, chilli powder and sesame oil in a flameproof casserole and bring to the boil. Add the vegetables and tofu (bean curd), reduce the heat, cover and simmer for 10 minutes.

4 Transfer to a warm serving dish and serve with rice.

COOK'S TIP

This recipe has a green vegetable theme, but alter the colour and flavour by adding your favourite vegetables, if you prefer.

VARIATION

Add 75 g/3 oz fresh or canned and drained straw mushrooms with the vegetables in step 2.

Marinated Beansprouts & Vegetables

Serves 4

INGREDIENTS

450 g/1 lb beansprouts
2 fresh red chillies, seeded and finely chopped
1 red (bell) pepper, seeded and thinly sliced
1 green (bell) pepper, seeded and thinly sliced
60 g/2 oz water chestnuts, quartered
1 celery stick, sliced
3 tbsp rice wine vinegar
2 tbsp light soy sauce
2 tbsp chopped chives
1 garlic clove, crushed
pinch of Chinese curry powder

1 Place the beansprouts, chilli, (bell) peppers, water chestnuts and celery in a bowl and mix well.

2 Mix together the rice wine vinegar, soy sauce, chives, garlic and Chinese curry powder in a bowl and pour over the prepared vegetables. Toss to mix thoroughly.

3 Cover the salad and leave to chill for at least 3 hours. Drain the vegetables thoroughly, transfer to a serving dish and serve.

COOK'S TIP

There are hundreds of varieties of chillies and it is not always possible to tell how hot they are going to be. As a general rule, dark green chillies are hotter than light green and red chillies. Thin, pointed chillies are usually hotter than fatter, blunter chillies. However, there are always exceptions and even chillies from the same plant can vary considerably in their degree of spiciness.

COOK'S TIP

This dish is delicious with Chinese roasted meats or served with the marinade and noodles.

Honey-Fried Chinese Leaves (Cabbage)

Serves 4

INGREDIENTS

450 g/1 lb Chinese leaves (cabbage)
1 tbsp peanut oil
1-cm/½-inch piece fresh root ginger, grated
2 garlic cloves, crushed
1 fresh red chilli, sliced
1 tbsp Chinese rice wine or dry sherry
4½ tsp light soy sauce
1 tbsp clear honey
125 ml/4 fl oz/½ cup orange juice
1 tbsp sesame oil
2 tsp sesame seeds
orange zest, to garnish

1 Separate the Chinese leaves (cabbage) and shred them finely.

2 Heat the peanut oil in a preheated wok. Add the ginger, garlic and chilli to the wok and stir-fry the mixture for 30 seconds.

3 Add the Chinese leaves (cabbage), Chinese rice wine or sherry, soy sauce, honey and orange juice to the wok. Reduce the heat and leave to simmer for 5 minutes.

4 Add the sesame oil, sprinkle the sesame seeds on top and mix to combine. Transfer to a warm serving dish, garnish with the orange zest and serve immediately.

COOK'S TIP

Single-flower honey has a better, more individual flavour than blended honey. Acacia honey is typically Chinese, but you could also try clover, lemon blossom, lime flower or orange blossom.

VARIATION

Use a cabbage, such as Savoy, instead of Chinese leaves (cabbage) if they are unavailable. The flavour will be slightly different and the colour darker, but it will still taste just as delicious.

Green Stir-Fry

Serves 4

INGREDIENTS

- 2 tbsp peanut oil
- 2 garlic cloves, crushed
- 1/2 tsp ground star anise
- 1 tsp salt
- 350 g/12 oz pak choi, shredded
- 225 g/8 oz baby spinach
- 25 g/1 oz mangetout (snow peas)
- 1 celery stick, sliced
- 1 green (bell) pepper, seeded and sliced
- 50 ml/2 fl oz/1/4 cup vegetable stock
- 1 tsp sesame oil

1 Heat the peanut oil in a preheated wok.

2 Add the crushed garlic to the wok and stir-fry for about 30 seconds. Stir in the star anise, salt, pak choi, spinach, mangetout (snow peas), celery and green (bell) pepper and stir-fry for 3–4 minutes.

3 Add the stock, cover and cook for 3–4 minutes.

4 Remove the lid from the wok and stir in the sesame oil. Mix together thoroughly

5 Transfer the stir-fry to a warm serving dish and serve.

COOK'S TIP

Serve this dish as part of a vegetarian meal or alternatively, with roast meats for non-vegetarians.

COOK'S TIP

Star anise is an important ingredient in Chinese cuisine. The attractive star-shaped pods are often used whole to add a decorative garnish to dishes. The flavour is similar to liquorice, but with spicy undertones and is quite strong. Together with cassia, cloves, fennel seeds and Szechuan pepper, dried star anise is used to make Chinese five spice powder.

Crisp Fried Cabbage & Almonds

Serves 4

INGREDIENTS

1.2 kg/2 lb pak choi or spring greens (collard greens)
700 ml/1 $^1/_4$ pints/3 cups vegetable oil
75 g/2 $^3/_4$ oz/$^3/_4$ cup blanched almonds
1 tsp salt
1 tbsp light brown sugar
pinch of ground cinnamon

1 Separate the leaves from the pak choi or spring greens (collard greens) and rinse them well. Pat dry with kitchen paper (paper towels).

2 Shred the greens into thin strips, using a sharp knife.

3 Heat the vegetable oil in a preheated wok until it is almost smoking.

4 Reduce the heat and add the greens. Cook for 2–3 minutes, or until the greens begin to float in the oil and are crisp.

5 Remove the greens from the oil with a slotted spoon and leave to drain thoroughly on absorbent kitchen paper (paper towels).

6 Add the almonds to the oil in the wok and cook for 30 seconds. Remove the almonds from the oil with a slotted spoon.

7 Mix the salt, sugar and cinnamon together and sprinkle on to the greens. Toss the almonds into the greens. Transfer to a warm serving dish and serve immediately.

COOK'S TIP

Ensure that the greens are completely dry before adding them to the oil, otherwise it will spit. The greens will not become crisp if they are wet when placed in the oil.

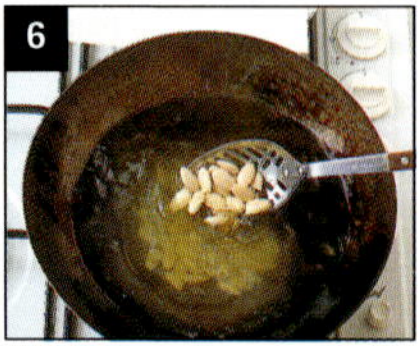

Creamy Green Vegetables

Serves 4

INGREDIENTS

450 g/1 lb Chinese leaves (cabbage), shredded
2 tbsp peanut oil
2 leeks, shredded
4 garlic cloves, crushed
300 ml/$^1/_2$ pint/1$^1/_4$ cups vegetable stock
1 tbsp light soy sauce
2 tsp cornflour (cornstarch)
4 tsp water
2 tbsp single (light) cream or natural (unsweetened) yogurt
1 tbsp chopped coriander (cilantro)

1 Blanch the Chinese leaves (cabbage) in boiling water for 30 seconds. Drain, rinse in cold water, then drain thoroughly again.

2 Heat the oil in a preheated wok and add the Chinese leaves (cabbage), leeks and garlic. Stir-fry for 2–3 minutes.

3 Add the vegetable stock and soy sauce to the wok, reduce the heat to low, cover and simmer for 10 minutes, or until the vegetables are tender.

4 Remove the vegetables from the wok with a slotted spoon and set aside. Bring the stock to the boil and boil vigorously until reduced by about half.

5 Blend the cornflour (cornstarch) with the water and stir the mixture into the stock. Bring to the boil, and cook, stirring constantly, until thickened and clear.

6 Reduce the heat and stir in the vegetables and cream or yogurt. Cook over a low heat for 1 minute.

7 Transfer to a serving dish, sprinkle over the chopped coriander (cilantro) and serve.

COOK'S TIP

Do not boil the sauce once the cream or yogurt has been added, as it will separate.

1

3

6

Stir-Fried Cucumber with Chillies

Serves 4

INGREDIENTS

2 medium cucumbers
2 tsp salt
1 tbsp vegetable oil
2 garlic cloves, crushed
1-cm/½-inch fresh root ginger, grated
2 fresh red chillies, chopped
2 spring onions (scallions), chopped
1 tsp yellow bean sauce
1 tbsp clear honey
125 ml/4 fl oz/½ cup water
1 tsp sesame oil

1 Peel the cucumbers and cut in half lengthways. Scrape the seeds from the centre with a teaspoon and discard.

2 Cut the cucumber into strips and place on a plate. Sprinkle the salt over the cucumber strips and set aside for 20 minutes. Rinse well under cold running water and pat dry with absorbent kitchen paper (paper towels).

3 Heat the oil in a preheated wok until it is almost smoking. Lower the heat slightly and add the garlic, ginger, chilli and spring onions (scallions) and stir-fry for 30 seconds.

4 Add the cucumbers to the wok, together with the yellow bean sauce and honey. Stir-fry for a further 30 seconds.

5 Add the water and cook over a high heat until most of the water has evaporated.

6 Sprinkle the sesame oil over the cucumber and chilli stir-fry. Transfer to a warm serving dish and serve immediately.

COOK'S TIP

The cucumber is sprinkled with salt and left to stand in order to draw out the excess water, thus preventing a soggy meal!

Spicy Mushrooms

Serves 4

INGREDIENTS

2 tbsp peanut oil
2 garlic cloves, crushed
3 spring onions (scallions), chopped
300 g/10 oz button mushrooms
2 large open-cap mushrooms, sliced
125 g/4$^1/_2$ oz oyster mushrooms
1 tsp chilli sauce
1 tbsp dark soy sauce
1 tbsp hoisin sauce
1 tbsp wine vinegar
$^1/_2$ tsp ground Szechuan pepper
1 tbsp dark brown sugar
1 tsp sesame oil
chopped parsley, to garnish

1 Heat the oil in a wok until almost smoking. Reduce the heat slightly, add the garlic and spring onions (scallions) and stir-fry for 30 seconds.

2 Add the mushrooms, chilli sauce, soy sauce, hoisin sauce, vinegar, pepper and sugar and stir-fry for 4–5 minutes, or until the mushrooms are cooked through.

3 Sprinkle the sesame oil on top. Transfer to a warm serving dish, garnish with parsley and serve immediately.

COOK'S TIP

This dish is ideal served with rich meat or fish dishes.

COOK'S TIP

Chinese mushrooms are used more for their unusual texture than for their flavour. Wood (tree) ears are widely used and are available dried from Chinese food stores. They should be rinsed, soaked in warm water for about 20 minutes and rinsed again before use. Straw mushrooms are available fresh or canned from Chinese food stores and some supermarkets. They have a slippery texture.

Garlic Spinach

Serves 4

INGREDIENTS

900 g/2 lb fresh spinach
2 tbsp peanut oil
2 garlic cloves, crushed
1 tsp chopped lemon grass
pinch of salt
1 tbsp dark soy sauce
2 tsp brown sugar

1 Carefully remove the stems from the spinach. Rinse the spinach leaves and drain them thoroughly, patting them dry with absorbent kitchen paper (paper towels).

2 Heat the oil in a preheated wok until it is almost smoking.

3 Reduce the heat slightly, add the garlic and lemon grass and stir-fry for 30 seconds.

4 Add the spinach and salt to the wok and stir-fry for 2–3 minutes, or until the spinach has wilted.

5 Stir in the dark soy sauce and brown sugar and cook for a further 3–4 minutes. Transfer to a warm serving dish and serve immediately.

COOK'S TIP

Lemon grass is widely used in Asian cooking. It is available fresh, dried and canned or bottled. Dried lemon grass must be soaked for 2 hours before using. The stems are hard and are usually used whole and removed from the dish before serving. The roots can be crushed or finely chopped.

COOK'S TIP

Use baby spinach, if possible, as the leaves have a better flavour and look more appealing. If using baby spinach, the stems may be left intact.

Chinese Fried Vegetables

Serves 4

INGREDIENTS

2 tbsp peanut oil
350 g/12 oz broccoli florets
1 tbsp chopped fresh root ginger
2 onions, cut into 8
3 celery sticks, sliced
175 g/6 oz baby spinach
125 g/4$^{1}/_{2}$ oz mangetout (snow peas)
6 spring onions (scallions), quartered
2 garlic cloves, crushed
2 tbsp light soy sauce
2 tsp caster (superfine) sugar
2 tbsp dry sherry
1 tbsp hoisin sauce
150 ml/$^{1}/_{4}$ pint/$^{2}/_{3}$ cup vegetable stock

1 Heat the peanut oil in a preheated wok until it is almost smoking.

2 Add the broccoli florets, ginger, onions and celery and stir-fry for 1 minute.

3 Add the spinach, mangetout (snow peas), spring onions (scallions) and garlic and stir-fry for 3–4 minutes.

4 Mix the soy sauce, sugar, sherry, hoisin sauce and stock and pour into the wok, mixing well to coat the vegetables. Cover and cook over a medium heat for 2–3 minutes, or until the vegetables are cooked through, but still crisp. Transfer to a serving dish and serve.

VARIATION

Any vegetables may be used in this recipe, depending on your preference and their seasonal availability.

COOK'S TIP

You could use this mixture to fill Chinese pancakes. They are available from Chinese food stores and can be reheated in a steamer in 2–3 minutes.

Vegetable Chop Suey

Serves 4

INGREDIENTS

1 yellow (bell) pepper, seeded
1 red (bell) pepper, seeded
1 carrot
1 courgette (zucchini)
1 fennel bulb
1 onion
60 g/2 oz mangetout (snow peas)
2 tbsp peanut oil
3 garlic cloves, crushed
1 tsp grated fresh root ginger
125 g/4 1/2 oz beansprouts
2 tsp light brown sugar
2 tbsp light soy sauce
125 ml/4 fl oz/1/2 cup vegetable stock

1 Cut the (bell) peppers, carrot, courgette (zucchini) and fennel into thin slices. Cut the onion into quarters and then cut each quarter in half. Slice the mangetout (snow peas) diagonally to create the maximum surface area.

2 Heat the oil in a preheated wok until it is almost smoking. Add the garlic and ginger and stir-fry for 30 seconds. Add the onion and stir-fry for a further 30 seconds.

3 Add the (bell) peppers, carrot, courgette (zucchini), fennel and mangetout (snow peas) and stir-fry for 2 minutes.

4 Add the beansprouts to the wok and stir in the sugar, soy sauce and stock. Reduce the heat and simmer for 1–2 minutes, until the vegetables are tender and coated in the sauce.

5 Transfer the vegetables and sauce to a serving dish and serve immediately.

COOK'S TIP

Use any combination of colourful vegetables that you have to hand to make this versatile dish.

1

2

3

Vegetable Sesame Stir-Fry

Serves 4

INGREDIENTS

- 2 tbsp vegetable oil
- 3 garlic cloves, crushed
- 1 tbsp sesame seeds, plus extra to garnish
- 2 celery sticks, sliced
- 2 baby corn cobs, sliced
- 60 g/2 oz button mushrooms
- 1 leek, sliced
- 1 courgette (zucchini), sliced
- 1 small red (bell) pepper, sliced
- 1 fresh green chilli, sliced
- 60 g/2 oz Chinese leaves (cabbage), shredded
- $^1/_2$ tsp Chinese curry powder
- 2 tbsp light soy sauce
- 1 tbsp Chinese rice wine or dry sherry
- 1 tsp sesame oil
- 1 tsp cornflour (cornstarch)
- 4 tbsp water

1 Heat the oil in a preheated wok until it is almost smoking. Lower the heat slightly, add the garlic and sesame seeds and stir-fry for 30 seconds.

2 Add the celery, baby corn, mushrooms, leek, courgette (zucchini), (bell) pepper, chilli and Chinese leaves (cabbage) and stir-fry for 4–5 minutes, or until softened.

3 Mix the Chinese curry powder, soy sauce, Chinese rice wine or sherry, sesame oil, cornflour (cornstarch) and water and stir the mixture into the wok. Bring to the boil and cook, stirring, until the sauce thickens and clears. Cook for 1 minute, spoon into a warm serving dish, sprinkle sesame seeds on top and serve.

VARIATION

You could substitute oyster sauce for the soy sauce, if you prefer.

COOK'S TIP

The ingredients are fried in vegetable oil in this recipe and not peanut oil as this would overpower the wonderful flavour of the sesame seeds.

Green Bean Stir-Fry

Serves 4

INGREDIENTS

450 g/1 lb thin green beans
2 fresh red chillies
2 tbsp peanut oil
1/2 tsp ground star anise
1 garlic clove, crushed
2 tbsp light soy sauce
2 tsp clear honey
1/2 tsp sesame oil

1 Cut the green beans in half.

2 Slice the fresh chillies, seeding them first if you prefer a milder dish.

3 Heat the oil in a preheated wok until almost smoking.

4 Lower the heat slightly, add the green beans and stir-fry for 1 minute.

5 Add the sliced red chillies, star anise and garlic to the wok and stir-fry for a further 30 seconds.

6 Mix together the soy sauce, honey and sesame oil and stir into the wok. Cook for 2 minutes, tossing the beans in the sauce to coat. Transfer the beans to a warm serving dish and serve immediately.

COOK'S TIP

This dish makes a great accompaniment to fish or lightly cooked meats with a mild flavour.

VARIATION

This recipe is surprisingly delicious made with Brussels sprouts instead of green beans. Trim the sprouts, then shred them finely. Stir-fry the sprouts in hot oil for 2 minutes, then proceed with the recipe from step 5.

Vegetable Rolls

Serves 4

INGREDIENTS

8 large Chinese leaves (Chinese cabbage leaves)

FILLING:

2 baby corn cobs, sliced
1 carrot, finely chopped
1 celery stick, chopped
4 spring onions (scallions), chopped
4 water chestnuts, chopped
2 tbsp unsalted cashews, chopped
1 garlic clove, chopped
1 tsp grated fresh root ginger
25 g/1 oz canned bamboo shoots, drained, rinsed and chopped
1 tsp sesame oil
2 tsp soy sauce

1 Place the Chinese leaves (cabbage leaves) in a large bowl and pour boiling water over them to soften them. Leave for 1 minute and drain thoroughly.

2 Mix together the baby corn cobs, carrot, celery, spring onions (scallions), water chestnuts, cashews, garlic, ginger and bamboo shoots in a bowl.

3 Mix together the sesame oil and soy sauce and add to the vegetables, mixing well.

4 Spread out the Chinese leaves (cabbage leaves) on a board and spoon an equal quantity of the filling mixture on to each leaf.

5 Roll the leaves up, folding in the sides, to make neat parcels. Secure the parcels with cocktail sticks (toothpicks).

6 Place the filled rolls in a small heatproof dish in a steamer, cover and cook for 15–20 minutes, until the parcels are cooked. Serve with a sauce of your choice.

COOK'S TIP

Make the parcels in advance, cover and store in the refrigerator until required, then steam according to the recipe.

Eight Jewel Vegetables

Serves 4

INGREDIENTS

2 tbsp peanut oil
6 spring onions (scallions), sliced
3 garlic cloves, crushed
1 green (bell) pepper, seeded and diced
1 red (bell) pepper, seeded and diced
1 fresh red chilli, sliced
2 tbsp chopped water chestnuts
1 courgette (zucchini), chopped
125 g/4½ oz oyster mushrooms
3 tbsp black bean sauce
2 tsp Chinese rice wine or dry sherry
4 tbsp dark soy sauce
1 tsp dark brown sugar
2 tbsp water
1 tsp sesame oil

1 Heat the peanut oil in a preheated wok until it is almost smoking.

2 Lower the heat slightly, add the spring onions (scallions) and garlic and stir-fry for 30 seconds.

3 Add the (bell) peppers, chilli, water chestnuts and courgette (zucchini) to the wok and stir-fry for 2–3 minutes, or until the vegetables are just beginning to soften.

4 Add the mushrooms, black bean sauce, rice wine or sherry, soy sauce, sugar and water to the wok and stir-fry for 4 minutes.

5 Sprinkle with sesame oil and serve.

VARIATION

Add 225 g/8 oz diced, marinated tofu (bean curd) to this recipe for a main meal for 4 people.

COOK'S TIP

Eight jewels or treasures form a traditional part of the Chinese New Year celebrations, which start in the last week of the old year. The Kitchen God, an important figure, is sent to give a report to heaven, returning on New Year's Eve in time for the feasting.

2

3

4

Spicy Vegetarian Fried Triangles

Serves 4

INGREDIENTS

1 tbsp sea salt
$4^1/_2$ tsp Chinese five-spice powder
3 tbsp light brown sugar
2 garlic cloves, crushed
1 tsp grated fresh root ginger
2 x 225 g/8 oz cakes tofu (bean curd)
vegetable oil, for deep-frying
2 leeks, halved and shredded
shredded leek, to garnish

1 Mix the salt, Chinese five-spice, sugar, garlic and ginger in a bowl and transfer to a plate.

2 Cut the tofu (bean curd) cakes in half diagonally to form two triangles. Cut each triangle in half and then in half again to form 16 triangles.

3 Roll the tofu (bean curd) triangles in the spice mixture, turning to coat thoroughly. Set aside for 1 hour.

4 Heat the oil for deep-frying in a wok until it is almost smoking. Reduce the heat slightly, add the tofu (bean curd) triangles and fry for 5 minutes, until golden brown. Remove from the wok with a slotted spoon and set aside.

5 Add the leeks to the wok and stir-fry for 1 minute. Remove from the wok with a slotted spoon and drain on absorbent kitchen paper (paper towels).

6 Arrange the leeks on a warm serving plate and place the fried tofu (bean curd) on top. Garnish with the fresh shredded leek and serve immediately.

COOK'S TIP

Fry the tofu (bean curd) in batches and keep each batch warm until all of the tofu (bean curd) has been fried and is ready to serve.

2

3

4

Chinese Vegetable Casserole

Serves 4

INGREDIENTS

4 tbsp vegetable oil
2 medium carrots, sliced
1 courgette (zucchini), sliced
4 baby corn cobs, halved lengthways
125 g/4 1/2 oz cauliflower florets
1 leek, sliced
125 g/4 1/2 oz water chestnuts, halved
225 g/8 oz tofu (bean curd), diced
300 ml/1/2 pint/1 1/4 cups vegetable stock
1 tsp salt
2 tsp dark brown sugar
2 tsp dark soy sauce
2 tbsp dry sherry
1 tbsp cornflour (cornstarch)
2 tbsp water
1 tbsp chopped coriander (cilantro), to garnish

1 Heat the vegetable oil in a preheated wok until it is almost smoking.

2 Lower the heat slightly, add the carrots, courgette (zucchini), corn cobs, cauliflower florets and leek to the wok and stir-fry for 2–3 minutes.

3 Stir in the water chestnuts, tofu (bean curd), stock, salt, sugar, soy sauce and sherry and bring to the boil. Reduce the heat, cover and simmer for 20 minutes.

4 Blend the cornflour (cornstarch) with the water to form a paste.

5 Remove the lid from the wok and stir in the cornflour (cornstarch) mixture. Bring the sauce to the boil and cook, stirring until it thickens and clears.

6 Transfer the casserole to a warm serving dish, sprinkle with chopped coriander (cilantro) and serve immediately.

COOK'S TIP

If there is too much liquid remaining, boil vigorously for 1 minute before adding the cornflour (cornstarch) to reduce it slightly.

Bamboo Shoots, Ginger & (Bell) Peppers

Serves 4

INGREDIENTS

2 tbsp peanut oil
225 g/8 oz canned bamboo shoots, drained and rinsed
2.5-cm/1-inch piece fresh root ginger, finely chopped
1 small red (bell) pepper, seeded and thinly sliced
1 small green (bell) pepper, seeded and thinly sliced
1 small yellow (bell) pepper, seeded and thinly sliced
1 leek, sliced
125 ml/4 fl oz/$^1/_2$ cup vegetable stock
1 tbsp light soy sauce
2 tsp light brown sugar
2 tsp Chinese rice wine or dry sherry
1 tsp cornflour (cornstarch)
2 tsp water
1 tsp sesame oil

1 Heat the peanut oil in a preheated wok.

2 Add the bamboo shoots, ginger, (bell) peppers and leek to the wok and stir-fry for 2–3 minutes.

3 Stir in the stock, soy sauce, sugar and Chinese rice wine or sherry and bring to the boil, stirring. Reduce the heat and simmer for 4–5 minutes, or until the vegetables begin to soften.

4 Blend the cornflour (cornstarch) with the water to form a paste.

5 Stir the cornflour (cornstarch) paste into the wok. Bring to the boil and cook, stirring, until the sauce thickens and clears.

6 Sprinkle the sesame oil over the vegetables and cook for 1 minute. Transfer to a warm serving dish and serve.

COOK'S TIP

Add a chopped fresh red chilli or a few drops of chilli sauce for a spicier dish.

Bamboo Shoots with Spinach

Serves 4

INGREDIENTS

3 tbsp peanut oil
225 g/8 oz spinach, chopped
175 g/6 oz canned bamboo shoots, drained and rinsed
1 garlic clove, crushed
2 fresh red chillies, sliced
pinch of ground cinnamon
300 ml/$^1/_2$ pint/1 $^1/_4$ cups vegetable stock
pinch of sugar
pinch of salt
1 tbsp light soy sauce

1 Heat the peanut oil in a preheated wok.

2 Add the spinach and bamboo shoots to the wok and stir-fry for 1 minute.

3 Add the garlic, chilli and cinnamon to the mixture in the wok and stir-fry for a further 30 seconds.

4 Stir in the vegetable stock, sugar, salt and soy sauce, cover and cook over a medium heat for 5 minutes, or until the vegetables are cooked through and the sauce has reduced. Transfer the bamboo shoots and spinach to a warm serving dish and serve.

COOK'S TIP

If there is too much liquid after 5 minutes cooking in step 4, blend a little cornflour (cornstarch) with double the quantity of cold water and stir into the sauce.

COOK'S TIP

Fresh bamboo shoots are rarely available in the West and, in any case, are extremely time-consuming to prepare. Canned bamboo shoots are quite satisfactory, as they are used to provide a crunchy texture, rather than for their flavour, which is fairly insipid.

Sweet & Sour Tofu (Bean Curd) with Vegetables

Serves 4

INGREDIENTS

2 celery sticks
1 carrot
1 green (bell) pepper, seeded
75 g/3 oz mangetout (snow peas)
2 tbsp vegetable oil
2 garlic cloves, crushed
8 baby corn cobs
125 g/4 1/2 oz beansprouts
450 g/1 lb tofu (bean curd), cubed
rice or noodles, to serve

SAUCE:
2 tbsp light brown sugar
2 tbsp wine vinegar
225 ml/8 fl oz/1 cup vegetable stock
1 tsp tomato purée (paste)
1 tbsp cornflour (cornstarch)

1 Thinly slice the celery, cut the carrot into thin strips, dice the (bell) pepper and cut the mangetout (snow peas) in half diagonally.

2 Heat the oil in a preheated wok until it is almost smoking. Reduce the heat slightly, add the garlic, celery, carrot, (bell) pepper, mangetout (snow peas) and corn cobs and stir-fry for 3–4 minutes.

3 Add the beansprouts and tofu (bean curd) to the wok and cook for 2 minutes, stirring well.

4 To make the sauce, combine the sugar, wine vinegar, vegetable stock, tomato purée (paste) and cornflour (cornstarch), stirring well to mix. Stir into the wok, bring to the boil and cook, stirring, until the sauce thickens and clears. Continue to cook for 1 minute. Serve with rice or noodles.

COOK'S TIP

Be careful not to break up the tofu (bean curd) when stirring.

2

3

4

Gingered Broccoli

Serves 4

INGREDIENTS

2 tbsp peanut oil
1 garlic clove, crushed
5-cm/2-inch piece fresh root ginger, finely chopped
675 g/1 1/2 lb broccoli florets
1 leek, sliced
75 g/2 3/4 oz water chestnuts, halved
1/2 tsp caster (superfine) sugar
125 ml/4 fl oz/1/2 cup vegetable stock
1 tsp dark soy sauce
1 tsp cornflour (cornstarch)
2 tsp water

1 Heat the oil in a preheated wok. Add the garlic and ginger and stir-fry for 30 seconds. Add the broccoli, leek and water chestnuts and stir-fry for a further 3–4 minutes.

2 Add the sugar, stock and soy sauce, reduce the heat and simmer for 4–5 minutes, or until the broccoli is almost cooked.

3 Blend the cornflour (cornstarch) with the water to form a smooth paste and stir it into the wok. Bring to the boil and cook, stirring constantly, for 1 minute. Transfer to a serving dish and serve immediately.

COOK'S TIP

If you prefer a slightly milder ginger flavour, cut the ginger into larger strips, stir-fry as described and then remove from the wok and discard.

VARIATION

You could substitute spinach for the broccoli, if you prefer. Trim the woody ends and cut the remainder into 5-cm/2-inch lengths, keeping the stalks and leaves separate. Add the stalks with the leek in step 1 and add the leafy parts 2 minutes later. Reduce the cooking time in step 2 to 3–4 minutes.

Chinese Potato Sticks

Serves 4

INGREDIENTS

650 g/1 $^{1}/_{2}$ lb medium-size potatoes
8 tbsp vegetable oil
1 fresh red chilli, halved
1 small onion, quartered
2 garlic cloves, halved
2 tbsp soy sauce
pinch of salt
1 tsp wine vinegar
1 tbsp coarse sea salt
pinch of chilli powder

1 Peel the potatoes and cut into thin slices along their length. Cut the slices into matchsticks.

2 Blanch the potato sticks in boiling water for 2 minutes, drain, rinse under cold water and drain well again. Pat thoroughly dry with absorbent kitchen paper (paper towels).

3 Heat the oil in a preheated wok until it is almost smoking. Add the chilli, onion and garlic and stir-fry for 30 seconds. Remove and discard the chilli, onion and garlic.

4 Add the potato sticks to the oil and fry for 3–4 minutes, or until golden.

5 Add the soy sauce, salt and vinegar to the wok, reduce the heat and fry for 1 minute, or until the potatoes are crisp.

6 Remove the potatoes with a slotted spoon and leave to drain on absorbent kitchen paper (paper towels).

7 Transfer the potato sticks to a serving dish, sprinkle with the sea salt and chilli powder and serve.

VARIATION

Sprinkle other flavourings over the cooked potato sticks, such as curry powder, or serve with a chilli dip.

Cucumber & Beansprout Salad

Serves 4

INGREDIENTS

350 g/12 oz beansprouts
1 small cucumber
1 green (bell) pepper, seeded and cut into matchsticks
1 carrot, cut into matchsticks
2 tomatoes, finely chopped
1 celery stick, cut into matchsticks
1 garlic clove, crushed
dash of chilli sauce
2 tbsp light soy sauce
1 tsp wine vinegar
2 tsp sesame oil
16 fresh chives

1 Blanch the beansprouts in boiling water for 1 minute. Drain well and rinse under cold water. Drain thoroughly again.

2 Cut the cucumber in half lengthways. Scoop out the seeds with a teaspoon and discard. Cut the flesh into matchsticks and mix with beansprouts, green (bell) pepper, carrot, tomatoes and celery.

3 Mix together the garlic, chilli sauce, soy sauce, vinegar and sesame oil. Pour the dressing over the vegetables, tossing well to coat. Spoon on to 4 individual serving plates. Garnish with fresh chives and serve.

COOK'S TIP

The vegetables may be prepared in advance, but do not assemble the dish until just before serving, otherwise the beansprouts will discolour.

VARIATION

You could substitute 350 g/12 oz cooked, cooled green beans or mangetout (snow peas) for the cucumber. Vary the beansprouts for a different flavour. Try aduki (adzuki) bean or alfalfa sprouts, as well as the better-known mung and soya beansprouts.

Fried Rice with Spicy Beans

Serves 4

INGREDIENTS

3 tbsp sunflower oil
1 onion, finely chopped
225 g/8 oz/1 cup long-grain white rice
1 green (bell) pepper, deseeded and diced
1 tsp chilli powder
600 ml/1 pint/2½ cups boiling water
100 g/3½ oz canned sweetcorn
225 g/8 oz canned red kidney beans
2 tbsp chopped fresh coriander (cilantro)

1 Heat the sunflower oil in a large preheated wok.

2 Add the finely chopped onion to the wok and stir-fry for about 2 minutes or until the onion has softened.

3 Add the long-grain rice, diced (bell) pepper and chilli powder to the wok and stir-fry for 1 minute.

4 Pour 600 ml/1 pint/2½ cups of boiling water into the wok. Bring to the boil, then reduce the heat and leave the mixture to simmer for 15 minutes.

5 Add the sweetcorn, kidney beans and coriander (cilantro) to the wok and heat through, stirring occasionally.

6 Transfer to a serving bowl and serve hot, scattered with extra coriander (cilantro), if wished.

VARIATION

For extra heat, add 1 chopped red chilli as well as the chilli powder in step 3.

COOK'S TIP

For perfect fried rice, the raw rice should ideally be soaked in a bowl of water for a short time before cooking to remove excess starch. Short-grain Oriental rice can be substituted for the long-grain rice.

3

4

5

Coconut Rice

Serves 4

INGREDIENTS

275 g/9½ oz long-grain white rice
600 ml/1 pint/2½ cups water
½ tsp salt
100 ml/3½ fl oz/⅓ cup coconut milk
25 g/1 oz/¼ cup desiccated (shredded) coconut

1 Rinse the rice thoroughly under cold running water until the water runs clear.

2 Drain the rice thoroughly in a sieve set over a large bowl.

3 Place the rice in a wok with 600 ml/1 pint/2½ cups water.

4 Add the salt and coconut milk to the wok and bring to the boil. Cover the wok, reduce the heat and leave to simmer for 10 minutes.

5 Remove the lid from the wok and fluff up the rice with a fork – all of the liquid should be absorbed and the rice grains should be tender.

6 Spoon the coconut rice into a warm serving bowl and scatter with the desiccated (shredded) coconut. Serve immediately.

COOK'S TIP

The rice is rinsed under cold running water to remove some of the starch and to prevent the grains from sticking together.

COOK'S TIP

Coconut milk is not the liquid found inside coconuts – that is called coconut water. Coconut milk is made from the white coconut flesh soaked in water and milk and then squeezed to extract all of the flavour. You can make your own or buy it in cans.

Stir-Fried Onion Rice with Five-Spice Chicken

Serves 4

INGREDIENTS

1 tbsp Chinese five-spice powder
2 tbsp cornflour (cornstarch)
350 g/12 oz boneless, skinless chicken breasts, cubed
3 tbsp groundnut oil
1 onion, diced
225 g/8 oz/1 cup long-grain white rice
½ tsp tumeric
600 ml/1 pint/2½ cups chicken stock
2 tbsp snipped fresh chives

1 Place the Chinese five-spice powder and cornflour (cornstarch) in a large bowl. Add the chicken pieces and toss to coat all over.

2 Heat 2 tablespoons of the groundnut oil in a large preheated wok. Add the chicken pieces to the wok and stir-fry for 5 minutes. Using a slotted spoon, remove the chicken and set aside.

3 Add the remaining groundnut oil to the wok.

4 Add the onion to the wok and stir-fry for 1 minute.

5 Add the rice, tumeric and chicken stock to the wok and bring to the boil.

6 Return the chicken pieces to the wok, reduce the heat and leave to simmer for 10 minutes, or until the liquid has been absorbed and the rice is tender.

7 Add the chives, stir to mix and serve hot.

COOK'S TIP

Be careful when using turmeric as it can stain the hands and clothes a distinctive shade of yellow.

Chinese Chicken Rice

Serves 4

INGREDIENTS

- 350 g/12 oz/1¾ cups long-grain white rice
- 1 tsp turmeric
- 2 tbsp sunflower oil
- 350 g/12 oz skinless, boneless chicken breasts or thighs, sliced
- 1 red (bell) pepper, deseeded and sliced
- 1 green (bell) pepper, deseeded and sliced
- 1 green chilli, deseeded and finely chopped
- 1 medium carrot, coarsely grated
- 150 g/5½ oz/1½ cups beansprouts
- 6 spring onions (scallions), sliced, plus extra to garnish
- 2 tbsp soy sauce

1 Place the rice and turmeric in a large saucepan of lightly salted water and cook until the grains of rice are just tender, for about 10 minutes. Drain the rice thoroughly and press out any excess water with double thickness paper towels.

2 Heat the sunflower oil in a large preheated wok.

3 Add the strips of chicken to the wok and stir-fry over a high heat until the chicken is just beginning to turn a golden colour.

4 Add the (bell) peppers and chilli to the wok and stir-fry for 2–3 minutes.

5 Add the rice to the wok, a little at a time, tossing well after each addition until well combined.

6 Add the carrot, beansprouts and spring onions (scallions) to the wok and stir-fry for a further 2 minutes.

7 Drizzle with the soy sauce and mix well.

8 Garnish with extra spring onions (scallions), if wished and serve at once.

VARIATION

Use pork marinated in hoisin sauce instead of the chicken, if you prefer.

Sweet Chilli Pork Fried Rice

Serves 4

INGREDIENTS

- 450 g/1 lb pork tenderloin
- 2 tbsp sunflower oil
- 2 tbsp sweet chilli sauce, plus extra to serve
- 1 onion, sliced
- 175 g/6 oz carrots, cut into thin sticks
- 175 g/6 oz courgettes (zucchini), cut into sticks
- 100 g/3½ oz/1 cup canned bamboo shoots, drained
- 275 g/9½ oz/4¾ cups cooked long-grain rice
- 1 egg, beaten
- 1 tbsp chopped fresh parsley

1 Using a sharp knife, slice the pork thinly.

2 Heat the sunflower oil in a large preheated wok.

3 Add the pork to the wok and stir-fry for 5 minutes.

4 Add the chilli sauce to the wok and allow to bubble, stirring, for 2–3 minutes or until syrupy.

5 Add the onions, carrots, courgettes (zucchini) and bamboo shoots to the wok and stir-fry for a further 3 minutes.

6 Add the cooked rice and stir-fry for 2–3 minutes, or until the rice is heated through.

7 Drizzle the beaten egg over the top of the fried rice and cook, tossing the ingredients in the wok, until the egg sets.

8 Scatter with chopped fresh parsley and serve immediately, with extra sweet chilli sauce, if desired.

COOK'S TIP

For a really quick dish, add frozen mixed vegetables to the rice instead of the freshly prepared vegetables.

Egg Fried Rice with Seven-Spice Beef

Serves 4

INGREDIENTS

225 g/8 oz/1 cup long-grain white rice
600 ml/1 pint/2½ cups water
350 g/12 oz beef fillet
2 tbsp soy sauce
2 tbsp tomato ketchup
1 tbsp Thai seven-spice seasoning
2 tbsp groundnut oil
1 onion, diced
225 g/8 oz carrots, diced
100 g/3½ oz/¾ cup frozen peas
2 eggs, beaten
2 tbsp cold water

1 Rinse the rice under cold running water, then drain thoroughly. Place the rice in a saucepan with 600 ml/1 pint/2½ cups of water, bring to the boil, cover and leave to simmer for 12 minutes. Turn the cooked rice out on to a tray and leave to cool.

2 Using a sharp knife, thinly slice the beef.

3 Mix together the soy sauce, tomato ketchup and Thai seven-spice seasoning. Spoon this mixture over the beef and toss well to coat evenly.

4 Heat the groundnut oil in a large preheated wok.

5 Add the beef to the wok and stir-fry for 3–4 minutes.

6 Add the onion, carrots and peas to the wok and stir-fry for a further 2–3 minutes.

7 Add the cooked rice to the wok and stir to combine.

8 Beat the eggs with 2 tablespoons of cold water. Drizzle the egg mixture over the rice and stir-fry for 3–4 minutes, or until the rice is heated through and the egg has set.

9 Transfer to a warm serving bowl and serve immediately.

VARIATION

You can use pork fillet or chicken instead of the beef, if you prefer.

5

6

8

Stir-Fried Rice with Chinese Sausage

Serves 4

INGREDIENTS

350 g/12 oz Chinese sausage
2 tbsp sunflower oil
2 tbsp soy sauce
1 onion, sliced
175 g/6 oz carrots, cut into thin sticks
175 g/6 oz/1¼ cups peas
100 g/3½ oz/¾ cup canned pineapple cubes, drained
275 g/9½ oz/4¾ cups cooked long-grain rice
1 egg, beaten
1 tbsp chopped fresh parsley

1 Using a sharp knife, thinly slice the Chinese sausage.

2 Heat the sunflower oil in a large preheated wok.

3 Add the sausage to the wok and stir-fry for 5 minutes.

4 Stir in the soy sauce and allow to bubble for 2–3 minutes, or until syrupy.

5 Add the onion, carrots, peas and pineapple to the wok and stir-fry for a further 3 minutes.

6 Add the cooked rice to the ingredients in the wok and stir-fry for 2–3 minutes, or until the rice is completely heated through.

7 Drizzle the beaten egg over the top of the rice and cook, tossing the ingredients in the wok, until the egg sets.

8 Transfer the stir-fried rice to a large, warm serving bowl and scatter with plenty of chopped fresh parsley. Serve immediately.

COOK'S TIP

Cook extra rice and freeze it in prepration for some of the other rice dishes included in this book as it saves time and enables a meal to be prepared in minutes.

1
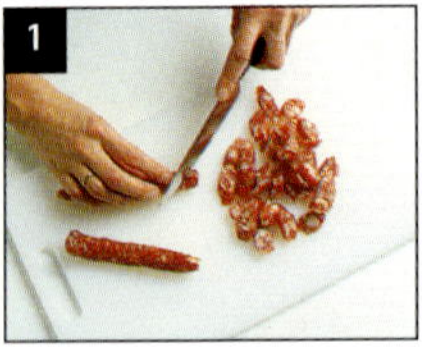

5

6

Chinese Risotto

Serves 4

INGREDIENTS

2 tbsp groundnut oil
1 onion, sliced
2 cloves garlic, crushed
1 tsp Chinese five-spice powder
225 g/8 oz Chinese sausage, sliced
225 g/8 oz carrots, diced
1 green (bell) pepper, deseeded and diced
275 g/9½ oz/1⅓ cups risotto rice
850 ml/1½ pint/1¾ cups vegetable or chicken stock
1 tbsp fresh chives, snipped

1 Heat the groundnut oil in a large preheated wok.

2 Add the onion, garlic and Chinese five-spice powder to the wok and stir-fry for 1 minute.

3 Add the Chinese sausage, carrots and green (bell) pepper to the wok and stir to combine.

4 Stir in the risotto rice and cook for 1 minute.

5 Gradually add the stock, a little at a time, stirring constantly until the liquid has been completely absorbed and the rice grains are tender.

6 Stir the snipped fresh chives into the wok with the last of the stock.

7 Transfer the Chinese risotto to warm serving bowls and serve immediately.

COOK'S TIP

Chinese sausage is highly flavoured and is made from chopped pork fat, pork meat and spices.

VARIATION

Use a spicy Portuguese sausage if Chinese sausage is unavailable.

Crab Congee

Serves 4

INGREDIENTS

225 g/8 oz/1 cup short-grain rice
1.5 litres/2¾ pints/6¼ cups fish stock
½ tsp salt
100 g/3½ oz Chinese sausage, thinly sliced
225 g/8 oz white crab meat
6 spring onions (scallions), sliced
2 tbsp chopped coriander (cilantro)

1 Place the short-grain rice in a large preheated wok.

2 Add the fish stock to the wok and bring to the boil. Reduce the heat, then simmer gently for 1 hour, stirring the mixture from time to time.

3 Add the salt, Chinese sausage, crab meat, spring onions (scallions) and coriander (cilantro) to the wok and heat through for about 5 minutes.

4 Add a little more water if the congee "porridge" is too thick.

5 Transfer the crab congee to warm serving bowls and serve immediately.

COOK'S TIP

Short-grain rice absorbs liquid more slowly than long-grain rice and therefore gives a different textured dish. A risotto rice, such as arborio, would also be ideal for this recipe.

COOK'S TIP

Always buy the freshest possible crab meat; fresh is best, although frozen or canned will work for this recipe. The delicate, sweet flavour of crab diminishes quickly: this is why many Chinese cooks make a point of buying live crabs. In the West, crabs are almost always sold ready-cooked. The crab should feel heavy for its size, and when it is shaken, there should be no sound of water inside.

2

2

3

Chicken Chow Mein

Serves 4

INGREDIENTS

250 g/9 oz packet of medium egg noodles
2 tbsp sunflower oil
275 g/9½ oz cooked chicken breasts, shredded
1 clove garlic, finely chopped
1 red (bell) pepper, deseeded and thinly sliced
100 g/3½ oz shiitake mushrooms, sliced
6 spring onions (scallions), sliced
100 g/3½ oz/1 cup beansprouts
3 tbsp soy sauce
1 tbsp sesame oil

1 Place the egg noodles in a large bowl or dish and break them up slightly.

2 Pour enough boiling water over the noodles to cover and leave to stand whilst preparing the other ingredients.

3 Heat the sunflower oil in a large preheated wok.

4 Add the shredded chicken, finely chopped garlic, (bell) pepper slices, mushrooms, spring onions (scallions) and beansprouts to the wok and stir-fry for about 5 minutes.

5 Drain the noodles thoroughly. Add the noodles to the wok, toss well and stir-fry for a further 5 minutes.

6 Drizzle the soy sauce and sesame oil over the chow mein and toss until well combined.

7 Transfer the chicken chow mein to warm serving bowls and serve immediately.

VARIATION

You can make the chow mein with a selection of vegetables for a vegetarian dish, if you prefer.

1

4

5

Egg Noodles with Chicken & Oyster Sauce

Serves 4

INGREDIENTS

250 g/9 oz egg noodles
450 g/1 lb chicken thighs
2 tbsp groundnut oil
100 g/3½ oz carrots, sliced
3 tbsp oyster sauce
2 eggs
3 tbsp cold water

1 Place the egg noodles in a large bowl or dish. Pour enough boiling water over the noodles to cover and leave to stand for 10 minutes.

2 Meanwhile, remove the skin from the chicken thighs. Cut the chicken flesh into small pieces, using a sharp knife.

3 Heat the groundnut oil in a large preheated wok.

4 Add the pieces of chicken and the carrot slices to the wok and stir-fry the mixture for about 5 minutes.

5 Drain the noodles thoroughly. Add the noodles to the wok and stir-fry for a further 2–3 minutes or until the noodles are heated through.

6 Beat together the oyster sauce, eggs and 3 tablespoons of cold water. Drizzle the mixture over the noodles and stir-fry for a further 2–3 minutes or until the eggs set. Transfer to warm serving bowls and serve hot.

VARIATION

Flavour the eggs with soy sauce or hoisin sauce as an alternative to the oyster sauce, if you prefer.

1

2
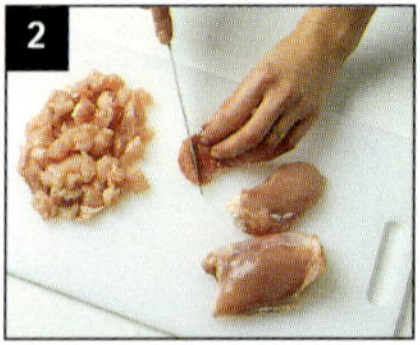

4

Ginger Chilli Beef with Crispy Noodles

Serves 4

INGREDIENTS

225 g/8 oz medium egg noodles
350 g/12 oz beef fillet
2 tbsp sunflower oil
1 tsp ground ginger
1 clove garlic, crushed
1 red chilli, deseeded and very finely chopped
100 g/3½ oz carrots, cut into thin sticks
6 spring onions (scallions), sliced
2 tbsp lime marmalade
2 tbsp soy sauce
oil, for frying

1 Place the noodles in a large dish or bowl. Pour over enough boiling water to cover the noodles and leave to stand for about 10 minutes while you stir-fry the rest of the ingredients.

2 Using a sharp knife, thinly slice the beef.

3 Heat the sunflower oil in a large preheated wok.

4 Add the beef and ginger to the wok and stir-fry for about 5 minutes.

5 Add the garlic, chilli, carrots and spring onions (scallions) to the wok and stir-fry for a further 2–3 minutes.

6 Add the lime marmalade and soy sauce to the wok and allow to bubble for 2 minutes. Remove the chilli beef and ginger mixture, set aside and keep warm.

7 Heat the oil for frying in the wok.

8 Drain the noodles thoroughly and pat dry with absorbent kitchen paper. Carefully lower the noodles into the hot oil and cook for 2–3 minutes or until crispy. Drain the noodles on absorbent kitchen paper.

9 Divide the noodles between 4 serving plates and top with the chilli beef and ginger mixture. Serve immediately.

VARIATION

Use pork or chicken instead of the beef, if you prefer.

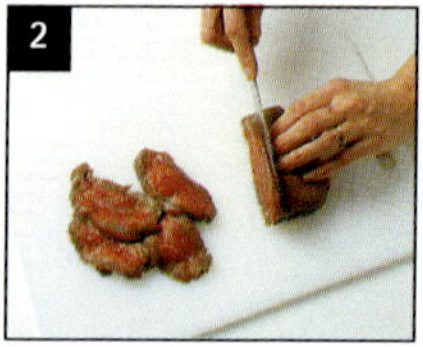
2

6

8

Twice-Cooked Lamb with Noodles

Serves 4

INGREDIENTS

250 g/9 oz packet egg noodles
450 g/1 lb lamb loin fillet, thinly sliced
2 tbsp soy sauce
2 tbsp sunflower oil
2 cloves garlic, crushed
1 tbsp caster (superfine) sugar
2 tbsp oyster sauce
175 g/6 oz baby spinach

1 Place the egg noodles in a large bowl and cover with boiling water. Leave to soak for about 10 minutes.

2 Bring a large saucepan of water to the boil. Add the lamb and cook for 5 minutes. Drain thoroughly.

3 Place the slices of lamb in a bowl and mix with the soy sauce and 1 tablespoon of the sunflower oil.

4 Heat the remaining sunflower oil in a large preheated wok.

5 Add the marinated lamb and garlic to the wok and stir-fry for about 5 minutes or until just beginning to brown.

6 Add the caster (superfine) sugar and oyster sauce to the wok and stir to combine.

7 Drain the noodles thoroughly. Add the noodles to the wok and stir-fry for a further 5 minutes.

8 Add the spinach to the wok and cook for 1 minute or until the leaves just wilt. Transfer the lamb and noodles to serving bowls and serve hot.

COOK'S TIP

If using dried noodles, follow the instructions on the packet as they require less soaking.

Singapore-Style Prawn (Shrimp) Noodles

Serves 4

INGREDIENTS

250 g/9 oz thin rice noodles
4 tbsp groundnut oil
2 cloves garlic, crushed
2 red chillies, deseeded and very finely chopped
1 tsp grated fresh ginger
2 tbsp Madras curry paste
2 tbsp rice wine vinegar
1 tbsp caster (superfine) sugar
225 g/8 oz cooked ham, finely shredded
100 g/3½ oz/1¼ cups canned water chestnuts, sliced
100 g/3½ oz mushrooms, sliced
100 g/3½ oz/¾ cup peas
1 red (bell) pepper, deseeded and thinly sliced
100 g/3½ oz peeled prawns (shrimp)
2 large eggs
4 tbsp coconut milk
25 g/1 oz/¼ cup desiccated (shredded) coconut
2 tbsp chopped fresh coriander (cilantro)

1 Place the rice noodles in a large bowl, cover with boiling water and leave to soak for about 10 minutes. Drain the noodles thoroughly, then toss them with 2 tablespoons of groundnut oil.

2 Heat the remaining groundnut oil in a large preheated wok. Add the garlic, chillies, ginger, curry paste, wine vinegar and sugar to the wok and stir-fry for 1 minute.

3 Add the ham, water chestnuts, mushrooms, peas and red (bell) pepper to the wok and stir-fry for 5 minutes.

4 Add the noodles and prawns (shrimps) to the wok and stir-fry for 2 minutes.

5 Beat together the eggs and coconut milk. Drizzle the mixture into the wok and stir-fry until the egg sets.

6 Add the desiccated (shredded) coconut and chopped coriander (cilantro) to the wok and toss to combine. Transfer the noodles to warm serving dishes and serve immediately.

VARIATION

Egg noodles may be used instead of rice noodles, if preferred.

Sweet & Sour Noodles

Serves 4

INGREDIENTS

3 tbsp fish sauce
2 tbsp distilled white vinegar
2 tbsp caster (superfine) or palm sugar
2 tbsp tomato purée
2 tbsp sunflower oil
3 cloves garlic, crushed
350 g/12 oz rice noodles, soaked in boiling water for 5 minutes
8 spring onions (scallions), sliced
175 g/6 oz carrot, grated
150 g/5½ oz/1¼ cups beansprouts
2 eggs, beaten
225 g/8 oz peeled king prawns (shrimp)
50 g/1¾ oz/½ cup chopped peanuts
1 tsp chilli flakes, to garnish

1 Mix together the fish sauce, vinegar, sugar and tomato purée in a small bowl. Set aside until required.

2 Heat the sunflower oil in a large preheated wok.

3 Add the garlic to the wok and stir-fry for 30 seconds.

4 Drain the noodles thoroughly and add them to the wok together with the fish sauce and tomato purée mixture. Mix well to combine.

5 Add the spring onions (scallions), carrot and beansprouts to the wok and stir-fry for 2–3 minutes.

6 Move the contents of the wok to one side, add the beaten eggs to the empty part of the wok and cook until the egg sets. Add the noodles, prawns (shrimp) and peanuts to the wok and toss together until well combined.

7 Transfer to warm serving dishes and garnish with chilli flakes. Serve hot.

COOK'S TIP

Chilli flakes may be found in the spice section of large supermarkets.

1

4

6

Noodles with Chilli & Prawns (Shrimp)

Serves 4

INGREDIENTS

- 250 g/9 oz thin glass noodles
- 2 tbsp sunflower oil
- 1 onion, sliced
- 2 red chillies, deseeded and very finely chopped
- 4 lime leaves, thinly shredded
- 1 tbsp fresh coriander (cilantro)
- 2 tbsp palm or caster (superfine) sugar
- 2 tbsp fish sauce
- 450 g/1 lb raw tiger prawns (large shrimp), peeled

1 Place the noodles in a large bowl. Pour over enough boiling water to cover the noodles and leave to stand for 5 minutes. Drain the noodles thoroughly.

2 Heat the sunflower oil in a large preheated wok.

3 Add the onion, chillies and lime leaves to the wok and stir-fry for 1 minute.

4 Add the coriander (cilantro), palm or caster (superfine) sugar, fish sauce and prawns (shrimp) to the wok and stir-fry for a further 2 minutes or until the prawns (shrimp) turn pink.

5 Add the drained noodles to the wok, toss to mix well, and stir-fry for 1–2 minutes or until heated through.

6 Transfer to warm serving bowls and serve immediately.

COOK'S TIP

Fish sauce is an essential staple throughout Thailand. You will usually find this labelled as nam pla.

COOK'S TIP

If you cannot buy raw tiger prawns (large shrimp), use cooked prawns (shrimp) instead and cook them with the noodles for 1 minute only, just to heat through.

Stir-Fried Cod & Mango with Noodles

Serves 4

INGREDIENTS

250 g/9 oz packet egg noodles
450 g/1 lb skinless cod fillet
1 tbsp paprika
2 tbsp sunflower oil
1 red onion, sliced
1 orange (bell) pepper, deseeded and sliced
1 green (bell) pepper, deseeded and sliced
100 g/3½ oz baby corn cobs, halved
1 mango, sliced
100 g/3½ oz/1 cup beansprouts
2 tbsp tomato ketchup
2 tbsp soy sauce
2 tbsp medium sherry
1 tsp cornflour (cornstarch)

1 Place the egg noodles in a large bowl and cover with boiling water. Leave to stand for about 10 minutes.

2 Rinse the cod fillet and pat dry with absorbent kitchen paper. Using a sharp knife, cut the cod flesh into thin strips.

3 Place the cod in a large bowl. Add the paprika and toss well to combine.

4 Heat the sunflower oil in a large preheated wok.

5 Add the onion, (bell) peppers and baby corn cobs to the wok and stir-fry for about 5 minutes.

6 Add the cod to the wok together with the mango and stir-fry for a further 2–3 minutes or until the fish is tender.

7 Add the beansprouts to the wok and toss well to combine.

8 Mix together the tomato ketchup, soy sauce, sherry and cornflour (cornstarch). Add the mixture to the wok and cook, stirring occasionally, until the juices thicken.

9 Drain the noodles thoroughly and transfer to serving bowls. Transfer the cod and mango stir-fry to separate serving bowls and serve immediately.

VARIATION

Use other white fish, such as monkfish or haddock, instead of the cod, if you prefer.

3

5

6

Japanese Noodles with Spicy Vegetables

Serves 4

INGREDIENTS

- 450 g/1 lb fresh Japanese noodles
- 1 tbsp sesame oil
- 1 tbsp sesame seeds
- 1 tbsp sunflower oil
- 1 red onion, sliced
- 100 g/3½ oz mangetout, (snow peas)
- 175 g/6 oz carrots, thinly sliced
- 350 g/12 oz white cabbage, shredded
- 3 tbsp sweet chilli sauce
- 2 spring onions (scallions), sliced, to garnish

1 Bring a large saucepan of water to the boil. Add the Japanese noodles to the pan and cook for 2–3 minutes. Drain the noodles thoroughly.

2 Toss the noodles with the sesame oil and sesame seeds.

3 Heat the sunflower oil in a large preheated wok.

4 Add the onion slices, mangetout (snow peas), carrot slices and shredded cabbage to the wok and stir-fry for about 5 minutes.

5 Add the sweet chilli sauce to the wok and cook, stirring occasionally, for a further 2 minutes.

6 Add the sesame noodles to the wok, toss well to combine and heat through for a further 2–3 minutes. (You may wish to serve the noodles separately, so transfer them to the serving bowls.)

7 Transfer the Japanese noodles and spicy vegetables to warm serving bowls and garnish with sliced spring onions (scallions). Serve immediately.

COOK'S TIP

If fresh Japanese noodles are difficult to get hold of, use dried rice noodles or thin egg noodles instead.

Stir-Fried Rice Noodles with Green Beans & Coconut Sauce

Serves 4

INGREDIENTS

275 g/10 oz rice sticks (wide, flat rice noodles)
3 tbsp groundnut oil
2 cloves garlic, crushed
2 shallots, sliced
225 g/8 oz green beans, sliced
100 g/3¾ oz cherry tomatoes, halved
1 tsp chilli flakes
4 tbsp crunchy peanut butter
150 ml/¼ pint/⅔ cup coconut milk
1 tbsp tomato purée
sliced spring onions (scallions), to garnish

1 Place the rice sticks (wide, flat rice noodles) in a large bowl and pour over enough boiling water to cover. Leave to stand for 10 minutes.

2 Heat the groundnut oil in a large preheated wok.

3 Add the garlic and shallots and stir-fry for 1 minute.

4 Drain the rice sticks (wide, flat rice noodles) thoroughly.

5 Add the green beans and drained noodles to the wok and stir-fry for 5 minutes.

6 Add the cherry tomatoes to the wok and mix well.

7 Mix together the chilli flakes, peanut butter, coconut milk and tomato purée.

8 Pour the chilli mixture over the noodles, toss well to combine and heat through.

9 Transfer to warm serving dishes and garnish with spring onion (scallion) slices. Serve immediately.

VARIATION

Add slices of chicken or beef to the recipe and stir-fry with the beans and noodles in step 5 for a more substantial main meal.

Noodle & Mango Salad

Serves 4

INGREDIENTS

250 g/9 oz thread egg noodles
2 tbsp groundnut oil
4 shallots, sliced
2 cloves garlic, crushed
1 red chilli, deseeded and sliced
1 red (bell) pepper, deseeded and sliced
1 green (bell) pepper, deseeded and sliced
1 ripe mango, sliced into thin strips
25 g/1 oz/¼ cup salted peanuts, chopped
4 tbsp peanut butter
100 ml/3½ fl oz/⅓ cup coconut milk
1 tbsp tomato purée

1 Place the egg noodles in a large dish or bowl. Pour over enough boiling water to cover the noodles and leave to stand for 10 minutes.

2 Heat the groundnut oil in a large preheated wok.

3 Add the shallots, garlic, chilli and (bell) pepper slices to the wok and stir-fry for 2–3 minutes.

4 Drain the egg noodles thoroughly.

5 Add the drained noodles and mango slices to the wok and heat through for about 2 minutes.

6 Transfer the noodle and mango salad to warmed serving dishes and scatter with chopped peanuts.

7 Mix together the peanut butter, coconut milk and tomato purée until well combined and then spoon over the noodle salad as a dressing. Serve immediately.

COOK'S TIP

If preferred, gently heat the peanut dressing before pouring over the noodle salad.

1

3

5

Egg Fried Rice

Serves 4

INGREDIENTS

- 150 g/5½ oz/⅔ cup long-grain rice
- 3 eggs, beaten
- 2 tbsp vegetable oil
- 2 garlic cloves, crushed
- 4 spring onions (scallions), chopped
- 125 g/4½ oz/1 cup cooked peas
- 1 tbsp light soy sauce
- pinch of salt
- shredded spring onion (scallion), to garnish

1 Cook the rice in a saucepan of boiling water for 10-12 minutes, until almost cooked, but not soft. Drain well, rinse under cold water and drain thoroughly again.

2 Place the beaten eggs in a saucepan and cook over a gentle heat, stirring until softly scrambled.

3 Heat the oil in a preheated wok. Add the garlic, spring onions (scallions) and peas and sauté, stirring occasionally, for 1-2 minutes.

4 Stir the rice into the mixture in the pan, mixing to combine.

5 Add the eggs, soy sauce and salt to the wok and stir to mix the egg in well.

6 Transfer to serving dishes and garnish with the spring onion (scallion).

COOK'S TIP

The rice is rinsed under cold water to wash out the starch and prevent it from sticking together.

VARIATION

You may choose to add prawns (shrimp), ham or chicken in step 3, if you wish.

Fried Rice with Pork

Serves 4

INGREDIENTS

- 150 g/5 1/2 oz/2/3 cup long-grain rice
- 3 tbsp peanut oil
- 1 large onion, cut into 8
- 225 g/8 oz pork tenderloin, thinly sliced
- 2 open-cap mushrooms, sliced
- 2 garlic cloves, crushed
- 1 tbsp light soy sauce
- 1 tsp light brown sugar
- 2 tomatoes, skinned, seeded and chopped
- 60 g/2 oz/1/2 cup cooked peas
- 2 eggs, beaten

1 Cook the rice in a saucepan of boiling water for 15 minutes, until tender, but not soft. Drain well, rinse under cold running water and drain again thoroughly.

2 Heat the oil in a preheated wok. Add the sliced onion and pork and stir-fry for 3-4 minutes, or until just beginning to colour.

3 Add the mushrooms and garlic to the wok and stir-fry for 1 minute.

4 Add the soy sauce and sugar to the mixture in the wok and stir-fry for a further 2 minutes.

5 Stir in the rice, tomatoes and peas, mixing well. Transfer the mixture to a warmed dish.

6 Stir the eggs into the wok and cook, stirring for 2-3 minutes, until just beginning to set.

7 Return the rice mixture to the wok and mix well. Transfer to serving dishes and serve immediately.

COOK'S TIP

You can cook the rice in advance and chill or freeze it until required.

Vegetable Fried Rice

Serves 4

INGREDIENTS

- 125 g/5 oz/2/3 cup long-grain white rice
- 3 tbsp peanut oil
- 2 garlic cloves, crushed
- 1/2 tsp Chinese five-spice powder
- 60 g/2 oz/1/3 cup green beans
- 1 green (bell) pepper, seeded and chopped
- 4 baby corn cobs, sliced
- 25 g/1 oz bamboo shoots, chopped
- 3 tomatoes, skinned, seeded and chopped
- 60 g/2 oz/1/2 cup cooked peas
- 1 tsp sesame oil

1 Cook the rice in a saucepan of boiling water for 15 minutes. Drain well, rinse under cold running water and drain thoroughly again.

2 Heat the peanut oil in a preheated wok.

3 Add the garlic and Chinese five spice and stir-fry for 30 seconds.

4 Add the green beans, (bell) pepper and corn cobs and stir-fry for 2 minutes.

5 Stir the bamboo shoots, tomatoes, peas and rice into the mixture in the wok and stir-fry for 1 minute.

6 Sprinkle the vegetable fried rice with sesame oil and transfer to serving dishes. Serve immediately.

VARIATION

You could add cashew nuts, dry-fried until lightly browned, in step 5 if you prefer.

COOK'S TIP

Use a selection of vegetables of your choice in this recipe, cutting them to a similar size in order to ensure that they cook in the same amount of time.

Green-Fried Rice

Serves 4

INGREDIENTS

150 g/5½ oz/⅔ cup long-grain rice
2 tbsp vegetable oil
2 garlic cloves, crushed
1 tsp grated fresh root ginger
1 carrot, cut into matchsticks
1 courgette (zucchini), diced
225 g/8 oz baby spinach
2 tsp light soy sauce
2 tsp light brown sugar

1 Cook the rice in a saucepan of boiling water for 15 minutes. Drain the rice well, rinse under cold running water and then rinse the rice thoroughly again.

2 Heat the vegetable oil in a preheated wok.

3 Add the garlic and ginger to the wok and stir-fry for about 30 seconds.

4 Add the carrot and courgette (zucchini) to the mixture in the wok and stir-fry for 2 minutes.

5 Add the baby spinach and stir-fry for 1 minute, until wilted.

6 Add the rice, soy sauce and sugar to the wok and mix together well.

7 Transfer the green-fried rice to warm serving dishes and serve immediately.

VARIATION

Chinese leaves may be used instead of the spinach, giving a lighter green colour to the dish.

COOK'S TIP

Light soy sauce has more flavour than the sweeter, dark soy sauce, which gives the food a rich, reddish colour.

Special Fried Rice

Serves 4

INGREDIENTS

150 g/5½ oz/⅔ cup long-grain rice
2 tbsp vegetable oil
2 eggs, beaten
2 garlic cloves, crushed
1 tsp grated fresh root ginger
3 spring onions (scallions), sliced
75 g/3 oz/¾ cup cooked peas
150 g/5½ oz/⅔ cup beansprouts
225 g/8 oz/1⅓ cups shredded ham
150 g/5½ oz peeled, cooked prawns (shrimp)
2 tbsp light soy sauce

1 Cook the rice in a saucepan of boiling water for 15 minutes. Drain well, rinse under cold water and drain thoroughly again.

2 Heat 1 tablespoon of the oil in a preheated wok and add the beaten eggs and a further 1 teaspoon of oil. Tilt the wok so that the egg covers the base to make a thin pancake. Cook until lightly browned on the underside, then flip the pancake over and cook on the other side for 1 minute. Remove from the wok and leave to cool.

3 Heat the remaining oil in the wok. Add the garlic and ginger and stir-fry for 30 seconds.

4 Add the spring onions (scallions), peas, beansprouts, ham and prawns (shrimp) and stir-fry for 2 minutes.

5 Stir in the soy sauce and rice and cook for a further 2 minutes. Transfer the rice to serving dishes.

6 Roll up the pancake, slice it very thinly and use to garnish the rice. Serve immediately.

COOK'S TIP

As this recipe contains meat and fish, it is ideal served with simpler vegetable dishes.

Chicken & Rice Casserole

Serves 4

INGREDIENTS

150 g/5½ oz/⅔ cup long-grain rice
1 tbsp dry sherry
2 tbsp light soy sauce
2 tbsp dark soy sauce
2 tsp dark brown sugar
1 tsp salt
1 tsp sesame oil
900 g/2 lb skinless, boneless chicken meat, diced
850 ml/1½ pints/3¾ cups chicken stock
2 open-cap mushrooms, sliced
60 g/2 oz water chestnuts, halved
75 g/3 oz broccoli florets
1 yellow (bell) pepper, sliced
4 tsp grated fresh root ginger
whole chives, to garnish

1 Cook the rice in a saucepan of boiling water for about 15 minutes. Drain well, rinse under cold water and drain again thoroughly.

2 Place the sherry, soy sauces, sugar, salt and sesame oil in a large bowl and mix until combined.

3 Stir the chicken into the soy mixture, turning to coat well. Leave to marinate for about 30 minutes.

4 Bring the chicken stock to the boil in a large saucepan or preheated wok.

5 Add the chicken with the marinade, mushrooms, water chestnuts, broccoli, (bell) pepper and ginger.

6 Stir in the rice, reduce the heat, cover and cook for 25-30 minutes, or until the chicken and vegetables are completely cooked through.

7 Transfer to serving plates, garnish with chives and serve.

VARIATION

This dish would work equally well with beef or pork. Chinese dried mushrooms may be used instead of the open-cap mushrooms, if rehydrated before adding to the dish.

Crab Fried Rice

Serves 4

INGREDIENTS

150 g/$5\frac{1}{2}$ oz/$\frac{2}{3}$ cup long-grain rice
2 tbsp peanut oil
125 g/$4\frac{1}{2}$ oz canned white crabmeat, drained
1 leek, sliced
150 g/$5\frac{1}{2}$ oz/$\frac{2}{3}$ beansprouts
2 eggs, beaten
1 tbsp light soy sauce
2 tsp lime juice
1 tsp sesame oil
sliced lime, to garnish

1 Cook the rice in a saucepan of boiling salted water for about 15 minutes. Drain well, rinse under cold running water and drain again thoroughly.

2 Heat the peanut oil in a preheated wok.

3 Add the crabmeat, leek and beansprouts to the wok and stir-fry for 2-3 minutes. Remove the mixture with a slotted spoon and set aside until required.

4 Add the eggs to the wok and cook, stirring occasionally, for 2-3 minutes, until they begin to set.

5 Stir the rice and the crabmeat, leek and beansprout mixture into the eggs in the wok.

6 Add the soy sauce and lime juice to the crabmeat mixture in the wok. Cook for 1 minute, stirring to combine, and then sprinkle with the sesame oil.

7 Transfer the crab fried rice to a serving dish, garnish with the sliced lime and serve immediately.

VARIATION

Cooked lobster may be used instead of the crab for a really special dish.

Fried Vegetable Noodles

Serves 4

INGREDIENTS

350 g/12 oz/3 cups dried egg noodles
2 tbsp peanut oil
2 garlic cloves, crushed
½ tsp ground star anise
1 carrot, cut into matchsticks
1 green (bell) pepper, cut into matchsticks
1 onion, quartered and sliced
125 g/4½ oz broccoli florets
75 g/3 oz bamboo shoots
1 celery stick, sliced
1 tbsp light soy sauce
150 ml/¼ pint/⅔ cup vegetable stock
oil, for deep-frying
1 tsp cornflour (cornstarch)
2 tsp water

1 Cook the noodles in boiling water for 1-2 minutes. Drain well and rinse under cold running water. Leave to drain in a colander.

2 Heat the oil in a preheated wok until smoking. Reduce the heat, add the garlic and star anise and stir-fry for 30 seconds. Add the remaining vegetables and stir-fry for 1-2 minutes.

3 Add the soy sauce and stock to the wok and cook over a low heat for 5 minutes.

4 Heat the oil for deep-frying to 180°C/350°F, or until a cube of bread browns in 30 seconds.

5 Form the drained noodles into rounds and deep-fry them in batches until crisp, turning once. Leave to drain on absorbent kitchen paper (paper towels).

6 Blend the cornflour (cornstarch) with the water to form a paste and stir into the wok. Bring to the boil, stirring until the sauce is thickened and clear.

7 Arrange the noodles on a warm serving plate, spoon the vegetables on top and serve.

COOK'S TIP

Make sure that the noodles are very dry before adding them to the hot oil, otherwise the oil will spit.

2

3

5

Chicken Noodles

Serves 4

INGREDIENTS

225 g/8 oz rice noodles
2 tbsp peanut oil
225 g/8 oz skinless, boneless chicken breast, sliced
2 garlic cloves, crushed
1 tsp grated fresh root ginger
1 tsp Chinese curry powder
1 red (bell) pepper, seeded and thinly sliced
75 g/3 oz mangetout (snow peas), shredded
1 tbsp light soy sauce
2 tsp Chinese rice wine
2 tbsp chicken stock
1 tsp sesame oil
1 tbsp chopped fresh coriander (cilantro)

1 Soak the rice noodles for 4 minutes in warm water. Drain thoroughly and set aside.

2 Heat the oil in a preheated wok. Add the chicken and stir-fry for 2-3 minutes.

3 Add the garlic, ginger and curry powder and stir-fry for 30 seconds.

4 Add the (bell) pepper and mangetout (snow peas) to the mixture in the wok and stir-fry for 2-3 minutes.

5 Add the noodles, soy sauce, Chinese rice wine and chicken stock to the mixture in the wok and mix well, stirring occasionally, for 1 minute.

6 Sprinkle the sesame oil and chopped coriander (cilantro) over the noodles.

7 Transfer the noodles to warmed serving plates and serve.

VARIATION

You can use pork or duck in this recipe instead of the chicken, if you prefer.

Curried Prawn (Shrimp) Noodles

Serves 4

INGREDIENTS

225 g/8 oz rice noodles
4 tbsp vegetable oil
1 onion, sliced
2 ham slices, shredded
2 tbsp Chinese curry powder
150 ml/$^1/_4$ pint/$^2/_3$ cups fish stock
225 g/8 oz peeled, raw prawns (shrimp)
2 garlic cloves, crushed
6 spring onions (scallions), chopped
1 tbsp light soy sauce
2 tbsp hoisin sauce
1 tbsp dry sherry
2 tsp lime juice
fresh snipped chives, to garnish

1 Cook the rice noodles in a pan of boiling water for 3-4 minutes. Drain well, rinse under cold water and drain thoroughly again. Set aside.

2 Heat 2 tbsp of the oil in a preheated wok.

3 Add the onion and ham and stir-fry for 1 minute.

4 Add the curry powder to the wok and stir-fry for 30 seconds.

5 Stir the noodles and stock into the wok and cook for 2-3 minutes. Remove the noodles from the wok and keep warm.

6 Heat the remaining oil in the wok. Add the prawns (shrimp), garlic and spring onions (scallions) and stir-fry for about 1 minute.

7 Add the soy sauce, hoisin sauce, sherry and lime juice and stir to combine. Pour the mixture over the noodles, toss to mix and garnish with fresh chives.

VARIATION

You can use cooked prawns (shrimp) if you prefer, but toss them into the mixture at the last minute – long enough for them to heat right through. Overcooking will result in tough, inedible prawns (shrimp).

Singapore Noodles

Serves 4

INGREDIENTS

225 g/8 oz dried egg noodles
6 tbsp vegetable oil
4 eggs, beaten
3 garlic cloves, crushed
1 1/2 tsp chilli powder
225 g/8 oz skinless, boneless chicken, cut into thin strips
3 celery sticks, sliced
1 green (bell) pepper, seeded and sliced
4 spring onions (scallions), sliced
25 g/1 oz water chestnuts, quartered
2 fresh red chillies, sliced
300 g/10 oz peeled, cooked prawns (shrimp)
175 g/6 oz/3/4 cup beansprouts
2 tsp sesame oil

1 Soak the noodles in boiling water for 4 minutes, or until soft. Leave to drain on kitchen paper (paper towels).

2 Heat 2 tablespoons of the oil in a preheated wok. Add the eggs and stir until set. Remove the cooked eggs from the wok, set aside and keep warm.

3 Add the remaining oil to the wok. Add the garlic and chilli powder and stir-fry for 30 seconds.

4 Add the chicken and stir-fry for 4-5 minutes, until just beginning to brown.

5 Stir in the celery, (bell) pepper, spring onions (scallions), water chestnuts and chillies and cook for 8 minutes, or until the chicken is cooked through.

6 Add the prawns (shrimp) and the reserved noodles to the wok, together with the bean-sprouts, and toss to mix.

7 Break the cooked egg with a fork and sprinkle over the noodles, together with the sesame oil. Serve immediately.

COOK'S TIP

When mixing precooked ingredients into the dish, such as the egg and noodles, ensure that they are heated right through and are hot when ready to serve.

Chilli Pork Noodles

Serves 4

INGREDIENTS

350 g/12 oz minced (ground) pork
1 tbsp light soy sauce
1 tbsp dry sherry
350 g/12 oz egg noodles
2 tsp sesame oil
2 tbsp vegetable oil
2 garlic cloves, crushed
2 tsp grated fresh root ginger
2 fresh red chillies, sliced
1 red (bell) pepper, seeded and finely sliced
25 g/1 oz/1/4 cup unsalted peanuts
3 tbsp peanut butter
3 tbsp dark soy sauce
dash of chilli oil
300 ml/1/2 pint/1 1/4 cups pork stock

1 Mix together the pork, light soy sauce and dry sherry in a large bowl. Cover and leave to marinate for 30 minutes.

2 Meanwhile, cook the noodles in a pan of boiling water for 4 minutes. Drain well, rinse in cold water and drain again.

3 Toss the noodles in the sesame oil.

4 Heat the vegetable oil in a preheated wok. Add the garlic, ginger, chillies and red (bell) pepper and stir-fry for 30 seconds.

5 Add the pork to the mixture in the wok, together with the marinade. Continue cooking for about 1 minute, until the pork is sealed.

6 Add the peanuts, peanut butter, soy sauce, chilli oil and pork stock and cook for 2-3 minutes.

7 Toss the noodles in the mixture and serve at once.

VARIATION

Minced (ground) chicken or lamb would also be excellent in this recipe instead of the pork.

Chicken on Crispy Noodles

Serves 4

INGREDIENTS

225 g/8 oz skinless, boneless chicken breasts, shredded
1 egg white
5 tsp cornflour (cornstarch)
225 g/8 oz thin egg noodles
320 ml/11 fl oz/1 2/3 cups vegetable oil
600 ml/1 pint/2 1/2 cups chicken stock
2 tbsp dry sherry
2 tbsp oyster sauce
1 tbsp light soy sauce
1 tbsp hoisin sauce
1 red (bell) pepper, seeded and very thinly sliced
2 tbsp water
3 spring onions (scallions), chopped

1 Mix the chicken, egg white and 2 tsp of the cornflour (cornstarch) in a bowl. Let stand for at least 30 minutes.

2 Blanch the noodles in boiling water for 2 minutes, then drain. Heat 300 ml/1/2 pint of the oil in a preheated wok. Add the noodles, spreading them to cover the base of the wok. Cook over a low heat for about 5 minutes, until the noodles are browned on the underside. Flip the noodles over and brown on the other side. Remove from the wok when crisp and browned, place on a serving plate and keep warm. Drain the oil from the wok.

3 Add 300 ml/1/2 pint/ 1 1/4 cups of the stock to the wok. Remove from the heat and add the chicken, stirring well so that it does not stick. Return to the heat and cook for 2 minutes. Drain, discarding the stock.

4 Wipe the wok with kitchen paper (paper towels) and return to the heat. Add the sherry, oyster, soy, and hoisin sauces, (bell) pepper and the remaining stock and bring to the boil. Blend the remaining cornflour (cornstarch) with the water to form a paste and stir it into the mixture. Return the chicken to the wok and cook over a low heat for 2 minutes. Place the chicken on top of the noodles and sprinkle with spring onions (scallions).

Cellophane Noodles with Yellow Bean Sauce

Serves 4

INGREDIENTS

- 175 g/6 oz cellophane noodles
- 1 tbsp peanut oil
- 1 leek, sliced
- 2 garlic cloves, crushed
- 450 g/1 lb minced (ground) chicken
- 450 ml/$^{3}/_{4}$ pint/1 cup chicken stock
- 1 tsp chilli sauce
- 2 tbsp yellow bean sauce
- 4 tbsp light soy sauce
- 1 tsp sesame oil
- chopped chives, to garnish

1 Soak the noodles in boiling water for 15 minutes. Drain the noodles thoroughly and cut them into short lengths with a pair of kitchen scissors.

2 Heat the oil in a preheated wok. Add the leek and garlic and stir-fry for 30 seconds.

3 Add the chicken to the mixture in the wok and stir-fry for 4-5 minutes, until the chicken is completely cooked through.

4 Add the chicken stock, chilli sauce, yellow bean sauce and soy sauce to the wok and cook for 3-4 minutes.

5 Add the drained noodles and sesame oil to the wok and cook, tossing to mix well, for 4-5 minutes.

6 Spoon the cellophane noodles and yellow bean sauce into warm serving bowls, sprinkle with chopped chives and serve immediately.

COOK'S TIP

Cellophane noodles are available from many supermarkets and all Chinese supermarkets.

Noodles with Prawns (Shrimp)

Serves 4

INGREDIENTS

225 g/8 oz thin egg noodles
2 tbsp peanut oil
1 garlic clove, crushed
1/2 tsp ground star anise
1 bunch spring onions (scallions), cut into 5-cm/2-inch pieces
24 raw tiger prawns (jumbo shrimp), peeled with tails intact
2 tbsp light soy sauce
2 tsp lime juice
lime wedges, to garnish

1 Blanch the noodles in a saucepan of boiling water for about 2 minutes. Drain well, rinse under cold water and drain again.

2 Heat the oil in a preheated wok until almost smoking.

3 Add the garlic and star anise to the wok and stir-fry for 30 seconds.

4 Add the spring onions (scallions) and prawns (shrimp) to the wok and stir-fry for 2-3 minutes.

5 Stir in the soy sauce, lime juice and noodles and mix well. Cook for 1 minute, then spoon into a warm serving dish. Transfer to serving bowls, garnish with lime wedges and serve immediately.

VARIATION

This dish is just as tasty with smaller cooked prawns (shrimp), but it is not quite so visually appealing.

COOK'S TIP

Chinese egg noodles are made from wheat or rice flour, water and egg. Noodles are a symbol of longevity, and so are always served at birthday celebrations – it is regarded as bad luck to cut them.

1

4

5

Beef Chow Mein

Serves 4

INGREDIENTS

450 g/1 lb egg noodles
4 tbsp peanut oil
450 g/1 lb lean beef steak, cut into thin strips
2 garlic cloves, crushed
1 tsp grated fresh root ginger
1 green (bell) pepper, thinly sliced
1 carrot, thinly sliced
2 celery sticks, sliced
8 spring onions (scallions)
1 tsp dark brown sugar
1 tbsp dry sherry
2 tbsp dark soy sauce
few drops of chilli sauce

1 Cook the noodles in a pan of boiling salted water for 4-5 minutes. Drain well, rinse under cold running water and drain thoroughly again.

2 Toss the noodles in 1 tablespoon of the oil.

3 Heat the remaining oil in a preheated wok. Add the beef and stir-fry for 3-4 minutes, stirring.

4 Add the garlic and ginger and stir-fry for 30 seconds.

5 Add the (bell) pepper, carrot, celery and spring onions (scallions) and stir-fry for 2 minutes.

6 Add the sugar, sherry, soy sauce and chilli sauce and cook, stirring, for 1 minute.

7 Stir in the noodles, mixing well, and cook until completely warmed through.

8 Transfer the noodles to warm serving bowls and serve immediately.

VARIATION

A variety of different vegetables may be used in this recipe for colour and flavour – try broccoli, red (bell) peppers, green beans or baby sweetcorn cobs.

2

5

7

Cantonese Fried Noodles

Serves 4

INGREDIENTS

350 g/12 oz egg noodles
3 tbsp vegetable oil
675 g/1 1/2 lb lean beef steak, cut into thin strips
125 g/4 1/2 oz green cabbage, shredded
75 g/3 oz bamboo shoots
6 spring onions (scallions), sliced
25 g/1 oz green beans, halved
1 tbsp dark soy sauce
2 tbsp beef stock
1 tbsp dry sherry
1 tbsp light brown sugar
2 tbsp chopped parsley, to garnish

1 Cook the noodles in a saucepan of boiling water for 2-3 minutes. Drain well, rinse under cold running water and drain thoroughly again.

2 Heat 1 tablespoon of the vegetable oil in a preheated wok.

3 Add the noodles to the wok and stir-fry for 1-2 minutes. Drain and set aside until required.

4 Heat the remaining oil in the wok. Add the beef and stir-fry for 2-3 minutes.

5 Add the cabbage, bamboo shoots, spring onions (scallions) and beans to the wok and stir-fry for 1-2 minutes.

6 Add the soy sauce, stock, sherry and sugar to the wok, stirring to mix well.

7 Stir the noodles into the mixture in the wok, tossing to mix together well.

8 Transfer to serving bowls, garnish with chopped parsley and serve immediately.

VARIATION

You can use lean pork or chicken instead of the beef in this recipe, if you prefer – remember to alter the stock accordingly.

Fried Noodles with Mushrooms & Pork

Serves 4

INGREDIENTS

- 450 g/1 lb thin egg noodles
- 2 tbsp peanut oil
- 350 g/12 oz pork fillet (tenderloin), sliced
- 2 garlic cloves, crushed
- 1 onion, cut into 8 pieces
- 225 g/8 oz oyster mushrooms
- 4 tomatoes, skinned, seeded and thinly sliced
- 2 tbsp light soy sauce
- 50 ml/2 fl oz/$^1/_4$ cup pork stock
- 1 tbsp chopped fresh coriander (cilantro)

1 Cook the noodles in a saucepan of boiling water for 2-3 minutes. Drain well, rinse under cold running water and drain thoroughly again.

2 Heat 1 tablespoon of the peanut oil in a preheated wok.

3 Add the noodles to the wok and stir-fry for 2 minutes.

4 Using a slotted spoon, remove the noodles from the wok, drain well and set aside until required.

5 Heat the remaining oil in the wok. Add the pork and stir-fry for 4-5 minutes.

6 Stir in the garlic and onion and stir-fry for a further 2-3 minutes.

7 Add the mushrooms, tomatoes, soy sauce, pork stock and noodles. Stir well and cook for 1-2 minutes.

8 Sprinkle with chopped coriander (cilantro) and serve immediately.

COOK'S TIP

For crisper noodles, add 2 tbsp of oil to the wok and fry the noodles for 5-6 minutes, spreading them thinly in the wok and turning half-way through cooking.

3

7

7

Lamb with Cellophane Noodles

Serves 4

INGREDIENTS

150 g/5$^1/_2$ oz cellophane noodles
2 tbsp peanut oil
450 g/1 lb lean lamb, thinly sliced
2 garlic cloves, crushed
2 leeks, sliced
3 tbsp dark soy sauce
250 ml/8 fl oz/1 cup lamb stock
dash of chilli sauce
red chilli strips, to garnish

1 Bring a large pan of water to the boil. Add the noodles and cook for 1 minute. Drain the noodles well, rinse under cold running water and drain thoroughly again.

2 Heat the peanut oil in a preheated wok. Add the lamb to the wok and stir-fry for 2 minutes.

3 Add the garlic and leeks to the wok and stir-fry for 2 minutes.

4 Stir in the soy sauce, stock and chilli sauce and cook for 3-4 minutes, until the meat is cooked.

5 Add the noodles to the wok and cook for 1 minute, until heated through. Transfer to serving plates, garnish and serve.

COOK'S TIP

Transparent noodles are available in Chinese supermarkets. Use egg noodles instead if transparent noodles are unavailable, and cook them according to the packet instructions.

COOK'S TIP

Chilli sauce is a very hot sauce made from chillies, vinegar, sugar and salt and should be used sparingly. Tabasco sauce can be used as a substitute.

Cellophane Noodles with Prawns (Shrimp)

Serves 4

INGREDIENTS

175 g/6 oz cellophane noodles
1 tbsp vegetable oil
1 garlic clove, crushed
2 tsp grated fresh root ginger
24 raw tiger prawns (jumbo shrimp), peeled and deveined
1 red (bell) pepper, seeded and thinly sliced
1 green (bell) pepper, seeded and thinly sliced
1 onion, chopped
2 tbsp light soy sauce
juice of 1 orange
2 tsp wine vinegar
pinch of brown sugar
150 ml/¼ pint/⅔ cup fish stock
1 tbsp cornflour (cornstarch)
2 tsp water
orange slices, to garnish

1 Cook the noodles in a saucepan of boiling water for 1 minute. Drain well, rinse under cold water and then drain thoroughly again.

2 Heat the oil in a preheated wok. Add the garlic and ginger and stir-fry for 30 seconds.

3 Add the prawns (shrimp) and stir-fry for 2 minutes. Remove the prawns (shrimp) with a slotted spoon and keep warm.

4 Add the (bell) peppers and onion to the wok and stir-fry for 2 minutes. Stir in the soy sauce, orange juice, vinegar, sugar and stock.

5 Return the prawns (shrimp) to the wok and cook for 8-10 minutes, until cooked through.

6 Blend the cornflour (cornstarch) with the water and add to the wok. Bring to the boil, add the noodles and cook for 1-2 minutes. Garnish and serve.

VARIATION

Lime or lemon juice and slices may be used instead of the orange. Use 3-5½ tsp of these juices.

Sweets & Desserts

Desserts are almost unheard of in many Oriental households and the following recipes are either adaptations of Imperial recipes or use Chinese cooking methods and ingredients to produce delicious desserts which would round off any meal perfectly.

The Chinese do not usually have desserts to finish off a meal, except at banquets and special occasions. Sweet dishes are usually served in between main meals as snacks, but fresh fruit is considered to be very refreshing at the end of a big meal.

Rice is cooked with fruits, lychees are spiced with ginger and served with a refreshing orange sorbet, and wonton wrappers are sealed around a sweet date filling and laced with honey, to name but a few of the tempting treats that follow in this chapter.

Sweet Fruit Wontons

Serves 4

INGREDIENTS

12 wonton wrappers
2 tsp cornflour (cornstarch)
6 tsp cold water
oil, for deep-frying
2 tbsp clear honey

selection of fresh fruit (such as kiwi fruit, limes, oranges, mango and apples), sliced, to serve

FILLING:
175 g/6 oz/1 cup chopped dried, stoned (pitted) dates
2 tsp dark brown sugar
1/2 tsp ground cinnamon

1 To make the filling, mix together the dates, sugar and cinnamon in a bowl.

2 Spread out the wonton wrappers on a chopping board and spoon a little of the filling into the centre of each wrapper.

3 Mix together the cornflour (cornstarch) and water and brush this around the edges of the wrappers.

4 Fold the wrappers over the filling, bringing the edges together, then bring the two corners together, sealing with the cornflour (cornstarch) mixture.

5 Heat the oil for deep-frying in a wok to 180°C/350°F, or until a cube of bread browns in 30 seconds. Fry the wontons, in batches, for 2-3 minutes, until a golden brown colour.

6 Remove the wontons from the oil with a slotted spoon and leave to drain on absorbent kitchen paper (paper towels).

7 Place the honey in a bowl and stand it in warm water, to soften it slightly. Drizzle the honey over the wontons and serve with a selection of fresh fruit.

Banana Pastries

Serves 4

INGREDIENTS

DOUGH:
450 g/1 lb/4 cups plain (all-purpose) flour
60 g/2 oz/4 tbsp lard (shortening)
60 g/2 oz/4 tbsp unsalted butter
125 ml/4 fl oz/$^1/_2$ cup water
1 egg yolk, beaten
icing (confectioner's) sugar, for dusting
cream or ice cream, to serve

FILLING:
2 large bananas
75 g/2$^3/_4$ oz/$^1/_3$ cup finely chopped no-need-to-soak dried apricots
pinch of nutmeg
dash of orange juice

1 To make the dough, sift the flour into a large mixing bowl. Add the lard (shortening) and butter and rub into the flour with the fingertips until the mixture resembles breadcrumbs. Gradually blend in the water to make a soft dough. Wrap in cling film (plastic wrap) and chill in the refrigerator for 30 minutes.

2 Mash the bananas in a bowl with a fork and stir in the apricots, nutmeg and orange juice, mixing together well.

3 Roll the dough out on a lightly floured surface and cut out 16 × 10-cm/4-inch rounds.

4 Spoon a little of the banana filling on to one half of each round and fold the dough over the filling to make semi-circles. Pinch the edges together and seal them by pressing with the prongs of a fork.

5 Arrange the pastries on a non-stick baking tray (cookie sheet) and brush them with the beaten egg yolk.

6 Cut a small slit in each pastry and cook in a preheated oven, 180°C/350°F/Gas 4, for about 25 minutes, or until golden brown.

7 Dust with icing (confectioner's) sugar and serve with cream or ice cream.

Mango Dumplings

Serves 4

INGREDIENTS

DOUGH:
2 tsp baking powder
1 tbsp caster (superfine) sugar
150 ml/$^1/_4$ pint/$^2/_3$ cup water
150 ml/$^1/_4$ pint/$^2/_3$ cup milk
400 g/14 oz/3$^1/_2$ cups plain (all-purpose) flour

FILLING AND SAUCE:
1 small mango
100 g/4 oz can lychees, drained
1 tbsp ground almonds
4 tbsp orange juice
ground cinnamon, for dusting

1 To make the dough, place the baking powder and sugar in a mixing bowl. Mix the water and milk together and then stir this mixture into the baking powder and sugar mixture until well combined. Stir in the flour to make a soft dough. Set the dough aside in a warm place for about 1 hour.

2 To make the filling, peel the mango and cut the flesh from the stone (pit). Roughly chop the mango flesh; reserve half and set aside for the sauce.

3 Chop the lychees and add to half of the chopped mango, together with the ground almonds. Let stand for 20 minutes.

4 To make the sauce, blend the reserved mango and the orange juice in a food processor until smooth. Press the mixture through a sieve to make a smooth sauce.

5 Divide the dough into 16 equal pieces. Roll each piece out on a lightly floured surface into 7.5-cm/ 3-inch rounds.

6 Spoon a little of the mango and lychee filling on to the centre of each round and fold the dough over the filling to make semi-circles. Pinch the edges together to seal.

7 Place the dumplings on a heatproof plate in a steamer, cover and steam for 20-25 minutes, or until cooked through.

8 Remove the dumplings from the steamer, dust with ground cinnamon and serve with the mango sauce.

2

4

6

Sweet Rice

Serves 4

INGREDIENTS

175 g/6 oz/¾ cup pudding rice
25 g/1 oz/2 tbsp unsalted butter
1 tbsp caster (superfine) sugar
8 dried dates, pitted and chopped
1 tbsp raisins
5 glacé (candied) cherries, halved
5 pieces angelica, chopped
5 walnut halves
125 g/4 oz/½ cup canned chestnut purée

SYRUP:
150 ml/¼ pint/⅔ cup water
2 tbsp orange juice
4½ tsp light brown sugar
1½ tsp cornflour (cornstarch)
1 tbsp cold water

1 Put the rice in a pan, cover with cold water and bring to the boil. Reduce the heat, cover and simmer for 15 minutes, or until the water has been absorbed. Stir in the butter and sugar. Grease a 600 ml/ 1 pint heatproof pudding basin (bowl). Cover the base and sides with a thin layer of the rice, pressing with the back of a spoon.

2 Mix the fruit and walnuts and press them into the rice.

3 Spread a thicker layer of rice on top and then fill the centre with the chestnut purée. Cover with the remaining rice, pressing the top down to seal in the purée. Cover the basin (bowl) with pleated greaseproof (wax) paper and foil and secure with string. Place in a steamer, or stand the basin (bowl) in a pan and fill with hot water until it reaches halfway up the sides of the basin (bowl). Cover and steam for 45 minutes. Let stand for 10 minutes.

4 Before serving, gently heat the water and orange juice. Add the sugar and stir to dissolve. Bring the syrup to the boil. Mix the cornflour (cornstarch) with the cold water to form a smooth paste, then stir into the boiling syrup. Cook for 1 minute until thickened and clear.

5 Turn the pudding out on to a serving plate. Pour the syrup over the top, cut into slices and serve.

1

3

3

Honeyed Rice Puddings

Serves 4

INGREDIENTS

300 g/10 oz/$1\frac{1}{2}$ cups pudding rice
2 tbsp clear honey, plus extra for drizzling
large pinch of ground cinnamon
15 no-need-to-soak dried apricots, chopped
3 pieces stem (preserved) ginger, drained and chopped
8 whole no-need-to-soak dried apricots, to decorate

1 Put the rice in a saucepan and just cover with cold water. Bring to the boil, reduce the heat, cover and cook for 15 minutes, or until the water has been absorbed.

2 Stir the honey and cinnamon into the rice.

3 Grease 4 × 150 ml/¼ pint/⅔ cup ramekin dishes.

4 Blend the apricots and ginger in a food processor to make a paste. Divide the paste into 4 equal portions and shape each into a flat round to fit into the base of the ramekins.

5 Divide half of the rice between the ramekins and place the apricot paste on top.

6 Cover the apricot paste with the remaining rice. Cover the ramekins with greaseproof (wax) paper and foil and steam for 30 minutes, or until set.

7 Remove the ramekins from the steamer and leave to stand for 5 minutes.

8 Turn the puddings out on to warm serving plates and drizzle with clear honey. Decorate with dried apricots and serve.

COOK'S TIP

The puddings may be left to chill in their ramekin dishes in the refrigerator, then turned out and served with ice cream or cream.

2

4

6

Mango Mousse

Serves 4

INGREDIENTS

400 g/14 oz can mangoes in syrup
2 pieces stem (preserved) ginger, chopped
200 ml/7 fl oz/1 cup double (heavy) cream
20 g/$^3/_4$ oz/4 tsp powdered gelatine
2 tbsp water
2 egg whites
1$^1/_2$ tbsp light brown sugar
stem (preserved) ginger and lime zest, to decorate

1 Drain the mangoes, reserving the syrup. Blend the mango pieces and ginger in a food processor or blender for 30 seconds, or until smooth.

2 Measure the purée and make up to 300 ml/ $^1/_2$ pint/1$^1/_4$ cups with the reserved mango syrup.

3 In a separate bowl, whip the cream until it forms soft peaks. Fold the mango mixture into the cream until well combined.

4 Dissolve the gelatine in the water and leave to cool slightly. Pour the gelatine into the mango mixture in a steady stream, stirring constantly. Leave to cool in the refrigerator for about 30 minutes, until almost set.

5 Beat the egg whites in a clean bowl until they form soft peaks, then beat in the sugar. Gently fold the egg whites into the mango mixture with a metal spoon.

6 Spoon the mousse into individual serving dishes and decorate with stem (preserved) ginger and lime zest. Serve immediately.

COOK'S TIP

The gelatine must be stirred into the mango mixture in a gentle, steady stream to prevent it from setting in lumps when it comes into contact with the cold mixture.

3

4

5

Poached Allspice Pears

Serves 4

INGREDIENTS

4 large, ripe pears
300 ml/$^1/_2$ pint/1 $^1/_4$ cups orange juice
2 tsp ground allspice
60 g/2 oz/$^1/_3$ cup raisins
2 tbsp light brown sugar
grated orange rind, to decorate

1 Using an apple corer, core the pears. Using a sharp knife, peel the pears and cut them in half.

2 Place the pear halves in a large saucepan.

3 Add the orange juice, allspice, raisins and sugar to the pan and heat gently, stirring, until the sugar has dissolved. Bring the mixture to the boil for 1 minute.

4 Reduce the heat to low and leave to simmer for about 10 minutes, or until the pears are cooked, but still fairly firm – test them by inserting the tip of a sharp knife.

5 Remove the pears from the pan with a slotted spoon and transfer to serving plates. Decorate and serve hot with the syrup.

VARIATION

Use cinnamon instead of the allspice and decorate with cinnamon sticks and fresh mint sprigs, if you prefer.

COOK'S TIP

The Chinese do not usually have desserts to finish off a meal, except at banquets and special occasions. Sweet dishes are usually served in between main meals as snacks, but fruit is refreshing at the end of a big meal.

Chinese Custard Tarts

Makes 15

INGREDIENTS

DOUGH:
175 g/6 oz/1 1/2 cups plain (all-purpose) flour
3 tbsp caster (superfine) sugar
60 g/2 oz/4 tbsp unsalted butter
25 g/1 oz/2 tbsp lard (shortening)
2 tbsp water

CUSTARD:
2 small eggs
60 g/2 oz/1/4 cup caster (superfine) sugar
175 ml/6 fl oz/3/4 cup pint milk
1/2 tsp ground nutmeg, plus extra for sprinkling
cream, to serve

1 To make the dough, sift the flour into a bowl. Add the sugar and rub in the butter and lard (shortening) until the mixture resembles breadcrumbs. Add the water and mix to form a dough.

2 Transfer the dough to a lightly floured surface and knead for 5 minutes, until smooth. Cover with cling film (plastic wrap) and leave to chill in the refrigerator while you prepare the filling.

3 To make the custard, beat the eggs and sugar together. Gradually add the milk and nutmeg and beat until well combined.

4 Separate the dough into 15 even-sized pieces. Flatten the dough pieces into rounds and press into shallow patty tins (pans).

5 Spoon the custard into the pastry cases (tart shells) and cook in a preheated oven, at 150°C/300°F/Gas Mark 2, for 25-30 minutes.

6 Transfer the tarts to a wire rack, leave to cool slightly, then sprinkle with nutmeg. Serve with cream.

COOK'S TIP

For extra convenience, make the dough in advance, cover and leave to chill in the refrigerator until required.

3

4

6

Ginger Lychees with Orange Sorbet

Serves 4

INGREDIENTS

SORBET:
225 g/8 oz/1¼ cups caster (superfine) sugar
450 ml/¾ pint/2 cups cold water
350 g/12 oz can mandarins, in natural juice
2 tbsp lemon juice

STUFFED LYCHEES:
425 g/15 oz can lychees, drained
60 g/2 oz stem (preserved) ginger, drained and finely chopped
lime zest, cut into diamond shapes, to decorate

1 To make the sorbet, place the sugar and water in a saucepan and stir over a low heat until the sugar has dissolved. Bring the mixture to the boil and boil vigorously for 2-3 minutes.

2 Meanwhile, blend the mandarins in a food processor or blender until smooth. Press the blended mandarin mixture through a sieve until smooth. Stir the mandarin sauce into the syrup, together with the lemon juice. Set aside to cool.

3 Pour the mixture into a rigid, plastic container suitable for the freezer and freeze until set, stirring occasionally.

4 Meanwhile, drain the lychees on absorbent kitchen paper (paper towels).

5 Spoon the chopped ginger into the centre of the lychees.

6 Arrange the lychees on serving plates, garnish and serve with scoops of orange sorbet.

COOK'S TIP

It is best to leave the sorbet in the refrigerator for 10 minutes, so that it softens slightly, allowing you to scoop it to serve.

Battered Bananas

Serves 4

INGREDIENTS

8 medium bananas
2 tsp lemon juice
75 g/2 3/4 oz/2/3 cup self-raising flour
75 g/2 3/4 oz/2/3 cup rice flour
1 tbsp cornflour (cornstarch)
1/2 tsp ground cinnamon
250 ml/8 fl oz/1 cup water
oil, for deep-frying
4 tbsp light brown sugar

1 Cut the bananas into chunks and place them in a large mixing bowl.

2 Sprinkle the lemon juice over the bananas to prevent discoloration.

3 Sift the self-raising flour, rice flour, cornflour (cornstarch) and cinnamon into a mixing bowl. Gradually stir in the water to make a thin batter.

4 Heat the oil in a preheated wok until almost smoking, then reduce the heat slightly.

5 Place a piece of banana on the end of a fork and carefully dip it into the batter, draining off any excess. Repeat with the remaining banana pieces.

6 Sprinkle the sugar on to a large plate.

7 Carefully place the banana pieces in the oil and cook for 2-3 minutes, until golden. Remove the banana pieces from the oil with a slotted spoon and roll them in the sugar. Transfer to bowls and serve with cream or ice cream.

COOK'S TIP

Rice flour can be bought from wholefood shops or from Chinese supermarkets.

Index